The Grove Press

GUIDE
TO THE
BLUES
ON CD

The Grove Press

GUIDE

TO THE

BLUES

ON CD

Frank-John Hadley

GROVE PRESS
New York

Published by Grove Press
A division of Grove Press, Inc.
841 Broadway
New York, NY 10003-4793

Published in Canada by General Publishing Company, Ltd.

LIBRARY OF CONGRESS CATALOGING-IN-PUBLICATION DATA

Hadley, Frank-John.
    The Grove Press guide to the blues on CD / Frank-John Hadley.—
    1st ed.
        p.   cm.
    Includes index.
    ISBN 0-8021-3328-2
    1. Blues (Music)—Discography.   2. Compact discs—Reviews.
I. Title.   II. Title: Guide to the blues on CD.
ML156.4.B6H3   1993
016.781643'026'6—dc20
                                                    92-17305
                                                    CIP
                                                    MN

Manufactured in the United States of America

Printed on acid-free paper

First Edition 1993

1 3 5 7 9 10 8 6 4 2

To George W. Travis and Miriam Hadley

Acknowledgments

I want to thank Grove editors Rose Marie Morse and Marc Romano, especially for their good cheer and clearheadedness.

With sincere gratitude I acknowledge the support and/or assistance given me by Darren Allen, Ann Braithwaite, Robert Brant, Donna and Ray Charbonneau, Mike Fagien, Frank Hadley, Jr., Holly Harris, John Jackimowicz, Larry Jacobs, Paul Julian, Ross Kolhonen, Karen Leipziger, Abe and Marlene Lenobel, David Leonhard, Dennis MacDonald, Ted Norton, Allen Perakis, Joe Phillips, Harvey Rabenold, Fred Reiss, Stan Rogers, Hope Travis, and Elaine Wing.

I should also like to thank the following writers, publicists, and record company people for their valuable assistance: Peter R Aschoff, Bob Blumenthal, Fred Bouchard, Bill Dahl, Jake Guralnick, Peter Guralnick, Patricia Jones, Jim Trageser; Doctor Jazz, Chris Kamatani, Peter Levenson, Robert S. Levinson, Don Lucoff, Ora Nance, Mark Pucci, Lisa Shively, Kat Stratton; Bruce Iglauer and Ken Morton (Alligator), Jim Bateman (Amazing), Ellen Battle (Antilles), Sally King (Antone's), Chris Strachwitz (Arhoolie), Peter Bullis (Black Eagle), Edward Chmelewski (Blind Pig), Jalila Larsuel

(Blue Note), Betsy Mahoney (Charisma), Barry Feldman, Joanne Sloan, Arthur Levy, and Monica Shovlin (CBS Records), Susan Swain (da Music), Steve Wagner and Jennifer Dirkes (Delmark), Michael Frank (Earwig), Sherry Ring Ginsberg (Elektra), Terri Hinte (Fantasy), Seymour Guenther and Mike Fleischer (Flying Fish), Joel Slotnikoff (Genes), Gene Norman (GNP Crescendo), Larry Sloven and Woody Chansky (Hightone), Helen Urriola (Ichiban), the Jewel Records staff, Orrin Keepnews (Landmark), Daniel Lester (LRC), Melanie and Floyd Soileau (Maison de Soul), Thomas Couch (Malaco), Andy McKaie (MCA/Chess), Cheryl Cross (Mesa/Bluemoon), Phyllis Schwartz and Pat Weaver (MFSL), Daniel Jacoubovitch (Modern Blues Recordings), Charlie Lourie (Mosaic), Barney Fields (Muse), B. J. Garrett (Powerhouse), Marilyn Lipsius (RCA), Jim Fouratt (Rhino), Bob Rivera (Rivera), Jim O'Neil (Rooster Blues), Brad Paul and Marian Leighton Levy (Rounder), Carrie Anne Svingen (Rykodisc), Andrew Seidenfeld (Shanachie), Suzanne Langille (St. Joan), Richard Rosenblatt (Tone-Cool), Kent Crawford and Bernice McGeehan (Vanguard), Sonia Crocker (Verve), Bill Bentley and the Warner Brothers publicity f-f-folks, and Kathi Sweet (Windham Hill). Not to forget a tip of the fedora to hundreds of musicians and the late Sanford Berman, who introduced me to the music of Helen Humes and Blind John Davis.

Contents

Foreword

I once asked Miles Davis about a jazz pianist of astonishing technical skills. Miles dismissed him. "Hell, he can't play the blues, so how can he play jazz?"

The blues is the common language not only of jazz but of the western swing of Merle Haggard and Bob Wills. It is also at the molten core of that rock music which lasts beyond a minute on the charts. The blues is much, much more American than apple pie.

Jimmy Rushing, long with Count Basie and so compelling a blues singer that you could hear him long after you'd gone home, used to say, "Anytime a person can play the blues he has a soul, and that gives him a sort of lift to play anything else he wants to play. The blues are sort of a base, like a foundation to a building, because any time you get into trouble playing a number, you curve the blues down and get out of it."

The blues can stir your soul and relax it too. When I was an A&R man for a jazz label, the musicians every once in a while would get stuck—like in flypaper—as they worked on an elaborate arrangement. I would then walk into the studio and suggest they take a break and just play the blues. Those sounds, those feelings, were so satisfying that usually they never went back to all that paper; instead, the improvised blues became part of the album.

Another boundless benefit of the blues is its diversity, its scope. Billie Holiday once told me, "You sing the blues when you're sad, but you can also sing blues very well when you're feeling good, because you can tell another kind of story about the blues then."

It is this vivid, continually surprising variety of the blues that has been carefully, lovingly illustrated in Frank-John Hadley's *The Grove Press Guide to the Blues on CD.* From Bessie Smith to Marcia Ball, he and his contributing writers have presented not only an extraordinarily wide-ranging series of blues illuminations, but they have also documented much of this multicultural nation that doesn't make *The New York Times* or the network news.

If I were teaching American history or political science or sociology or poetry, I would play recordings from this compendium in every class. The blues tells a story, it always tells a story. That's what the blues is. And the stories in these recordings—from originators who are now ghosts to young disciples who have grown into the blues—tell so much about this nation and its future that this guide should be in every school, from middle schools through universities.

"The last thing Charlie Parker said to me," Art Blakey recalled when Bird died, "was he wondered when the young people would come back to playing the blues."

A good many have come back, and they're here. So are the blues bards who reached them so deeply that they had to find the blues. And once the blues gets you, it doesn't let go. And you don't want it to let go, because it has become an essential part of your life, of how you understand where you've been and where you want to go.

—Nat Hentoff

Preface

> "I feel like the wisdom of the blues is the greatest thing
> the world can have."
> —Willie Dixon, bluesman
> December 1, 1988, to the author

No one should look upon *The Grove Press Guide to the Blues on CD* as a complete, inclusive, exhaustive handbook to what's currently available by recording artists in the compact disc configuration. This humble scribe and a few colleagues have attempted to provide an escort or entry point into the bewildering maze of hundreds and hundreds of six-inch discs one might encounter in a well-stocked CD emporium. Undaunted by the continuing avalanche of releases from all over, we've concentrated on reviewing a goodly number of domestic titles along with a scant smattering of import titles in hopes of making the aisle search somewhat easier.

Anyone wanting to take full measure of the innumerable CDs in print is advised to seek out the catalogs and/or "updates" offered by the following mail order firms:

- Bose Express Music—The Mountain, Framingham, MA 01701 phone: 1-800-451-BOSE
- Roundup Records—P.O. Box 154, Cambridge, MA 02140
- Shanachie Records—P.O. Box 208, Newton, NJ 07860
- Stackhouse/Delta Record Mart—232 Sunflower Avenue, Clarksdale, MS 38614 phone: (601) 627-2209

Self-righteous purists may take umbrage at the *Guide's* inclusion of artists generally designated as exponents of jazz, rock, R&B, and so forth. No apologies here. Blues belongs to the common language of virtually all American musics, and countless performers rely on imparting moods through the telling or slapdash use of its timbral and harmonic elements. We hope future editions of the *Guide* can take stock of many other artists conversant or purportedly comfortable with the twelve-bar form and/or blues feeling.

Does this book imply the full endorsement of digital reproduction of sound? Should the phonograph record, with its analog sound, be thrown on the scrapheap? No and no. Record albums, to these ears, often have a more authentic sonic presence/spatial depth than CDs, with the analog (AAD) mode's reduced dynamic range and deeper, fatter low ends especially flattering to the music built on the three basic chords of the diatonic system. Digital technology (look for the DAT imprint) hasn't the "dirtiness" of the analog format, but digital's sonic reproductions are usually more than acceptable when employed by respectful, intelligent engineers and producers. That laser light scanning the audio information living in the plastic structure of the six-inch discs isn't to be feared. One should always bear in mind, however, that the results of the recording process are but a simulacrum of how the artists actually sound or sounded like.

Lastly, the blues is not a spent force as naysayers are wont to state. To be sure, there are a skulk of thieves flying the blues banner who mindlessly rehash the past, their "riffs so old they got whiskers," as Jelly Roll Morton once put it. Yet sincerity in tandem with fresh impulses and the wisdom the late Willie Dixon claimed truck with is not something uncommon. Look to Lonnie Pitchford's interpretations of Robert Johnson songs, octogenarian Jack Owens's pitch shadings, vibraphonist Milt Jackson's stately blues phrases, Melvin Taylor's distorted guitar tones, T-Bone Ford's Delta wail, Leroy Jenkins's earthy violin, Dave Van Ronk's application to his craft, Duke Ellington's rich palette of blue hues (savor his 1940 minor blues "Ko-Ko," for one) . . . and the music of a boxcar-load of performers mentioned in the pages to come.

Key to This Book

The time-honored star rating system has been adopted from *Down Beat* magazine. The designations after the celestial figures most definitely owe nothing to the aforementioned music publication. As a rule of thumb, anything awarded at least two and a half stars is worth hearing.

★★★★★ Sterling   ★★✔ Moderately interesting

★★★★✔ Gilt-edged   ★★ Decent

★★★★ Splendid   ★✔ Beastly

★★★✔ Better-than-good ★ Accurst

★★★ Enjoyable

The listed CD running time is given in hours, minutes, and seconds: e.g., 3:25:09. The hour is included only when there are two or more CDs belonging to the reviewed entry; in such cases the running times of all discs in the set have been combined. Where review CDs have been unavailable (only in a few cases) the time has been determined by consulting records or cassette.

"Reissue" means that the disc has formerly enjoyed shelf life as a record album and/or cassette. The listing of a specific year points to a fresh session or collection that, as best can be determined, was originally issued in the CD configuration.

The reviews are arranged alphabetically, by artist, and then chronologically, according to recording dates—earliest to most recent; anthologies are alphabetized by title.

Contributors

Bill Dahl (B.D.) has written about blues, soul, and rock for *Living Blues* (where he's currently record reviews editor), *Goldmine*, *Down Beat*, *Guitar World*, and the *Chicago Tribune*.

Jake Guralnick (J.G.) works for Rounder Records and writes about music for the *Boston Phoenix*.

Jim Trageser (J.T.) is a regular contributor to *Living Blues* and *Blues Revue Quarterly*. He is presently working as an editor at the *Oceanside Blade–Citizen* (Ca.).

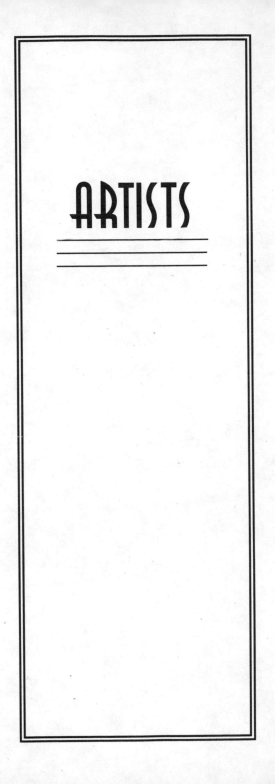

ARTISTS

Johnny Ace
Memorial Album (MCA) ★★★✔

Johnny Ace (John Alexander, Jr.) used his slightly unsteady baritone to intone sad blues ballads that raced up the R&B charts between 1952 and 1955. "Pledging My Love"—released shortly after he accidentally took his life on Christmas Eve 1954—is the one for all time, and nine of the other eleven tracks have aged with nearly equal grace. (32:39/Reissue)

Faye Adams
Golden Classics (Collectables) ★★★

This heavily gospel-influenced vocalist scored three R&B chart-toppers in 1953–54 for the Herald label; strangely, only two are included here ("Shake a Hand" and "I'll Be True"). The rest of the set is evenly varied between ballads and up-tempo material. Sound quality isn't the greatest, obviously from vinyl. (B.D.) (31:38/Reissue)

Johnny Adams
Room with a View of the Blues (Rounder)   ★★★

Adept at essaying a variety of musical styles, the New Orleans singer known as the "Tan Canary" dons his sharpest blues clothes for his third Rounder release. Adams's handsomely expressive voice wins out over some questionable material and home turf accompanists who are more often loose and perfunctory than tightknit and involved.   (46:02/1988)

Walking on a Tightrope (Rounder)   ★★★★♪

Johnny Adams singing Percy "Poet Laureate of the Blues" Mayfield is about the soul blues equivalent to jazz first lady Ella Fitzgerald singing Cole Porter—a sublime occasion for hoisting the tankards. Forty years committed to Louisiana R&B, Adams endows his swinging phrases with all the warmth and surety of a mature master. Adams finds revelatory shades of meaning in the lyrics of Mayfield, and his penchant for slow tempos stands him in good stead. Tasteful arrangements flatter his regular Crescent City support team, decidedly more responsive this time out. A smart and stylish triumph.   (43:38/1989)

Johnny Adams Sings Doc Pomus: The Real Me (Rounder)   ★★★★

Ever the winsome embodiment of blues urbanity, Adams gives eleven Doc Pomus songs a warm, inviting glow just weeks after the redoubtable New York songwriter's death in April 1991. The singer reads his friend's lyrics on bittersweet romance as if he'd lived them, while coproducer/keyboardist Dr. John and fellow New Orleans musicians sensitively echo a similar understanding of words and sentiment. The music has harmonious design and seductive colors.   (46:29/1991)

Cannonball Adderley

The Cannonball Adderley Collection, Volume One: Them ★★★✦
Dirty Blues (Landmark)

Blues coursed through the veins of Cannonball Adderley, the late saxophonist who sprung out of a Miles Davis band to lead an outfit through the 1960's soulful hard bop boom into the 1970s. On his quintet's first recording, the Tampa native speaks a lexicon of blues phrases, in keeping with his brother Nat on cornet and Bobby Timmons on piano. The program includes previously unreleased takes of classics "Work Song" and "Dat Dere." (50:40/Reissue)

Henry "Red" Allen

World on a String (RCA/Bluebird) ★★★★

A superb New Orleans trumpeter, Allen reunited with fellow Fletcher Henderson Orchestra alumnus Coleman Hawkins in 1957 to cut this engaging jazz session. Showing remarkable command of bends, smears, and blues tonality, he brings to "I Cover the Waterfront," "Algiers Bounce," and nine more songs a sense of triumph and beauty. Few have played blues and jazz with the note-perfect surety of performance of clarinetist Buster Bailey. (61:23/1991)

Lee Allen

Walkin' with Mr. Lee (Collectables) ★★★★

Lee Allen was so profoundly busy as the top session tenor saxman in New Orleans during the 1950s that he had precious little time to record under his own name. In fact, this rocking 1958 all-instrumental set, first released on Ember, represents nearly everything he cut as a front man, including the jumping hit title track and the fiery follow-up, "Boppin' at the Hop." (B.D.) (33:39/Reissue)

Mose Allison
Back Country Suite (Fantasy)   ★★★★✦

Mose Allison's seminal debut recording from 1959 launched his career as a singular interpreter of American musical styles. The Mississippi pianist wraps country blues and modern jazz together in a series of autobiographical pastoral dance sketches, serving them up in his trademark low-key approach. He sings only on the brief "Blues," a Delta dreamer evoking something unfamiliar and fascinating, especially to young English musicians gearing up for R&B anarchy.   (34:07/Reissue)

My Backyard (Blue Note)   ★★★✦

On this album, recorded in New Orleans with local jazz players, Allison's mature style intertwines his signature pithy, sardonic lyrics and harmonic dissonance with classic Big Easy street rhythm. An icon to a generation of rockers, he still writes songs that span the broad emotional and musical spectrum; his originals, notably the satirical "Ever Since I Stole the Blues" and a comical rumination on mortality titled "Was," join his cover of the standard "Your Red Wagon" to reveal that after thirty years the hep cat's message still brings it home.   (43:47/1990)

The Allman Brothers Band
At Fillmore East (Mobile Fidelity)   ★★★✦

According to blues-rock hagiography, the Allmans' March 1971 New York City performance—seven songs elongated over two discs—belongs to the canon. Secularists, however, hear a singer (brother Gregg) with a narrow emotional frame of reference and a fair amount of directionless instrumental crowing. Most everyone reveres those relatively compact covers of material from Elmore James, T-Bone Walker, and Blind Willie McTell.   (1:18:47/Reissue)

Eat a Peach (Mobile Fidelity) ★★★

The sweetest fruit here—transformations of Sonny Boy Williamson's "One Way Out" and Muddy Waters's "Trouble No More"—comes from that fraternal 1971 Fillmore show, which also yields one long yawn, the thirty-five-minute "Mountain Jam." The three selections recorded after Duane Allman's death are of little appeal to blues fans.

(69:59/Reissue)

Seven Turns (Epic) ★★★

Singer Gregg Allman, guitarist Dickey Betts, and trap drummers Butch Trucks and Jai Jaimoe are tirelessly ambitious instigators who know how to fire up the old engines without being enslaved to recidivist tendencies. Three fresh faces have saddled up with the original members, yet everybody's playing modulates with assurance and without showiness.

(48:21/1990)

Shades of Two Worlds (Epic) ★★★♩

Gregg Allman's wear 'n' tear voice is forthright and his organ is unrepentant. Betts's guitar rips with hair-raising voltage. The drummers cannonade as though Fort Sumter were theirs for the taking. The new hands further acclimate themselves to their roles. If only their collective imagination rivaled their fervid spirit. The top displays of kith-and-kin sincerity are "Get on with Your Life" and an acoustic interpretation of Robert Johnson's "Come on in My Kitchen," the latter featuring Betts's slide guitar.

(52:38/1991)

Gene Ammons
Greatest Hits, Volume One: The Sixties (Prestige) ★★★

Gene "Jug" Ammons—son of boogie-woogie pianist Albert—
lived hard, so it's not surprising that a wealth of tortured
subtleties inform his weighty Chicago tenor saxophone sound.
Between prison stints, 1960–62, he cut these blues-steeped
jazz sides for Prestige, and best seller "Jungle Soul" remains
the sempiternal delight.   (39:57/Reissue)

Louis Armstrong
The Hot Fives & Hot Sevens, Volume Three (Columbia) ★★★★★

Perhaps Gabriel heralded better news than Satchmo, but no
trumpet-touting seraph (let alone mortal) had half the New
Orleans waif's musical genius. This collection of 1927 recordings by his famed outfits are by and large superb, his singing
and playing shot through with joy and pain all at once. Guitarist Lonnie Johnson, heard on three songs, propounds an innately keen sensitivity to turning blues into jazz.
                                                      (50:12/Reissue)

The Best of the Decca Years, Volume One: The ★★★★✦
   Composer (MCA/Decca)

Trombonist Kid Ory once said, "You can't go wrong with
Louis." This program of 1935–57 material emphasizes his
brilliance as songwriter *and* singer *and* trumpeter. Great
blues entertainment.   (47:02/1990)

The Assassins
Cut Me Loose (Seymour) ★★

Passably interesting blues/soul/rock group from Virginia features guitarist Jim Thackery and singer Tom Lepson on ten

songs. They want you to crank the volume and meet the neighbors. (46:52/1989)

Marcia Ball

Soulful Dress (Rounder) ★★★

Bayou-reared Marcia Ball, formerly a country singer, has parlayed her ardor for R&B into a successful career as the effervescent queen regnant of the Austin blues scene. On this 1983 album her high, understated voice reveals a strong and resilient woman who uses songs like Sugar Pie DeSanto's "Soulful Dress" and Smiley Lewis's "Jailbird" to serve notice that she can handle herself. Her piano playing asserts the same—but with less subtlety. Guitar hero Stevie Ray Vaughan joins Ball and her able band on the title track.

(35:38/Reissue)

Hot Tamale Baby (Rounder) ★★★

Never at a loss for picking good material, Ball electrifies out-of-the-way soul, R&B, and zydeco songs identified with such worthies as Laura Lee, Little Willie John, and Clifton Chenier. By understanding her source material so well, knowing what emotions went into the originals and what arrangements are most fitting, she stands tall as a torchbearer who enlivens the musical past for self-liberating purposes. Professor Longhair would love her piano stomping on this 1985 album. (32:01/Reissue)

Gatorhythms (Rounder) ★★★♩

In the late 1980s, Ball's voice and piano conveyed an even stronger sense of musical self-assurance than before. Just when you think the Louisiana romps peg her as a good-time mama, she delivers strong blows to the solar plexus with ballads that fulminate her independence and emotional constancy. Of the seven she wrote, "Find Another Fool" is the standout. (34:11/1989)

Marcia Ball/Lou Ann Barton/Angela Strehli
Dreams Come True (Antone's) ★★★★

This album, an exaltation of the Texas blues tradition, took longer to make than the Astrodome and reportedly involved more temper tantrums than you'd find in a week's worth of daytime soaps. Bolstered by the backing of keyboardist/guitarist/producer Dr. John and assorted Lone Star firebrands, each of the three Austin belles, singing either lead or harmony, concentrates emotion in her voice. Marcia Ball takes her wickedly understated approach, Lou Ann Barton tantalizes with lusty tones, and Angela Strehli's graceful phrasing exudes friendliness. The sagebrush trinity's rendition of Ike and Tina Turner's "A Fool in Love," in particular, delivers the shared joy of R&B harmonizing—bowie knives held to each other's throats or not. (40:22/1990)

Tom Ball and Kenny Sultan
Too Much Fun (Flying Fish) ★★

Country blues stylings performed by two Santa Barbara musicologists bent on supplying smile-inducing entertainment. Sultan is a guitar virtuoso, and Ball plays a spry harmonica and sings well. The problem is they demean the blues by disavowing its pain and sensuality. (38:03/1990)

Roosevelt "Booba" Barnes and the Playboys
The Heartbroken Man (Rooster Blues)

This studio set gives some idea of the roughhouse pleasure to be found in Barnes's Greenville, Mississippi, Playboy Club on most Friday and Saturday nights. Decidedly unconcerned with structure or niceties, Barnes throttles songs about forlorn romance and wayward libido with clamant singing, an unforgiving electric guitar, and a restless harmonica. His Delta sidemen, too, are all the better for their inartistic bent.

(54:41/1990)

Lou Ann Barton
Read My Lips (Antone's) ★★★

Lou Ann Barton, a sultry Texas trouper who's worked with early editions of the Fabulous Thunderbirds and Roomful of Blues, coils her voice through the songs here like a rattlesnake looking for a fight. At other times her drawl smacks of coquettish come-on. There's no faulting her song selection, a gaggle of little-known swamp and city blues. She also knows how to pick her men, notably guitarists Denny Freeman and Jimmie Vaughan. (50:05/1989)

• See also **Marcia Ball/Lou Ann Barton/Angela Strehli**

Count Basie
One O'Clock Jump (MCA/Decca) ★★★★

William "Count" Basie's first big band sides, in 1937, are fraught with exemplary Kansas City blues spirit, always more jubilation than sadness. Of seventeen selections, "Boogie Woogie" and "One O'Clock Jump" are the swinging riff-blues masterpieces, with trumpeter Buck Clayton soloing on both. The original analog recordings have some rough sections.

(49:26/Reissue)

Brand New Wagon (RCA/Bluebird) ★★✦

The Basie full band and small groups recorded by RCA in 1947 weren't on the order of his earlier and later outfits. Still, two Jimmy Rushing vocals and bushels of blue notes make this twenty-one-song compilation interesting. (59:32/1990)

The Complete Roulette Live Recordings of Count Basie ★★★★★ and His Orchestra (1959–1962) (Mosaic)

This wonderful eight-CD boxed set has 137 Miami, New York, or Sweden performances by Basie's creatively fecund orchestra, of which only twenty-eight have appeared before. Blues has a prominent role, from Joe Williams's urbane vocals to Basie's piano plinks and from corked-volcano section calls-and-responses to the down 'n' nasty solos of trombonist Quentin Jackson and other workhorses. The CDs are accompanied by an informative twenty-four-page booklet. (8:40:33/1991)

Fun Time (Pablo) ★★★

Blues, of course, is a great part of the pleasure generated by the Count and his court at the Montreaux Jazz Festival in July 1975. Adequate twelve-bar belter Bill Caffey helps out on two of the previously unissued songs. (49:00/1991)

Mostly Blues . . . and Some Others (Pablo) ★★★✦

A better-than-good septet date with the puckishly perceptive pianist featured with guitarist Joe Pass and tenor saxophonist Eddie "Lockjaw" Davis. Even near the end, here in June 1983, the seventy-nine-year–old Kid from Red Bank spread news of the blues with fresh splendor. (41:41/Reissue)

• See also **Teresa Brewer and Count Basie**

Joe Beard
No More Cherry Rose (King Snake) ★★✦

Decent singer/guitarist gets it off his chest while backed by pianist Lucky Peterson and other sessionmen affiliated with King Snake Records. His song "Heaven of My Own" invites repeated plays. (41:52/1990)

Sidney Bechet
The Victor Sessions: Master Takes 1932–43 ★★★★★
(RCA/Bluebird)

One of jazz's giants, Creole Sidney Bechet combined musical sophistication with pained blues feeling in the bells of his soprano saxophone and clarinet. Sixty tracks grouped on three discs cover an artistically fertile period in his career when he romped and swayed with the likes of Jelly Roll Morton, Earl Hines, and Red Allen. (2:59:35/1990)

Carey Bell
Mellow Down Easy (Blind Pig) ★★★✦

Trained in the advanced principles of raw-boned harp playing by giants Walter Horton and Little Walter, Bell is hardly a dilettante. He blows his chromatic instrument (and sings) with an outstanding balance of power and discipline on a program heavily tilted toward 1950s and 1960s Chicago blues. His Baltimore support band, Tough Luck, is too enamored of the style to be authoritative but manages to get by. (47:11/1991)

• See also **James Cotton/Junior Wells/Carey Bell/Billy Branch**

Jesse Belvin
The Blues Balladeer (Specialty) ★★★★

Crooner Jesse Belvin, a key figure on the 1950s West Coast R&B scene, had a special way with slow and medium ballads; his adoration of melody and lyrics was stirringly dramatic yet never bathetic. This collection of released tracks and long-lost demos and alternate takes does not have his signature piece, "Goodnight My Love," which was made for another label.

(66:12/Reissue)

Chuck Berry
The Chess Box (MCA/Chess) ★★★★★

Not *all* the Chuck Berry you'll ever need to hear, but close. Three pristine-sounding discs house seventy-one songs from the rock guitar pioneer's 1955–66 and 1969–73 reigns on Chess. Beginning with the country/R&B hybrid smash "Maybellene," Berry's twangy trademark licks and witty, literate lyrics have come to define rock's first generation, and the prototypical classics are all included: "Rock and Roll Music," "Sweet Little Sixteen," and, of course, "Johnny B. Goode." Berry's blues content is also showcased, notably his first B-side, "Wee Wee Hours," and mellow remakes of Charles Brown's "Merry Christmas Baby" and Guitar Slim's "Things that I Used to Do." The boxed set includes a thirty-six-page booklet. (B.D.) (3:21:56/1989)

Missing Berries: Rareties, Volume Three (MCA/Chess) ★★★

Casual Berry enthusiasts may be disappointed, but hard-core fans will be thrilled by these 1956–64 leftovers from the Chess vaults. "21 Blues," from the guitarist's 1957 rocking heyday, is a minor revelation, while the jumping "Big Ben Blues" and "The Little Girl from Central" date from Berry's 1964 comeback period. (B.D.) (31:08/1990)

Big Bad Smitty
Mean Disposition (Genes)   ★★★♪

St. Louis singer/guitarist John Howard Smith, aka Big Bad Smitty, born and bred in Mississippi, doesn't take kindly to decorum, and he messes up electrified Chicago-style originals and evergreens from the likes of Muddy Waters, Howlin' Wolf, and Albert King with a stentorian fervency. Underrated harmonica player Arthur Williams and a petulant rhythm section join Smitty in turning incivilities into dark truths that resound with the immediacy of those early 1950s rabble-rousers they admire so devotedly.   (49:10/1991)

Elvin Bishop
Big Fun (Alligator)   ★★★

When Bishop played guitar with Paul Butterfield in the 1960s he fancied himself a countrified hippie named Pig Boy Cranshaw. His sense of humor remains intact decades later, evidenced on a relaxed blues-oriented rock program shot through with a smart sort of bumpkin levity. He never could sing (it was Mickey Thomas on his 1970s smash "Fooled Around and Fell in Love"), but his guitar rides roughshod over those of many a better-known blues artist. (36:00/1988)

Don't Let the Bossman Get You Down! (Alligator)   ★♪

Let Bishop ruin your day instead. This time around his guitar flourishes are excessively self-conscious, his songs are an indifferent lot—weighted with forced aw-shucks humor—and his vocals are barnyard slop. The regeneration of Jimmy McCracklin's "Steppin' " is the saving grace.   (39:47/1991)

Billy Bizor
Blowing My Blues Away (Collectables)   ★★★⭒

This unjustly obscure Texas harmonica wizard recorded these unkempt sides shortly before his passing in April 1969. As illness scourged his body, Bizor gave a foreboding sense of resignation to his singing in "When I'm Dead"; his harmonica, in defiance, flaunts his love of life. He's accompanied by hand-picked Houston players, and Lightnin' Hopkins appears on two forgettable numbers.   (48:59/Reissue)

Blind Blake
Ragtime Guitar's Foremost Fingerpicker (Yazoo)   ★★★★⭒

The mysterious Blind Blake was a guitar marvel and good singer whose recording career lasted just a few years, 1926–32. These twenty-three titles on the Paramount label, most of them blessed with clear sound, are as much about his easeful control over picking technique as his emotional outlook. Blake's blues, ragtime, and unclassifiable tunes are interestingly written, with melodies, improvisations, and rhythms taking unexpected routes. The music always has a certain charm to it, even when lachrymose (e.g., "Chump Man Blues," "Rope Stretching Blues").   (66:30/Reissue)

Bobby Bland
The 3B Blues Boy—The Blues Years: 1952–1959   ★★★★★
(Ace import)

A superlative reissue, this twenty-five-track collection traces the highly influential vocalist's formative years from 1952–59 on the Duke label. With Clarence Hollimon providing searing guitar, Bland absolutely tears up "I Smell Trouble," "Further Up the Road," and "Loan a Helping Hand," while the last half-minute of the impassioned "Little Boy Blue" is an altar full of consecrated melodic pleas and screams. These belong to Bland's best blues and R&B sides, in breathtakingly crisp mono. (B.D./F.J.H.)   (66:34/1991)

Two Steps from the Blues (MCA)   ★★★★★

Originally issued in 1961, this sublime album has Bland merging precise and eloquent vocals with an exceptional musical imagination on "I Pity the Fool," "Don't Cry No More," and nine more enthralling songs. Sympathetic producer Joe Scott never lets the brass section hinder the upsurge of Bland's phrases.   (30:17/Reissue)

The Best of Bobby Bland (MCA)   ★★★★★

This reissue is a casually packaged collection of Bland's Duke hits of the late 1950s and early 1960s—to wit, twelve of the finest tunes anywhere. The potentate's strong, gospel-trained baritone expressively works over every word to achieve remarkable shadings of emotional intent. Joe Scott's sophisticated arrangements are often wonders in themselves, supporting either the vocalist's reflective or upbeat moods. Wayne Bennett, Mel Brown, and Clarence Hollimon fret the classic guitar parts.   (31:13/Reissue)

Touch of the Blues/Spotlighting the Man (Mobile Fidelity)   ★★★

On two 1969 recordings, Bland gives a gully-low panache to the soul and pop sentiments of Duke/Peacock sessions players (including horns, strings, and female warblers). It's a measure of his talent that he can sing mawkish songs and yet make them appealing.   (61:25/Reissue)

His California Album (MCA)

With his magnificently mature baritone, Bland tries his damnedest to extract meaning from clichéd lyric in mostly dismal songs. Meantime, Los Angeles studio hacks feign involvement on the 1973 session that introduced him to mainstream America. (38:11/Reissue)

Dreamer (MCA) ★★

Any pop reverie induced by Bobby Bland deserves better than lifeless CD sound and songs a minor league soul bluesman would snub. His musicians? The Sid Sharp strings and other 1974 studio clock-punchers. (36:18/Reissue)

Blues You Can Use (Malaco) ★★★★

Thirty years since his career kicked into gear, Bland still has a deep-felt aptitude for understanding the melancholic side of love. His interpretations of the intelligent verse supplied by Malaco's stable of songwriters wrench the heart. And that ultrarich voice is no less for barroom snorts having replaced Sunday morning shouts. Tasteful charts, too. (37:10/1987)

Portrait of the Blues (Malaco) ★★★★

Bland paints intoxicating blue moods with his tender, yearning vocal lines above steadily flowing rhythms. The material from the Malaco songwriting clerisy is musically and lyrically sound, although a few numbers have arrangements teetering on emotional falsehood. (44:52/1991)

• See also **B. B. King and Bobby Bland**

The Blasters

The Blasters Collection (Warner Brothers/Slash) ★★★

Uncompromising Los Angeles rockers, the Blasters knew that the relaxed but relentless "crazy beat" they advocated had its genesis in Chicago and Delta blues, R&B, rockabilly, and country and western. This post-mortem compilation proffers twenty songs (three previously unheard) that are lyrically specific and musically compelling, planted deep in that soil of American culture worked by Muddy Waters, Carl Perkins, and Roy Orbison. (64:19/1991)

Rory Block

Mama's Blues (Rounder) ★★✦

Block is a white country blues stylist whose singing and guitar playing teem with honest empathy for past masters such as Bessie Smith, Tommy Johnson, and Robert Johnson. As an interpretive singer, however, she conveys little sense of the pained emotionality of her mentors—her inflections are noticeably secondhand—and only when she handles unexceptional originals does her character begin to emerge. This recent outing, recorded for arcane reasons in Chatham, New York's Payne A.M.E. church, joins five earlier Block efforts, 1992's *Ain't I a Woman*, and a compilation disc—all fair to middling—in the Rounder catalog. (38:46/1991)

The Bluerunners

The Bluerunners (Island) ★★★

In the early 1990s these Louisianian hellriders who play guitar, bass, washboard, accordion, and drums stomp the dance floors of rock clubs around the country, but it's no surprise to learn the adventurous foursome caught dance fever growing up in zydeco halls. (40:32/1991)

Bluesiana Triangle

Bluesiana Triangle (Windham Hill)

An attractive studio jam. Gris-gris pianist Dr. John preaches the jazz gospel, the great jazz drummer Art Blakey superintends the inflections and accents of down-home blues, and Texas reed player David "Fathead" Newman carves a bluesy niche between R&B and jazz. Blakey's croaky vocal on Cousin Joe's "Life's a One-Way Ticket" takes on an ironic poignancy, as he severed his mortal coil just months after the session.

(43:03/1990)

Bluesiana II

Bluesiana II (Windham Hill)   ★★

Dr. John and Newman carry the Bluesiana banner, enlisting jazz trombone king Ray Anderson (whose royal power encompasses blues) and Living Colour drummer Will Calhoun (who likes his funk). Too many songs glissade beneath the weight of well-intentioned but long-winded solos, save for Anderson's marvelously gritty choruses.   (55:52/1991)

Deanna Bogart

Out to Get You (Blind Pig)   ★★

A favorite in the mid-Atlantic region, Bogart sings neatly, hammers the boogie piano keys with reasonable authority, and has fun recording her debut album. Unfortunately her concept of swing best suits an old Daffy Duck cartoon played too fast on the projector.   (39:26/1990)

Zuzu Bollin
Texas Bluesman (Antone's)   ★★★

Bollin was a T-Bone Walker–inspired singer/guitarist who contributed to the lustre of the postwar swinging blues language and who later worked with Jimmy Reed. After a long retirement from music he played around Austin in the late 1980s and made this agreeable big band blues session—failing health and personal demons notwithstanding. Reissue bonuses are two tracks from a 1988 Doug Sahm album he performed on.   (40:34/Reissue)

Juke Boy Bonner
The Texas Blues Troubadour (Collectables)   ★↙

Weldon "Juke Boy" Bonner was a spirited one-man band (vocals, guitar, harmonica), but only die-hard aficionados of Lone Star sounds need to hear these plodding late 1960s and 1970s recordings, nearly all unissued at the time for obvious reasons.   (42:24/Reissue)

James Booker
Classified (Rounder)   ★★★★

James Booker, a lifelong New Orleans resident, was someone special. His R&B piano playing was on a par with Professor Longhair's: more dazzling than liquid mercury, rock-ribbed, painterly, drenched in gospel and classical. His singing? Fibrillating melismas and glides hinting of Ray Charles, but all his own. Recording in late 1982, Booker is joined on five of the dozen tracks by bassist James Singleton and drummer John Vidacovich, with local legend Red Tyler lending tenor saxophone to four.   (37:30/Reissue)

Teresa Brewer and Count Basie
The Songs of Bessie Smith (Sony Music) ★★

Teresa Brewer's thin, pixyish voice isn't suited to hard-nosed Bessie Smith originals, though she is less the kewpie doll here than back in her pop early 1950s. The Basie bandmembers, playing good Thad Jones arrangements, are wise and careful collaborators on this 1983 release.   (39:01/Reissue)

Lonnie Brooks
Bayou Lightning (Alligator) ★★★★

On his first widely available album, guitarist/vocalist Brooks slams through the 1979 stylistic barriers separating Chicago blues, early rock 'n' roll, Louisiana swamp pop, funk, and Southern soul. For all the fulgurations of his fretted conductor, he maintains a degree of control and reserve that instantly stamps him a noble bluesman—as if anyone who'd encountered him in any Chicago bar during the past twenty years had any doubts. Casey Jones expertly mans the drums.
                                                          (41:43/Reissue)

Turn On the Night (Alligator) ★★★

Brooks's treatment of "I'll Take Care of You," a Brook Benton slow blues, involves understated vocals and guitar just this side of despair. That performance leaves an impression long after the studio houserocking has gone loudly into the night. First released in 1981.   (39:06/Reissue)

Wound Up Tight (Alligator) ★★★

The hook on this 1986 album is having Brooks and onetime idolator Johnny Winter knock heads on two rave-ups. Elsewhere it's business as usual. His working band chugs along

with the tireless determination of a Lafayette–Chicago locomotive, and the man at the throttle unleashes guitar solos that
merge West Side blues and rock 'n' roll.   (39:48/Reissue)

Live from Chicago: Bayou Lightning Strikes (Alligator)   ★★★

Alligator finally records him in a speakeasy—only a few thou-
sand gigs after signing him. With just a dream of flashy mind-
lessness, the Brooks outfit get Chicagoans dancing on their
chairs with repertoire staples and new songs. Keep a fire
extinguisher next to your stereo setup.   (46:07/1988)

Satisfaction Guaranteed (Alligator)   ★★♪

Well, yes, assuming tried-and-true blues rock with a pinch of
Tabasco is your passion. His son Ronnie now helps out on
guitar, and Koko Taylor has been enlisted to jolt the good
times into "If the Price Is Right."   (58:46/1991)

Big Bill Broonzy
The Young Big Bill Broonzy (Yazoo)   ★★★★

This Chicago prewar great's rapid-fire single-string guitar
style was very advanced for its time, and these 1928–35
tracks, dubbed from 78s, spotlight his dazzling instrumental
skill and sturdy vocals. (B.D.)   (39:41/Reissue)

Do That Guitar Rag (1928–1935) (Yazoo)   ★★★★

A first-generation bluesman, Broonzy's career stretched from
the earliest blues recordings to the electric era of Muddy
Waters and Howlin' Wolf. His rich tenor voice and melodic
acoustic guitar were consistent throughout, and this second
Yazoo collection of his early material is highly recommended.
(J.T.)   (40:35/Reissue)

Good Time Tonight (Columbia/Legacy) ★★★★

Broonzy's unflagging gift for felicitous storytelling—purveyed by a sure and steady voice and facile guitar technique—made him one of the notable talents in his adopted home of Chicago throughout the period covered by this twenty-song compilation, 1930–40. These ensemble performances, most lost till now, benefit supremely from Columbia's state-of-the-art methods of sound restoration. Note: This set is a fine companion volume to the Yazoo compilations, as most of the material postdates those discs. (57:18/1990)

Big Bill Broonzy (1934–1947) (Story of Blues) ★★★

More Big Bill blues, this time with pianist Memphis Slim among his accompanists. Only two songs overlap with the Columbia set, and many of the eighteen selections are interesting. Not-so-pleasing sound quality. (53:30/Reissue)

Big Bill Broonzy Sings Folk Songs (Smithsonian/Folkways) ★★★★

An icon of American folk music to reverent Europeans, Broonzy proves himself in his 1956 performances to be a vibrant blues gentleman, not a stylized stick figure in his dotage. The folk-pop numbers (say, "Bill Bailey" and "Glory of Love") may have been topical concessions to admirers, but his electrifying guitar playing and singing on the three songs given over to woman-trouble serve only himself and his Maker. (34:41/Reissue)

Big Bill Broonzy and Washboard Sam

Big Bill Broonzy and Washboard Sam (MCA/Chess) ★★★♪

Washboard Sam (Robert Brown) and Bill Broonzy's 1953 Chicago sides are forceful reminders that voice and rhythm are the very substance of the blues. Each of the team's adequate lead singing is inextricably tied to Sam's rubboard scraping, Big Crawford's upright bass pulse, and modern guitar from Broonzy and Lee Cooper (who at times sounds like Chuck Berry). (34:26/1987)

Charles Brown
Driftin' Blues (DCC) ★★✦

Brown is the paragon of smooth West Coast piano blues, but this 1963 small combo set crowned him King of Schmaltz. The singer's phrasing is snail-pace laborious and his organ playing is funereal. Moreover, he slobbers over the lovey-dovey lyric of banal pop tunes to the point of devastating self-parody. Still, his extreme involvement with good songs—his old hit "Driftin' Blues" and Buddy Johnson's "Since I Fell for You"—is as haunting as a sad dream about a long lost love that's hard to shake. (42:27/Reissue)

One More for the Road (Alligator) ★★★★

The low-key blues-streaked balladry of Charles Brown found favor among black listeners in the late 1940s and early 1950s, then lost its commercial footing when shoved aside by a more declarative, tougher R&B. This 1986 album, reissued three years later with added tracks and improved sound, evidences little if any change in his quiet, wistful music over the decades. Backed by four upscale saloon players, Brown gives poignant readings of songs identified with Frank Sinatra, Bobby Bland, Billy Eckstine, and himself, gliding his baritone from note to note so sincerely and so seductively. (44:22/Reissue)

All My Life (Rounder) ★★★★

To immensely pleasing end, the dapper gent on the piano bench revisits treasures from the golden R&B past (e.g., Amos Milburn's "Bad Bad Whiskey") and scrutinizes new compositions. A few songs go up-tempo, giving necessary variety to the finger-snapping set; and the newly popular friend of Bonnie Raitt is put at ease by guest vocalists Dr. John and Ruth Brown on a number apiece, and by congenial musicians such as Charles Brown's favorite guitarist, Danny Caron, and ex–Ray Charles saxophonist Clifford Solomon.   (52:28/1990)

Clarence "Gatemouth" Brown
The Original Peacock Recordings (Rounder) ★★★★

This grouping of twelve tunes released on Don Robey's label in the 1950s covers the jump blues turf of Brown's Great Plains–wide musical vision, which also takes in Cajun and Anglo-American country musics. His driving T-Bone Walker–type guitar ignites jazz sparks in the prototypical shuffle "Okie Dokie Stomp" and slows down to shed real tears during "Sad Hour." Throughout the disc his singing is earnest but unexceptional, while his fiddle has the slippery and spry moves of a horned toad in "Just Before Dawn" and his harmonica adds black pepper to "Gate's Salty Blues."   (32:43/Reissue)

Pressure Cooker (Alligator) ★★★

Nine good tracks pulled from several French albums recorded in the early 1970s, when Brown and other stalwarts from the early R&B/jazz campaigns had to travel to Europe for proper respect. The highlight is Brown and legendary pianist Jay McShann doing the slow boil in "Deep Deep Water."

(41:11/Reissue)

Texas Swing (Rounder)   ★★★✦

Here are good-sized portions of Brown's Rounder albums *Alright Again!* (1982) and *One More Mile* (1983). The Lone Star State sage scourges lyrics with conviction, and he carves his intelligent solos on guitar and fiddle with the effortless surety of a master woodcutter. He's the show as two different horn sections and rhythm teams codify the ostensibly special Texas grooves with a stilted propriety.   (66:40/1987)

Real Life (Rounder)   ★★★★

Brown knows exactly what he likes, and his telling his musicians that "We finally got us a thing going" during this 1985 Fort Worth performance is not to be taken lightly. The bandleader dips and thrusts his jazzy, disciplined guitar phrases through everything from Duke Ellington to W. C. Handy to Percy Mayfield, and his vocals and violin pizzicato are every bit as intelligent and rousing. On one of those rare live albums free of longueur and superfluity, saxophonist Dennis Taylor and the rest of the alert band deserve a tip of his ten-gallon hat.   (42:55/Reissue)

Standing My Ground (Alligator)   ★★★★

Brown continues his sui generis way with blues and other American musics. Relying on a top-flight horn section for chatoyance, he blends his fervency and lyricism into some of the most fetching songs he's recorded in his Rounder years, from "Got My Mojo Working" to "Never Unpack Your Suitcase." And for someone who hates easy categorization, the eccentric Texan has given a few of his songs revealing titles: "Cool Jazz" and "Louisiana Zydeco."   (37:00/1989)

No Looking Back (Alligator) ★★★

Far from Brown's own standards, this overproduced effort has flashes of the old "Gate," but too much is buried under heavy horn choruses. Brown's fame is based on his distinctive vocals and incisive guitar playing; neither is heard enough here. (J.T.)   (41:34/1992)

James Brown
20 All-Time Greatest Hits! (Polydor) ★★★★

Twenty of the funk and rhythm dynamo's points of light hark back to his upbringing in the poor, deep rural South for their poignant emotional framework. "Night Train," in particular, belongs in sound and feeling to postwar jump grooves, its explosive sexuality every bit equal to that of Jimmy Forrest's 1952 classic. More sizzle: Polydor's aptly titled two-CD *Messin' with the Blues* and the ultimate bacchanal, *Live at the Apollo: October 24, 1962.*   (70:26/1991)

Kevin Brown
Rust (Hannibal) ★↘

Corroded pop-blues by an Englishman who plays guitar better than he sings or writes songs. The guest appearance of Joe Louis Walker on Brown's half-baked salute to the San Francisco guitarist, "Hey Joe Louis," is mildly interesting. Mildly. (39:05/1990)

Nappy Brown
Don't Be Angry (Savoy Jazz) ★★↘

Napoleon "Nappy" Brown's signature is the title song, an undeniably catchy R&B hit in 1955 that had his vocal hijinks challenged by the tenor saxophone squalls of Sam "'The Man"

Taylor. Nineteen more songs from his Savoy 1950s have less
value as entertainment.   (52:30/Reissue)

Tore Up (Alligator)   ★★↗

In 1984, Brown surfaced after many years of gospel service
and hooked up with Atlanta's Heartfixers, a blues rock band
led by guitarist Tinsley Ellis. He's generally in strong voice,
managing to find freshness in Ray Charles's "Losing Hand"
and making the most of Bob Dylan and Gregg Allman songs
someone unwisely threw his way.   (38:00/Reissue)

Something Gonna Jump Out the Bushes (Black Top)   ★★★

Brown's voice strains at times. Yet the Black Top folks have
dealt him good material (from Percy Mayfield, Earl King, etc.)
and musical settings highly favorable to the rise of his robust
R&B spirit. Pay attention to guitarists Anson Funderburgh,
Ronnie Earl, and Eugene Ross, who know how to put their
shoulders to the wheel. Indulge the tall fellow his occasional
PG-13 naughtiness.   (40:59/1987)

Apples & Lemons (Ichiban)   ★

The tall fellow visits Atlanta and tosses off threadbare originals amid anonymous-sounding local bluesmen. One sour
mess, as was a second Ichiban issue, *Aw! Shucks*, two years
later.   (37:05/1989)

Ruth Brown
Miss Rhythm (Greatest Hits & More) (Atlantic)   ★★★★★

This exceptional two-CD set has forty songs recorded between 1949 and 1960 by a major R&B star: twenty-four hits,
twelve obscurities, four previously unreleased tracks. Even at

age twenty-two, when Brown's first hit, "Teardrops from My Eyes," brought her national prominence, she was an accomplished singer with a simon-pure feel for incipient rock 'n' roll. As the chronologically displayed material bears out, her voice becomes weightier and the "tear" at the end of lines more supercharged with accumulated life experience. Splitting hairs, maybe, but the jazz-oriented production of Atlantic's cofounder Herb Abramson on the earlier numbers seems to suit that semisophisticated voice even better than the R&B settings shaped years later by Jerry Wexler. Sessions heroes include pianist Harry Van Walls and guitarist Mickey Baker.
(1:49:31/1989)

Help a Good Girl Go Bad (DCC) ★★★

The girl, ahem, woman is in her element swinging and swaying alongside a studio big band and strings on this commercial 1964 session. The blues feeling she carries around envelops Nellie Lutcher's "Hurry On Down" and "He's a Real Gone Guy." Nice. (35:25/Reissue)

Have a Good Time (Fantasy) ★★★★

More than what's suggested by the title. Her voice agile and powerful, Miss Brown holds a late 1980s hotel club audience in fear of their lives through three of her Atlantic classics and several standards. Bobby Forrester's Hammond organ and Charles Williams's alto saxophone heighten the tension and further deepen her sense of selfhood. (52:44/1988)

Blues on Broadway (Fantasy) ★★↗

One of the stars of *Black and Blue,* the middle-aged singer encores stage favorites and standards. Fair enough, but her big voice has, well, a certain staginess, and her first-call accompanists play as if smug about receiving union scale.
(59:00/1989)

Fine and Mellow (Fantasy) ★★★★

Allegiant to jazz shading and accenting, Miss Brown offers a great number of blues revelations while essaying selections from the repertoires of Dinah Washington, Louis Jordan, Ray Charles, Jackie Wilson, and others. Sideman Rodney Jones is a marvelously understated blues guitarist.   (46:23/1991)

Ray Bryant
All Mine . . . and Yours (EmArcy) ★★★♪

Jazz pianist Ray Bryant has an uncanny feel for the happiness explicit in gospel and implicit in blues, as shown on this 1989 recording date with bassist Rufus Reid and drummer Winard Harper.   (43:46/1991)

Roy Buchanan
When a Guitar Plays the Blues (Alligator) ★★♪

In Buchanan's case, blues or not, wallpaper peels and mountains move. On this 1985 album the former rockabilly guitarist whose technique earned him wide acclaim in the early 1970s agitates the program with a virtuosity that defines the parameters of sonic extremism. Buchanan and Chicagoans Otis Clay and Gloria Hardiman provide a few vocals, the former ineptly and the latter two adequately.   (42:19/Reissue)

Dancing on the Edge (Alligator) ★★♪

On a 1986 album Buchanan takes a respite from his trebly fanfaronade and finds a balance between heartache and tenderness in "Baby, Baby, Baby" alongside honky-tonk singer Delbert McClinton.   (38:52/Reissue)

Hot Wires (Alligator)　★★★

The late guitarist's twelfth and last recording has stretches when he slows his attack down, thinks methodically, and takes heed of form and direction; at such times his storytelling is immensely more concise than usual. To hell with believable stories, though; the instrumental "High Wire" is wilder and more fantastic than a whirling dervish juggling knives on a trampoline.　(44:41/1987)

Buckwheat Zydeco

Waitin' for My Ya Ya (Rounder)　★★

Creole Southern soul/zydeco exponent Stanley "Buckwheat" Dural is self-deluded about his ascension to Clifton Chenier's throne, but the former Chenier organist sure knows what keys to press on his accordion during this 1985 session. His Ils Sont Partis swamp band, unfortunately, appears ill at ease with the faraway Boston studio.　(39:09/Reissue)

On a Night Like This (Island)　★★

On his initial crossover gambit, the leader's squeezebox launches riffs while washboard, rhythm guitar, bass, and drums thunder dance grooves with the subtlety of a drunken rhino tripping the light fantastic. Blame the big record company for the mix.　(34:43/1987)

Taking It Home (Island)　★★

The Ils Sont Paris Band drifts so far from Louisiana musically that at one point Dural has to recite the names of bayou towns for acclimation's sake. Eric Clapton, never mistaken for a bayou native, plays on the Derek and the Dominoes tune "Why Does Love Have to Be So Sad?"　(36:44/1988)

Where There's Smoke There's Fire (Island) ★★★★

Los Lobos guitarist (and zydeco fan) David Hidalgo signs on as producer and helps create a fun, intelligent "Creole blues" album. Dancing is encouraged: "What You Gonna Do?" is urged along by Dural's playful vocals and accordion; the traditional stomp "Pour Tout Quelque'un" has Wilbert Willis's corrugated washboard at the eye of its storm; and a heartfelt version of the Rolling Stones' "Beast of Burden" inspires close swaying. Eight more too; most smoke *and* fire. (41:36/1990)

On Track (Charisma) ★★★↓

A commercial entity, Dural takes over as producer for the first time in his long recording career. He chooses to treat songs he cares deeply for, such as Solomon Burke's "Cry to Me" and Texas work song "Midnight Special," and he never compromises his blues, soul, and traditional French roots for accessibility. The eight-minute version of "Hey Joe" is a mistake, though, fizzling when band guitarists Melvin Veazie, Joseph Chavis, and Mike Melchione take turns futilely emulating Jimi Hendrix. (43:56/1992)

Bumble Bee Slim
Bumble Bee Slim (1931–1937) (Story of Blues) ★★↓

Amos "Bumble Bee Slim" Easton, a peripatetic Georgian, was one of the most popular recording artists in Depression-era Chicago. His singing voice suggests Leroy Carr's in its tone and polite delivery but doesn't convey a similar authority. His guitar playing barely suffices. The eighteen songs here are interesting primarily for their lyrics on steady rolling mamas, floods, the hobo life, etc. (56:48/Reissue)

R. L. Burnside and the Sound Machine
Bad Luck City (Fat Possum) ★★

Raw contemporary Mississippi blues from this electric family-based unit, with far too many covers of the bandstand variety (including an odious "Outskirts of Town"). Guitarist Burnside's lusty vocals are generally convincing, though. (B.D.)
(59:02/1991)

Kenny Burrell
Midnight Blue (Blue Note) ★★★★

On a 1963 Blue Note session jazz guitarist Burrell, a precocious thirty-two-year-old, plays a world of nonclichéd blues figures that flow with rhythmic grace. The wonderfully colorful moods and varied tempi are intensified by low-flame passion from Stanley Turrentine on tenor saxophone, Major Holley on upright bass, and two percussionists. (44:04/Reissue)

Kenny Burrell and the Jazz Guitar Band
Pieces of Blue and the Blues (Blue Note) ★★★★

In a 1986 club appearance the middle-aged electric-guitar wizard taps personal reservoirs of blue feeling alongside talented guitar acolytes Bobby Broom and Rodney Jones, both of whom apply a deep-seated honesty to blues and bop.
(46:09/1988)

George "Wild Child" Butler
Keep On Doing What You're Doing (Black Magic) ★★★

George "Wild Child" Butler is an electrifying harmonica player who was long a staple of the Chicago blues scene. On this rerelease of a 1969 Mercury album he leads a tight band featuring guitarist Mighty Joe Young and pianist Lafayette Leake through some sizzling electric boogie and straight-ahead blues. (J.T.)   (41:54/1991)

These Mean Old Blues (Bullseye Blues)   ★★★✦

Based in southern Ontario, Butler deserves to be recognized as one of the most satisfying artists working. On a recent Chicago-style ensemble date in London he sings and plays harp with the pleasing kind of authority and scampish wit that suggests a natural raconteur. His personality would be even more distinct without the occasional Howlin' Wolf and Muddy Waters mimicries.   (45:10/1992)

Henry Butler
Blues & More, Volume One (Windham Hill Jazz)   ★★★

Building on the blues, New Orleans pianist Butler brings concentration, technical ease, sincerity, and an unfailing sense of composition to the eleven songs on his initial solo outing. On his game, his left hand hammers stride or barrel-house figures while his right explores the melodic byways of R&B, pop, or jazz. Good enough, but he needs to curb his mawkish tendencies and rein in his showy eclecticism. As a singer he's not a threat to any modestly gifted gospel choir member.   (59:09/1992)

Paul Butterfield
East-West (Elektra)   ★★★★

Wielding a harmonica honed under the supervision of South Side masters, Paul Butterfield popularized electric Chicago blues in the mid 1960s with a seemingly effortless ability to capture the spirit of Little Walter and Muddy Waters without copying their exact wording. The Butterfield Blues Band's second album, *East-West* (1966), is less hidebound stylistically than their eponymous first album and uses modern jazz and Indian music forms that encourage extended improvisations by the harmonica traditionalist and his superb blues rock guitarists Mike Bloomfield and Elvin Bishop. The thirteen-minute title track is the showpiece.   (44:57/Reissue)

Chris Cain
Cuttin' Loose (Blind Pig)   ★★↗

Stirred by two horns and a rhythm section, the San Francisco Bay Area club favorite lets fly with exciting guitar licks suggestive of B. B.'s and Albert King's. His well-plotted singing style, groomed band, and constricted arrangements contradict the claim of the title. Cain wrote all thirteen songs, none an eye-opener.   (45:43/1990)

J. J. Cale
Travel-Log (Silvertone)   ★★★★

Cale's ninth album is in keeping stylistically with all the previous ones: low-boil blues-based rock. The easygoing Tulsa native counterpoints his phlegmatic vocals with his stimulating guitar picking in some of his most homespun, charming songs ever. Bassist Tim Drummond and drummer Jim Keltner conjure the fetching grooves.   (42:50/1990)

John Campbell
One Believer (Elektra)   ★↗

A Shreveport native living in New York, John Campbell has spent too long staring at the skulls on his bookshelves. His sacred-versus-profane imagery is heavy-handed, and his tormented, doomsday voice is about as convincingly malevolent as Igor's in the grade-Z horror film *Jesse James Meets Frankenstein's Daughter.* His electric guitar casts a slightly more credible evil eye. (50:21/1991)

Canned Heat
Reheated (Chameleon) ★★★✦

Surprise. Canned Heat of the 1990s is more than a ghost band rocking out of the tie-dye past for (maybe) one more shot at the boogie big time. Old hands Fita de la Parra and Larry Taylor, on drums and bass fiddle respectively, clearly savor exploring a range of moods, sonorities, and rhythms on a thoughtful program of originals and covers. Singer James Thornbury isn't the front man the late Al Wilson and Bob Hite were, but Junior Watson on lead guitar evidences considerable facility and a quiet conviction that constantly impresses. (45:24/1990)

Canned Heat and John Lee Hooker
Hooker 'n' Heat (EMI) ★★★

Hooker permanently secured his reputation as the ultimate Boogie Man with this 1970 collaboration with Canned Heat on Liberty, although most of the best moments on this two-disc reissue take place when Hooker is alone or backed only by Alan Wilson's sensitive second guitar or piano. Canned Heat joins in at full strength with Hooker for the last five cuts, forgoing subtlety to produce some pretty decent rock-oriented blues. (B.D.) (86:34/Reissue)

Hooker 'n' Heat (Rhino) ★

Don't be misled. This Venice, California, concert recording was done a number of years after the similarly named album came out on Liberty. Hooker boogied all over that one, but here the elder statesman appears on just three of the ten numbers—not that he missed anything. Bob Hite, the only original bandmember present, died before the album hit the stores in 1981. (53:26/Reissue)

Captain Beefheart and the Magic Band
The Spotlight Kid/Clear Spot (Reprise) ★★★★

Unconventional to the nth power, Captain Beefheart (Don Van Vliet) constructed a gnostic blues world where Howlin' Wolf curls Salvador Dali's moustache and Little Walter espouses dadaism. Of the two early-1970s albums juxtaposed here, *The Spotlight Kid* most interestingly turns twelve-bar music on its head with Beefheart's multi-octave son-of-Wolf voice, his pixilated lyrics, his marvelous Chicago-style harp, and his specially instructed Magic Band's asymmetrical rhythms. Not to say the second heartfelt blues travesty, *Clear Spot*, scrimps on the quirky "low yo yo" either. (73:18/Reissue)

Chubby Carrier and the Bayou Swamp Band
Boogie Woogie Zydeco (Flying Fish) ★★★

High-energy zydeco with a contemporary rock/soul edge from this young Louisiana aggregation. Carrier's agreeable vocals and melodic accordion ride over an aggressive rhythm section and David LeJeune's rapid-fire lead guitar. (B.D.) (54:20/1991)

Clarence Carter
Between a Rock and a Hard Place (Ichiban) ★★

In recent years ladies' man Clarence Carter has evolved a taste for ironic self-pity in light of women's saying no to his machismo. Steer clear of his Ichiban funky blues and hope to

high heaven Atlantic reissues the singer's excellent late 1960s
Southern soul work.   (40:27/1990)

John Cephas and Phil Wiggins
Dog Days of August (Flying Fish)   ★★★✦

At a time when style counts more than meaning, singer/gui-
tarist Cephas and singer/harpist Wiggins, a team since the
mid 1970s, are a rarity. They love the folk blues of the Delta
and the low hills of the Piedmont region, and their renditions
of traditional tunes are at once emotional and artistically authoritative. Cephas is the better singer. Warm and inviting
first takes from 1986.   (40:54/Reissue)

Guitar Man (Flying Fish)   ★★★★✦

Cephas is even more wondrous here than on the Washingto-
nian's earlier album. Through voice and guitar he commandingly brings the songs of Blind Blake, Furry Lewis, and Blind
Boy Fuller into the present. Wiggins turns in a winning, work-
manly performance. Their music is sunshine flashing off wet
mountain foliage at the break of dawn.   (52:47/1989)

Ray Charles
The Birth of Soul (Atlantic)   ★★★★★

When aficionados call Ray Charles "the Genius," it's his
1952–59 Atlantic sides—the ones that altered the R&B idiom
forever—they're referring to. Charles's earthshaking blend of
gospel feeling and secular lyrics, typified by his mid-1950s
smashes "I Got a Woman" and "Hallelujah I Love Her So,"
jolted the R&B world. This three-disc set contains nearly all
of his R&B output on Atlantic (fifty-three tracks), and much
of the third disc from 1958–59 is in clean stereo (including
"What'd I Say"). No artist can lay more convincing claim to

inventing soul music than Ray Charles, and this box eloquently defines the genre. (B.D.)   (2:31:12/1991)

Boozoo Chavis
The Lake Charles Atomic Bomb (Rounder)   ★★★✦

Fourteen primitive sides made by zydeco cofounder Wilson
"Boozoo" Chavis some time between 1955 and 1960 for Gold-
band, the shoestring-budget Louisiana record company responsible for irking him into retirement for nearly three
decades. The accordionist's zydeco grill sauce consists of
cayenne pepper, Creole mustard, and country and western
and blues seasonings.   (32:55/1990)

Zydeco Trail Ride (Maison de Soul)   ★★★★

Saddle up and accompany Chavis and friends on a *joie de
zydeco* day trip complete with horse-drawn food and bever-
age wagons. The procession leader's diatonic accordion in-
tones the melodies with an insistent, sober-minded spirit,
while his breakdown boys blithely lay down shuffle rhythms.
Contained herein is the Creole's fourth album plus nine tracks
from two other late 1980s Maison de Soul records and an
obscurity titled "Went to New Orleans."   (65:11/1990)

Boozoo Chavis (Elektra Nonesuch)   ★★

The zydeco giant, now in his sixties, and his swamp syncopa-
tors don't take a shine to the New Orleans recording studio
hired out by the major record company from faraway climes.
They strain a bit, apparently cautious of the pressure to stay
in tune and otherwise measure up to musical standards not
enforced out Mamou way.   (43:53/1991)

Jeannie and Jimmy Cheatham
Sweet Baby Blues (Concord) ★★★★

Jeannie's full-throated vocals and rousing barrelhouse piano, along with Jimmy's charts providing just the right voicing, give Cheathams and Co. a big band blues sound as fat and sassy as the legendary bands of Jay McShann and Count Basie. This is their first album, released in 1985. (J.T.)

(41:43/Reissue)

Homeward Bound (Concord) ★★★✦

The Cheathams, that swinging couple from California, continue to construct their jazz style on the secure foundation of the blues. Jeannie sings and plays piano authoritatively, Jimmy growls way down low on his bass trombone, and their sextet, augmented by saxophonist/singer Eddie "Cleanhead" Vinson, has serious fun with originals and standards recorded in early 1987. (47:31/Reissue)

Basket Full of Blues (Concord) ★★★★

This sixth outing for the Cheathams is a departure from their earlier efforts, displaying a more jazzy, introspective mood. Jeannie's expressive vocals are just as well suited to the softer, slower material, and Count Basie alumnus Frank Wess lays down some wonderful blues passages on flute. The highlight may be the sequel to their classic "Meet Me With Your Black Drawers On." Ultimately this album blurs the lines between jazz and blues until they no longer exist, creating an evocative, melodious whole. (J.T.) (66:51/1992)

C. J. Chenier
Hot Rod (Slash) ★★★

Number one zydeco son C. J. Chenier and the Red Hot Louisiana Band, anchored by three holdovers from Clifton's reign,
speak the cypress R&B language with requisite excitability
and determined self-confidence. C. J.'s vocals start to take on
some of the rascally charm of his father's over an entertaining
program highlighted by the heir's blues tune that bears the
affectionate title "You're Still the King to Me." (45:20/1990)

Clifton Chenier
Louisiana Blues and Zydeco (Arhoolie) ★★★★

Opening with a series of waltzes and two-steps with brother
Cleveland's clattering rubboard to the fore, this collection of
1964–67 efforts by the inventor of zydeco soon shifts to a
bluesier feel. The program includes the rocking instrumental
"Hot Rod" and several tracks with only percussion backing
that emphasize Clifton's full-bodied accordion. (B.D.)
(64:40/Reissue)

Bon Ton Roulet (Arhoolie) ★★★★

Generous twenty-one-track sampling (three previously unissued) of Chenier's early tenure on Arhoolie, mostly centering
on the accordionist's mid–1960s output. He was still a regional
sensation at this point, and these unassuming tracks contain
few commercial concessions—this is authentic zydeco, steamy
and boisterous. (B.D.) (63:00/Reissue)

60 Minutes with the King of Zydeco (Arhoolie) ★★★★

Fifteen choice selections from Chenier's 1960s Arhoolie recordings, including "Blake Snake Blues," "Louisiana Blues,"

and "I'm a Hog for You." Pepper in his shoe, indeed. Dance-floor pauses for breath bring it up to the hour promised.
(58:03/Reissue)

Live at St. Mark's (Arhoolie)   ★★★

Cut live at a jumping Creole function in 1971, this is an atmospheric and accurate representation of the zydeco accordion pioneer in action, though there's little to make it stand out from Arhoolie's many other offerings except a preponderance of longer dance workouts and between-songs patter. (B.D.)
(60:57/Reissue)

The King of Zydeco Live at Montreux (Arhoolie)   ★★★♪

Previously issued on both Tomato and Arhoolie (in shorter form on the latter). Chenier turns the 1975 Montreux Jazz Festival into a down-home swampfest with his scorching accordion and tight combo. Many of the songs are staples of his repertoire, but there's a lot of energy throughout. (B.D.)
(68:08/Reissue)

Bogalusa Boogie (Arhoolie)   ★★★★

Zydeco pioneer Chenier fronted a killer band when this set was cut in 1975, including brother Cleveland on rubboard and John Hart on saxophone, and it shows why he can never be replaced as the idiom's monarch. Chenier blows harp on two selections in addition to wailing on accordion, and the disc is drenched in bayou funk, with lyrics evenly divided between French and English. (B.D./F.J.H.)
(50:22/Reissue)

I'm Here! (Alligator)   ★★★♪

The late zydeco man always remains present in the mind of anyone touched by the Fais-Do-Do sounds emanating from

Louisiana's French Triangle. At a 1982 record date Chenier and his sweaty outfit fill an imaginary dance floor. Note how his *blues* accordion has the harmonic density of the entire Glenn Miller Orchestra on "In the Mood."   (34:59/Reissue)

Eric Clapton
24 Nights (Reprise)   ★★

Clapton's 1990 and 1991 Royal Albert Hall concerts, filling these two discs, featured several blues numbers. Unfortunately the rock icon's singing and guitar playing suggests he was in dire need of bed rest, and as stage focal point he brags down the wide-awake work of Buddy Guy, Robert Cray, Johnnie Johnson, Jerry Portnoy, and Jimmie Vaughan.

                                                      (1:45:23/1991)

William Clarke
Blowin' Like Hell (Alligator)   ★★★♪

Los Angeleno Clarke has minuscule devils dancing on the metal reeds inside his chromatic harp. One of the instrument's consummate players, Clarke is concerned with the blues' intrinsic merit more than its surface detail, and he almost never showboats. Favoring jazzy West Coast rhythms, he employs a fine guitarist named Alex Schultz and a rhythm section that has imagination and taste to go along with technique. It should be noted that Clarke is an acceptable songwriter and an undistinguished singer.   (48:18/1990)

Serious Intentions (Alligator)   ★★★★

As the adopted son of the late harp master George "Harmonica" Smith, Clarke has familial instinct for conveying pain and loss through his visceral cadences. The songs, built on swing or postwar Delta rhythms, breathe a certain vitality as he and his friends perform attractive originals and versions of James Oden's "Soon Forgotten" and Nat Adderley's "The Work Song." His improving vocals are fillers while we await the harp commentaries. (49:01/1992)

Otis Clay
Soul Man: Live in Japan (Rounder) ★★

Clay has been singing soul music intertwined with gritty blues since 1965, when he crossed over from the gospel world, and his passion hasn't abated over the years. Yet the Chicagoan's 1983 performance, with his voice forcing its emotion and his ersatz Otis Redding, O. V. Wright, and Al Green moves, is of interest to admirers only. Clay's studio-recorded 1992 release *I'll Treat You* (Bullseye Blues CD) is better, though it can't touch his 1970s *I Can't Take It* LP on the Hi label, or his recent gospel sides. (65:15/Reissue)

Eddy Clearwater
A Real Good Time—Live! (Rooster Blues) ★★★★

Eddy Clearwater (Eddy Harrington) shakes the foundations of Midwest bars with riotous vocals and combative electric-guitar playing that evoke Chuck Berry, Magic Sam, and Jimmy Reed. The Mississippi native's high spirits have yet to flag almost forty years after he first began club campaigning. His ruffian band also raises Cain on a more than reliable program of originals and the occasional cover. (63:08/1990)

Help Yourself (Blind Pig) ★★★★

A man of conspicuous generosity, Clearwater wrestles feeling from every blue note that belongs to his compositions and his cover songs (e.g., Willie Mahon's "Poison Ivy"). His ardor for the primitive brazenness of rock 'n' roll brings the material up to contemporary speed. Harmonica player Carey Bell is among Clearwater's keening helpmates. (42:40/1992)

Jimmy Coe
After Hours Joint (Delmark) ★★⌐

Obscure jazz/R&B saxophonist Jimmy Coe replaced Charlie Parker in Jay McShann's 1942 band, then eleven years later cut these feature sides for the United Label. Unlike many tenor players of the time, he kept his cool and didn't blast into the stratosphere. (38:12/Reissue)

Nat King Cole Trio
Jumpin' at Capitol (Rhino) ★★★★

Cole's sophisticated vocals and brilliant jazz-laced piano plus the daring, innovative lead guitar of Oscar Moore deeply influenced the postwar West Coast club blues movement. This sparkling 1942–50 assortment of the pianist's precrooning trio days on Capitol spotlights some of his best and most popular material, including "Straighten Up and Fly Right" and "Route 66." (B.D.) (46:29/1990)

Gary B. B. Coleman
Dancin' My Blues Away (Ichiban) ★★

Guitarist Coleman parrots the single-string lines of his hero B. B. King as well as anyone. A great compliment, of sorts. Alas, "functional" is too kind a word for his singing, and his songwriting is as fresh as toast left two weeks on the counter. (41:09/1989)

Albert Collins

Truckin' with Albert Collins (MCA) ★★★★⁴

Collins, in his early thirties, was already a guitarist of considerable imagination and finesse when he recorded these dozen songs for a couple of Houston labels in 1962–63. "Frosty," "Sno-Cone," and "Don't Lose Your Cool" belong to the blues-instrumentals hall of fame, with two or three of the others perennially on the ballot. The *cool* breeze of his unusually pitched tones is a perfect foil to the warm feel of the three horns, organ, bass, and drums. Collins's one vocal, probably his first on tape, seconds the misery of his guitar entreaties in "Dyin' Flu," another classic. (32:52/Reissue)

The Complete Imperial Recordings (EMI) ★★★⁴

Houston's "Master of the Telecaster" made three albums for Imperial circa 1969–70, and all thirty-six tracks occupy this two-disc set. Collins's Imperial era wasn't his most consistent, as he experimented freely, but many of the instrumentals that predominate the set are solid examples of his patented icy sound, notably his version of Jimmy McGriff's "All About My Girl." (B.D.) (1:40:11/1991)

Ice Pickin' (Alligator) ★★★★★

The Cool Sound. Collins's first Alligator recording, in 1978, is impervious to wear, tear, or melting. His fretboard work is amazing: he builds suspense deliberately, letting ideas emerge at their own pace, eventually achieving release at the peak of hard-won excitement. His singing likewise displays interpretive keenness for control of pitch, dynamics, and blues inflections. Support players Casey Jones (drums), Larry Burton (second guitar), and Aaron Burton (bass) have exemplary command of rhythmic shadings. (38:09/Reissue)

Frostbite (Alligator) ★★★

The Telecaster Big Freeze continues in 1980. Those piercing, clipped high notes, wet-finger-in-light-socket riffs, and lucent lines are in abundance, lancing an assortment of originals and little-known R&B tunes. Collins's vocals, meantime, reflect the wit and seriousness of his guitar playing. Unfortunately he has to contend with a bumptious horn section. (41:04/Reissue)

Frozen Alive! (Alligator) ★★★★

The Union Bar in Minneapolis was a frigid zone for four nights in March 1981. Collins dignifies the proceedings by stating that it "ain't nothin' but the blues." Johnny B. Gayden's funky bass broadens the definition. There's stronger material and playing here than on his *Live in Japan* (see below). (38:36/Reissue)

Live in Japan (Alligator) ★★★

Collins's stage pyrotechnics endear him to a 1982 Tokyo audience ravished for more, more, more. As a master of pacing and the use of dynamics the guitarist also tells quietly suspenseful stories, notably "If Trouble Was Money." Either way he relies heavily on stock licks and phrases—not that they're lacking for emotional uprightness, mind you. Drummer Casey Jones is a powerhouse and saxophonist A. C. Reed would have been if miked properly. (40:13/Reissue)

Don't Lose Your Cool (Alligator) ★★★↗

Collins is never far in spirit from the 1940s and 1950s gin mills of his youth, where he soaked up blues, R&B, country and western, jazz, and all their various amalgams. On this 1983 date he impressively revitalizes his old Texas hit "Don't Lose Your Cool," turns the heat up on Guitar Slim's "Quicksand,"

and adds newfangled vocal and guitar insinuations to Big Walter Price's "Get to Gettin'." (40:09/Reissue)

Cold Snap (Alligator) ★★★♩

On the slickest of the Telecaster Master's seven Alligator discs (this one from 1986), Collins covers Clarence Carter's "Snatching It Back" and tries party-style sing-along R&B on Jimmy Liggins's "I Ain't Drunk." Some of the best moments occur on songs closer to the guitarist's customary output: the supercool blues "Lights Are On but Nobody's Home" and the Texas shuffle "A Good Fool Is Hard to Find" (although Morris Jenning's drums are mixed too loud). (B.D.) (42:47/Reissue)

Albert Collins (Pointblank/Charisma) ★★★

Goaded by the Uptown Horns and a small army of coconspirators, including faithful bassist Johnny B. Gayden, Collins plugs in his Telecaster and brings his barbed-wire vibrato to bear on likable funky blues that often tilt toward thermal Memphis soul—not exactly his natural climate. (43:21/1991)

Albert Collins/Robert Cray/Johnny Copeland
Showdown! (Alligator) ★★★

The title of this 1985 album leads one to think the three guitarists have engaged in an OK Corral shootout. Well, old Texas friends Collins and Copeland do scuffle, along with young firebrand Cray, but no one tries too hard to plant the other in Boot Hill. Alligator artist Collins fires the most rounds, soloing on all nine songs, and Copeland's vocals best kick up the dirt. (40:56/Reissue)

Sam Collins
Jail House Blues (Yazoo)   ★★★↓

Delta player Collins made only a few commercial recordings
(all in 1927 and 1931) before being lost to the mists of time.
On blues, spirituals, and pop bagatelles both his normal and
forced tenor voice have a ruminative preternaturalism, with
his bottleneck guitar seconding his sung plaints, affirmations,
and neutral observations. Try not to be scared off by the
surface noise of the 78s.   (44:03/1990)

John Coltrane
Coltrane Plays the Blues (Atlantic)   ★★★★

The depth and the breadth of modern jazz colossus John
Coltrane's blues feeling and technical virtuosity sustain the
music on this famous 1960 quartet recording. The tenor and
soprano saxophonist redesigns blues structure with stupen-
dous ideas about harmony. A nonblues tune, "Untitled Original," has been added to the original six-song program.
                                                (46:16/Reissue)

Joanna Connor
Believe It! (Blind Pig)   ★

Don't! This Chicago wild woman's electric guitar and vocals
clobber like a door slammed in the face. The same goes for her
late-1980s blues/rock/soul band. Lots of contrived drama
without any subtle depictions of mood or rhythmic incantation.   (41:25/Reissue)

Ry Cooder
Paradise and Lunch (Reprise)   ★★★★╛

Cooder is a masterful bottleneck guitarist and limited singer
with a penchant for revitalizing marvelous old songs, often of
the blues variety. Inventive arrangements and excellent ensemble musicianship on Blind Blake's "Diddie Wa Diddie"
(that's jazz giant Earl Hines on piano), Willie McTell's "Tat-
tler," and seven more from the American songbook carry the
charge through this delightful album from 1974.

(37:24/Reissue)

Johnny Copeland
Texas Twister (Rounder)   ★★★★

Johnny Clyde Copeland, a recording artist since the late
1950s, is one of the most imposing of the Texas blues singers
and guitarists. He and his synthesis of New Orleans funk and
Kansas City jazz only reached a sizable audience in the 1980s,
when he relocated to New York and landed a record deal with
Rounder. Parts of four albums for the Cambridge label ballast
this 1986 collection, a fine entry point for novitiates but something less for longtime admirers. The horn-sumptuous *Copeland Special*—one of the most poignant blues records of the
last twenty-five years and unavailable on CD—quits after
four opening tracks, and none of the ensuing eleven tunes
anneal the spirit equally. Which isn't to say they're less than
damn good.   (67:16/Reissue)

When the Rain Starts Fallin' (Rounder)   ★★★

Rounder raids the same four albums for another collection.
This time producer Dan Doyle has programmed his selections
willy-nilly rather than grouping them by album, as on *Texas
Twister*.   (65:24/1987)

Ain't Nothin' but a Party (Rounder) ★⌐

As the closest thing to a sonic hell in Rounder's R&B catalog, this indifferently recorded 1978 show in Houston clamors out of home speaker cabinets like an unruly and unwanted guest. Pianist Ken Vangel's arrangements are impossibly cluttered and Copeland struggles to rise above the din. (38:09/1988)

Boom Boom (Rounder) ★★

Jerry-built production puts a damper on Copeland's natural dynamism. He appears to be performing from a hole, beaten back at nearly every turn by a crash bang rhythm section. (35:49/1989)

• See also **Albert Collins/Robert Cray/Johnny Copeland**

Al Copley
Automatic Overdrive (Black Top) ★★

One day in the late 1980s, Copley, a cofounder of Roomful of Blues playing a stillborn solo career, surprised everyone by vanishing. He turned up in Europe, and this 1987 trio date is his musical postcard. Copley's boogie 'n' blues piano playing is passionate, witty, and intelligent, but his singing is toneless and without shading or sensitivity. Eight of nine songs have vocals. (32:09/1989)

Al Copley and Hal Singer
Royal Blue (Black Top) ★★⌐

Copley plays entertainingly, but he still can't sing a lick. The prominent roles of ex-Roomful guitarist Duke Robillard and Saxophonist Hal Singer, an R&B legend living in Europe since 1965, make this jump session tolerable. Lucky for us Robillard

kept *his* mouth closed. Lucky for us too that New Orleans guitarist Snooks Eaglin showed up to play on four tunes.
(42:08/1990)

James Cotton
Cut You Loose! (Vanguard)   ★★

Singer/harpist Cotton slips the moorings of his upbringing in the Howlin' Wolf and Muddy Waters bands, turning to faceless studio hacks and flat pop production in 1968.
(37:59/Reissue)

Take Me Back (Blind Pig)   ★★

This mid-1980s session tries lamely to evoke the plainspoken Chicago sound characteristic of Cotton's very first band twenty years earlier. Despite its gruff warmth, Cotton's voice is barely satisfactory in simple arrangements of material from Guitar Slim, Jimmy Reed, Little Walter, and Howlin' Wolf. His harp is seldom heard. Better his small ensemble weren't at all.
(34:55/1987)

Live at Antone's Nightclub (Antone's)   ★★✦

Wild and woolly nights at the Austin watering hole in the summer of 1987. A fairly predictable program is manhandled by the featured player and guitarists Matt Murphy and Luther Tucker, not to forget the indefatigable Muddy Waters alumni in the rhythm section.
(47:07/1988)

Mighty Long Time (Antone's)   ★★★✦

Star-time hubris often seems to block Cotton from finding the joy and/or sadness in songs, but that's not the case here, when he's in the studio next to fellow luminaries Luther Tucker,

Matt Murphy, Wayne Bennett, and Hubert Sumlin. The material has been chosen intelligently and performed effectively, highlighted by Cotton's rediscovery of early-1950s Sun gems "Straighten Up Baby" and "Hold Me in Your Arms." Even the leader's scorched vocals get over.   (52:47/1991)

James Cotton/Junior Wells/Carey Bell/Billy Branch
Harp Attack! (Alligator)   ★★★

The temptation must have been great for gamesmanship when the four big men of Chicago blues harmonica cut this onetime all-star session. The quadrumvirate, however, interacts on an even keel, the only duel a brief, inconclusive one between young torchbearer Branch and the grizzly Cotton in "Who." Each player gets about equal room in which to showcase his singing and reed bending, with Bell's less than workmanlike singing the only disappointment.   (53:59/1990)

• See also **Junior Parker/James Cotton/Pat Hare**

Hank Crawford
Portrait (Milestone)   ★★★♪

True for decades, Crawford's alto saxophone blends mirth with melancholy and sexy sauciness with gracious politeness, singing the verities of jazz, blues, and soul. The former Ray Charles musical director (1960–63) makes this effort a standout in his discography by empowering organist Johnny Hammond and guitarist Jimmy Ponder to share his special moods.   (43:46/1991)

Hank Crawford and Jimmy McGriff
On the Blue Side (Milestone) ★★★★

Organist Jimmy McGriff and alto saxophonist Hank Crawford define "soulfulness" on their third recording-studio collaboration. Bending musical genres they accentuate the pulse of their flowing originals and standards with a sort of sensible joyousness developed over long and estimable careers. Guitarist Jimmy Ponder also knows the meaning of that ineffable "s" word that many strive after but few get a hold on.

(41:00/1990)

Robert Cray
Too Many Cooks (Tomato) ★★✦

Cray stirs Southern soul music and blues for his first public feast, in 1980. At this point little known outside the Pacific Northwest, he utilizes his clean, clear, and boyish tenor voice and still-developing guitar style to inhabit a thoughtfully chosen program of covers (from Willie Dixon, Howlin' Wolf, etc.) and jealous-guy originals. (35:48/Reissue)

Bad Influence (Hightone) ★★★

A portent of impressive things to come. In 1983 Cray's second album trickled out of Oakland and turned a few heads. Here was a thirty-year-old unknown capable of co-writing articulate, absolutely gripping songs of forlornness ("Phone Booth") and complicated love-lust relationships ("The Grinder," "Bad Influence"). Less involving then were his spiky guitar work— too emulative of Albert King's—and his not-yet-ripe singing.

(34:30/Reissue)

False Accusations (Hightone)   ★★★⅃

In his precommercial days Robert Cray meshes up-tempo, syncopated, melodic musical themes with lyrics that examine the darker side of contemporary society. With his smooth vocals and imaginative guitar work, Cray emerges as one of the freshest musical voices of the new generation, predating the equally modern blues that Joe Louis Walker and Kenny Neal parlayed to such success a few years later. (J.T.)
(32:58/Reissue)

Strong Persuader (Mercury/Hightone)   ★★★★

Cray's commercial breakthrough. The single "Smokin' Gun" spearheaded yet another blues revival. This album is a strong collection of blues and R&B-based songs steeped in the tradition of Bobby Bland, O. V. Wright, Stax Records, and guitar stylings of equal parts Steve Cropper and Albert Collins. The songs are thematically linked—all deal with cheating and its ramifications—and give Cray an anguished, contemporary persona. (J.G.)
(39:03/1986)

Don't Be Afraid of the Dark (Mercury)   ★★★⅃

This is widely perceived as a sellout, but for no good reason. Cray continues to deliver the goods: great songs, great playing. If anything Cray is too consistent; the material stretches a bit. Cray tackles homelessness on "Night Patrol." His straight blues shuffle, "Across the Line," is a showpiece, as is the Stax-perfect ballad "At Last." "I Can't Go Home" is a masterpiece of dramatic soul singing and became a concert highlight. (J.G.)
(42:28/1988)

Midnight Stroll (Mercury) ★★★★

This album was honed by months on the road. By now the Memphis Horns receive star billing and achieve a perfect marriage with Cray's sound. Original members Peter Boe and David Olson are gone, and new keyboardist Jimmy Pugh favors a Hammond B-3 organ over synthesizers, a welcome move. Second guitarist Tim Kahaitsu offers interesting interplay with Cray. Also, Cray finally pushes his vocals over the edge. Highlights are "Bouncin' Back" and "Consequences." (J.G.) (50:06/1990)

• See also **Albert Collins/Robert Cray/Johnny Copeland**

Pee Wee Crayton
Things I Used to Do (Vanguard) ★★★

A guiding light of the postwar West Coast scene, Crayton was two decades past his salad days when he recorded this session in 1971. No matter. His guitar still rings with truths once shared with friend T-Bone Walker, and his vocals, less forcefully delivered but sunnier in mood, continue to do the job. He astutely refurbishes a few of his old R&B successes, including "Peace of Mind," and he stirringly adapts songs by Guitar Slim, Earl King, and others. Pedestrian backup playing hurts, though. (41:34/Reissue)

Cream
Strange Brew—The Very Best of Cream (Polydor) ★★★★

Cream's blues-rooted rock was free, loud, and excessive, notably in concert during the trio's 1966–68 lifetime. In the tracks on this compilation grandiloquence takes a backseat to serious, centralized musicmaking, from the straight blues of Robert Johnson's "Crossroads" (recorded live, with guitarist Eric

Clapton intelligently taking flight) and Willie Dixon's "Spoonful" (Jack Bruce is a better bassist than harp blower) to splendid chart-denting pop tunes. **(43:54/Reissue)**

Arthur "Big Boy" Crudup
That's All Right Mama (RCA/Bluebird)   ★★

In 1954, Elvis Presley reconstructed Crudup's "That's All Right Mama" and scored his first Memphis hit thanks to local disc jockey Dewey Phillips. The original and twenty-one other songs recorded by the Delta-born singer/guitarist for RCA's Lester Melrose between 1941 and 1953 are competently performed but unremarkable. Crudup's preening voice lacks heft and evocative power, and his small groups don't have a leavening sense of swing. **(62:41/1992)**

James "Thunderbird" Davis
Check Out Time (Black Top)   ★★★

Davis's claim to fleeting fame was "Blue Monday," a side issued by Duke Records in the early 1960s that charted in the South and was later covered by Z. Z. Hill. Resurfacing in 1988 after twenty-odd years of obscurity, the Louisiana soul blues singer works hard fattening up lyric with his deep tones, but he doesn't have the range and emotional depth to conjure the most transcendent Southern soul. The material is acceptable and the support supplied by old and new Gulf Coast friends pleases to no end. **(39:47/1989)**

Larry Davis
Sooner or Later (Bullseye Blues)   ★★★♪

Larry Davis, whose "Texas Flood" was covered by Stevie Ray Vaughan, pledged truth to the blues as far back as the early

1950s, and it has been a long, arduous haul to the belated recognition rightfully accorded him by this recent Memphis soul/blues session. His tenor voice is genuine, unclouded, resilient, carrying the meaning of the words of, for example, Little Milton's Stax Records–era "How Could You Do It to Me?" and heartsore Howlin' Wolf's 1954 song "Baby, How Long?" The interplay between his conscientiously played guitar and the irrepressible swell created by his skilled Tennessee sidemen further lends the tradition-bound material a new lease of believability. (46:13/1992)

Miles Davis
Kind of Blue (Columbia)   ★★★★★

This first-take, unrehearsed Miles Davis session from 1959, no less than a jazz/blues *succès d' estime,* offers stimulation for the mind and satisfaction for the soul. The late trumpeter and his fellow improvisers (notably John Coltrane and Bill Evans) create shifting prismatic colors, textures given over to lyricism, and intriguingly vague tonality within five compositions. A quiet, wondrous state of equilibrium between tension and repose. (45:11/Reissue)

Reverend Gary Davis
Pure Religion & Bad Company (Smithsonian/Folkways)   ★★★★

Gary Davis's bass runs and altogether winsome picking were in full blossom by the mid 1930s—and stayed that way for many years. This 1957 session has the ordained minister and father of the Piedmont blues guitar style performing blues, dance songs, and adaptations of Baptist church favorites without erring from his right course. Captivating. (59:28/Reissue)

Reverend Gary Davis at Newport (Vanguard)   ★★★

The folk blues revival of the 1960s saw Davis performing solo at the famous Newport Folk Festival that doubled as a campground meeting. Despite some rough going, the gospel bluesman's singing and playing shone as deep blue as the nearby Rhode Island Sound in the late afternoon sun.   (46:02/Reissue)

Jimmy Dawkins
All for Business (Delmark)   ★★↲

This 1971 studio meeting between West Side guitarists Jimmy Dawkins and Otis Rush makes a reasonably good impression for the two aces' ability to wrest affecting music from their instruments—even if each has a tendency to cruise on automatic pilot. Also, the recently departed Andrew "Big Voice" Odom handles a few vocals, matching the expressiveness of the guitarists' work with his own plangent phrasing. Two previously unreleased tracks are throwaways.   (59:57/Reissue)

Kant Sheck Dees Bluze (Earwig)   ★★★↲

The first domestic studio release in eons for this veteran of Chicago's West Side, and Fast Fingers responds with some dirty, distorted lead guitar and a program of intense originals with a crackling contemporary edge. Dawkins has progressed markedly as a singer from his early, less confident Delmark days, plus his protégé, Nora Jean Wallace, is showcased as vocalist on two tracks. (B.D.)   (70:38/1992)

John Delafose
Joe Pete Got Two Women (Arhoolie)   ★★★★

Around the Gulf Coast, John Delafose and the Eunice Playboys are known as leading exponents of zydeco *bons temps rouler.* This exceptional collection has twenty-two of their earliest recordings, drawn from two early-1980s sessions and a Lafayette concert of the same period. Six songs are feelingly sung in English by the accordion-playing leader; on the rest, several of which are two-steps, he uses his native Creole patois. (63:20/Reissue)

Sugar Pie DeSanto
Down in the Basement (MCA/Chess) ★★✦

Satisfactory R&B singer had commercial success with "I Want to Know" (included here), then tried unsuccessfully in the Chess 1960s to forge a career on par with that of her cousin Etta James. The single "Soulful Dress" was covered by Marcia Ball years later. (33:27/Reissue)

Vic Dickenson
Trombone Cholly (Gazell) ★★★✦

On this 1976 session the beloved jazz trombonist delivers a program of blues and pop songs associated with Bessie Smith using a deliciously tender attack, soft tone, and profound Juvenal wit. Still strong at sixty-nine, Dickenson gets expert blues help from former Basie-ites Joe Newman on trumpet and Frank Wess on tenor saxophone, along with the estimable string bassist Milt Hinton. (37:15/Reissue)

Bo Diddley
The Chess Box (MCA/Chess) ★★★★★

The extraordinary rhythmic sense of Ellas "Bo Diddley" McDaniel is evidenced on forty-five songs (classics and obscure gems alike) recorded between 1955 and 1969, one of the all-time peaks of creativeness in rock 'n' roll. The sides filling two discs in this handsome boxed set also show that the Mississippi native who was raised on Chicago's South Side has a guitar and voice acute in blues intonation and a penchant for lyrics that are barbed-wire sharp with irreverent humor. The accompanying twenty-two-page booklet includes a Robert Palmer essay, sessions details, and remembrances by Diddley.

(2:08:36/1990)

Rare & Well Done (MCA/Chess) ★★★

Those addicted to the "hambone beat" will rejoice over this unofficial supplement to the Chess box: five obscure Checker singles (including novelty item "Bo Meets the Monster") and eleven heretofore unreleased tracks all recorded between 1955 and 1968. (48:27/1991)

Floyd Dixon
Marshall Texas Is My Home (Specialty) ★★✦

West Coast R&B of the 1950s was all the richer for Dixon's piano, singing voice, songs, and band. This collection of twenty-two songs from his 1953–57 sessions for Specialty, however, gives an occluded glimpse of his value; about all of the eleven previously unreleased songs should have stayed locked up in the vault because his voice and/or accompaniment are abysmal. On the plus side, the lively classic "Hey Bartender," the sad Charles Brown–influenced ballad "Call Operator 210" (a demo), and a couple more winners are present. (58:00/Reissue)

Willie Dixon
The Chess Box (MCA/Chess) ★★★★★

This top-shelf tribute, two discs plus a twelve-page booklet, has three dozen acclaimed or forgotten tunes written by

Dixon that showcase the impudent urgency of electric Chicago blues between 1951 and 1968. Dixon, Howlin' Wolf,
Muddy Waters, Little Walter, Bo Diddley, Sonny Boy Williamson, and seven more singing headliners all vent their
respective optimism, disquietude, or resentment while treating his provocative lyrics. So do, in instrumental terms, a
passel of responsive musicians.   (1:49:01/1988)

The Big Three Trio (Columbia/Legacy)   ★★★

Twenty-one enjoyable light blues and pop numbers from 1947
to 1952 sway, sashay, or boogie—compliments of Leonard
Caston on piano, Bernardo Dennis or Ollie Crawford on guitar, and Dixon on bass fiddle. The three harmonize capably.
                                                   (56:16/1990)

I Am the Blues (Mobile Fidelity)   ★★✦

Originally released in 1970, this disc has the legendary songwriter singing nine of his classics as his hand-picked Chicago
band makes the changes. Dixon's nothing special, even if he
is the blues personified, since his dryly charming voice lacks
tonal inflections and his way with rhythm is less than fluent.
Whatever glimmers of expressivity these performances have
are due to harp player Carey Bell. In spite of Mobile
Fidelity's exemplary sound technology, the instruments at the
original session sound like mysterious things thumping on the
roof in the dead of night.   (43:54/Reissue)

Hidden Charms (Capitol)   ★★★★

Enjoying his first big label session since the late 1940s, Dixon
relies on his offhandedly magnetic semivocals to nuzzle
through the simple melodies of old and new songs from the
witty, bright side of his pen: "I Love the Life I Live," "Jungle
Swing," "Good Advice," "I Do the Job" (wink, wink), and

five more. Dixon's attendants include famous New Orleans drummer Earl Palmer, venerable Chicago pianist Lafayette Leake (a longtime friend of his), young harmonica player Sugar Blue, and dobroist T-Bone Burnett, who conscientiously produced the session.   (46:03/1988)

Dr. John and Chris Barber
On a Mardi Gras Day (Great Southern)   ★★★

The temporary partnership of New Orleans singer/pianist Mac Rebennack (aka Dr. John, the gris-gris jivester) and trombonist Chris Barber, an English jazz and blues institution, caused quite a media stir in Great Britain in the early 1980s. Recording at a club full of Londoners, the two principals and Barber's deft Bourbon Street–on-the-Thames septet get festive with tunes more or less appropriate for Shrove Tuesday. The headliners' duet blues "You Lie Too Much" is a keeper.
(60:22/Reissue)

Bill Doggett
The Right Choice (After Hours)   ★★★

Doggett is famous for the jump blues/rock 'n' roll instrumental "Honky Tonk, Parts 1 & 2," a huge 1956 hit that gets revived on this recent date. Still spry in his seventh decade, the organist lets his unending passion for blues and jazz color nine more songs that are further uplifted by jubilant players like saxophonist Bill Easley and blues guitarist Gregory Townson. A sleeper.   (49:27/1991)

Bo Dollis and the Wild Magnolias
I'm Back . . . at Carnival Time! (Rounder)　　★★★★

The Wild Magnolias are a traditional New Orleans "Indian" tribe featuring only vocals and percussion. Joined here by among others the potent New Rebirth Brass Band, the Magnolias provide a jumping, pulsating example of Mardi Gras celebration. In a just world their stellar 1974 eponymous album on Polydor would be out on CD. (J.T./F.J.H.)
(43:11/1990)

Don and Dewey
Jungle Hop (Specialty)　　★★★

The R&B duo of Don "Sugarcane" Harris (vocals, guitar, piano, electric violin) and Dewey Terry (vocals, guitar, piano) plied their trade in the late 1950s. Twenty-three songs from the period (seven formerly lost) and two 1964 tracks are by and large small treasures.　　　　(61:01/Reissue)

Champion Jack Dupree
Back Home in New Orleans (Bullseye Blues)　　★★★♪

This session was made during Dupree's long, long overdue return visit to his first blues turf. The seventy-nine-year-old Hamburg resident's fingers no longer drive the piano keys and his voice doesn't resonate as in years past, but the *feeling* is there in spades. His sincerity envelops songs about alcohol, paramours, life's downside, universal brotherhood—his words never come forth smug or perfunctory. Respectful New Orleans musicians aid and abet him on four tracks, with only Swedish guitarist Kenn Lending helping on the remaining half dozen.　　　　(43:42/1990)

Forever and Ever (Black Top)

The late dignitary offers a second recent New Orleans studio session that is as homey as a private parlor recital. Settle back in your armchair and let his entrancement work wonders. He sings and scats some, fingers a few barrelhouse patterns on his piano, and lets several solicitous colleagues add to the allurement of the mood. "Yella Pocahontas," with Mardi Gras Indian chief Bo Dollis, is an endearing glance back at his New Orleans youth.   (45:33/1991)

Cornell Dupree
Can't Get Through (Amazing) ★★★★

Guitarist Dupree belongs to the soul blues elite for his work with King Curtis's band and his estimable studio playing in the company of Aretha Franklin ("Rock Steady" still rivets twenty-odd years later) and innumerable others. (Let's not forget his out-of-print mid-1970s feature record *Teasin'*, either.) This recent headlining date has his well-ordered lines still impressing as models of creative fecundity and tastefulness, plus his working band comes by its complementary amiability naturally. Without a hint of false feeling, Dupree works restful miracles in "Could It Be."   (45:00/1991)

Snooks Eaglin
Baby, You Can Get Your Gun! (Black Top) ★★★

Eaglin never has had the strongest R&B voice in New Orleans, but his guitar shows why he's been a highly respected performer around town for thirty years plus. At his initial Black Top session in 1986 the eclectic's eclectic sings gamely and dips his furtive, barbed guitar into songs from James Brown, the Ventures, Professor Longhair, Earl King, the local Pentecostal church, and elsewhere. Fats Domino's rhythm section and noted saxman David Lastie are among those ably backing him. (32:43/Reissue)

Out of Nowhere (Black Top) ★★★✦

On this second Black Top feature session Eaglin redefines twelve of the thousands of songs he knows with characteristic unpredictability, twisting items from the books of Benny Spellman, Smiley Lewis, the Falcons, the Isleys, and others into inventive new shapes. Anson Funderburgh's group and Black Top hirelings follow his fey moves spiritedly and understandingly. (37:47/1989)

Teasin' You (Black Top) ★★★✦

Once again, Eaglin—he with the high-density expanded memory of an IBM—locates a common ground among New Orleans R&B, blues, jazz, soul, gospel, and his own guitar epiphanies. In control of guitar color and rhythmic form, he gives new shades of meaning to, in particular, four songs from the pen of Earl King, whom he calls "my lifelong friend and one of my greatest musical inspirations." The New Orleans rhythm section and horns, including Texas tenor soloist Grady Gaines, keep him engaged. (48:01/1992)

Ronnie Earl

Deep Blues (Black Top) ★★✦

Tracks off two Earl feature albums from the early 1980s make up this not-so-profound blues collection. The Roomful of Blues guitarist parties with Fabulous Thunderbird harmonica player Kim Wilson and several fast friends from Roomful and Sugar Ray and the Bluetones. His single-note lines are frequently skittish and forced, though he and vocalist Ray Norcia fidget to marvelous end in "Follow Your Heart" and "Some Day, Some Way." (66:30/1988)

I Like It When It Rains (Antone's) ★★⟩

Long a technically proficient player, Earl begins to speak from the heart with this mostly country blues set. Yet he appears hesitant to dig very far into his seven originals—maybe it hurt too much. Some of his lines have a self-reproachful cast.

(41:34/Reissue)

Soul Searchin' (Black Top) ★★★

In a recording contemporaneous with his departure from Roomful, the leader of the Broadcasters sizes up Texas and Chicago blues as well as Southern soul. More thoughtful than before, Earl has taken large strides toward natural fluency with the idiomatic expression of emotion. It's a crime that singer Darrell Nulisch offsets the guitarist's alluring soul investigations with his pallid, hollow voice. (42:55/1988)

Peace of Mind (Black Top) ★★★

With newfound poise and control—closer, apparently, to self-awareness—Earl fires off fast yet relaxed runs that prickle the skin. The most authentic excitement is generated in the title tune where he plays soft and slow while in the grip of serene feelings that have no fake sentiment about them. He well understands that sensitivity to timing and self-editing needs to accompany his command of timbral shadings. Unfortunately cold-wind vocalist Nulisch is present for one last Broadcasters session, partly freezing nine noninstrumentals.

(48:22/1990)

Surrounded by Love (Black Top) ★★★★

Songwriter/guitarist Earl covers his most sophisticated emotional terrain yet. Ever gaining in self-confidence and personality, he makes his guitar almost rival that of guest Robert Jr.

Lockwood's for communicative immediacy. Inspired by the Broadcasters, especially Tony Zamagni's warm organ and Sugar Ray Norcia's deep-hued vocals, Earl has a great deal to reveal in the centerpiece blues "That's When My Soul Comes Down," building tension slowly in increments until effecting sweet release. Another guitar highlight, of many, is his dutiful acoustic slide work on "Blues for Robert Jr." (54:34/1991)

Charles Earland
Whip Appeal (Muse) ★★★

Forget the tacky masochistic cover. The pleasure to be · derived from Earland's recording session comes from the happy flogging given our ears by his insistently swinging Hammond B-3 organ. The young turk of the late-1960s "soul jazz" genre, now middle-aged but ever so agile, creates his singing melodies and walking bass lines in a conservative septet setting. The rickety, frosty-toned soprano saxophonist is no fun of any kind. (41:48/1991)

Teddy Edwards
Mississippi Lad (Antilles) ★★★★

Not half as well known as he should be, Edwards is a Delta-born jazz saxophonist who impresses for his post-bop inventiveness and his predisposition to the blues. Allowed a rare feature date, he gives lessons in how to delve into a melody for meaning and then express the resulting revelations in down-home terms—relish the poetic beauty of the title song. Tom Waits, an original, molds his vocal excesses into triumphant blues declarations in Edwards's stunning composition "I'm Not Your Fool Anymore." Indeed. (57:50/1991)

Tinsley Ellis
Fanning the Flames (Alligator)   ★★

Ellis's leads and rhythm figures cause a conflagration, but all
the virtuosic excitement is secondary to his hit-or-miss attempts at expressing subtle shadings of emotional intent. His
voice doesn't have a clue.   (40:44/1989)

Trouble Time (Alligator)   ★

Make that *Debacle Time*. Almost an hour of Grand Guignol
swashbuckling, with Otis Redding's "Hey Hey Baby" con-
torted into grandioso nothingness and peacocky originals that
are unwittingly self-parodistic.   (53:07/1992)

Tinsley Ellis and the Heartfixers
Cool on It (Alligator)   ★★

The Heartfixers were Atlanta's hottest blues rock band in the
mid 1980s. Their creditable 1986 album, originally issued on
Landslide, convinced Alligator to sign guitarist Ellis to a solo
deal. The nine-minutes-plus slow blues "Time to Quit" is the
center of attention.   (39:01/Reissue)

Sleepy John Estes
I Ain't Gonna Be Worried No More, 1929–41 (Yazoo)   ★★★★✔

Favored with rare songwriting insight, John Adam Estes from
western Tennessee found his proper place among the country
blues illuminati because of his prewar 78s for Victor Records
and other labels. The quietly thunderous "Someday Baby"
and twenty-two more selections hinge on his high voice's
exquisite tonal clarity, his self-confident delivery, his bringing
intelligibility to the phrase "construction of music," and his
drawing of subtle yet great feelings from his own or tradi-

tional verses. The interaction of Estes's singing with Hammie Nixon's harmonica, James "Yank" Rachell's mandolin, and/or Jab Jones's piano results in textures that heighten the music's relaxed state of enchantment. On the minus side, the songs reveal Estes to have been an unremarkable guitarist.

(70:27/Reissue)

Electric Sleep (Delmark) ★

Electric narcosis. The 1967 Chicago meeting between country bluesman Estes, decades past his prime, and local modernists such as electric guitarist Jimmy Dawkins is the stuff of nightmares. (57:27/Reissue)

The Fabulous Thunderbirds
The Ultimate Collection (Chrysalis) ★★★★

This anthologizes the band's first four records for Takoma and Chrysalis. Present is Austin's number one band's recipe for success: lean arrangements, driven by Jimmie Vaughan's perfect guitar; hot harmonica licks from Kim Wilson; and a reverential view of obscure blues and R&B, Cajun, and other regional styles in a universally rockin' blend. Some of this album represents the original lineup featuring Keith Ferguson on bass and Mike Buck on drums—before they were replaced by Roomful of Blues alumni Preston Hubbard and Fran Christina. (J.G.) (58:31/1991)

Tuff Enuff (CBS) ★★★♪

This Dave Edmunds–produced album took Austin's best-known band and introduced them to the world in 1986. The two big hits, Kim Wilson's own "Tuff Enuff" and Sam and Dave's "Wrap It Up," move the band in a new R&B-flavored direction. This album encompasses the many influences that make up the T-Birds: zydeco on "Tell Me," soul music on "Two Time My Lovin' " (with Los Lobos), and a blues tribute to their home base, "Down at Antone's." This is easily the best of their three Epic releases with guitarist/singer Jimmie Vaughan. (J.G.) (32:47/Reissue)

Walk That Walk, Talk That Talk (CBS) ★★★✦

Thunderbirds cornerstone Jimmie Vaughan is replaced here by two notable figures from the New England blues scene, guitarists Duke Robillard and Kid Bangham. Stars of the show, their interweaved guitar textures are never flashy, always inventive, and, most importantly, they rock. The problem with this record is songwriting. Leader Kim Wilson seems obsessed with writing soul-type metaphors about how big his love is, but when placed next to a real example of this, like Sam and Dave's "Ain't That a Lot of Love," they pale in comparison. A cover of Junior Parker's John Lee Hooker interpolation "Feelin' Good" is excellent. (J.G.) (50:33/1991)

Georgie Fame
Cool Blues (Bluemoon/Go Jazz) ★★✦

A guiding light of 1960s British R&B, Fame has quietly cruised through a couple of decades as a jazz singer with a penchant for Mose Allison–style bluesiness. On his first America-distributed effort in eons he uses smooth phrasing to slip comfortably into his own songs and ones on loan from Allison, Willie Dixon, and Louis Jordan. His suave fervor is seconded by guitarist Robben Ford and other top-fee sessionsmen. The problem is Fame just doesn't have the natural *cool*, the distinctive qualities, of those whose material he embraces. (66:12/1991)

Fathers and Sons

Fathers and Sons (MCA/Chess)

Muddy Waters and Otis Spann ceremoniously took young white Chicago bluesmen Paul Butterfield and Mike Bloomfield under their wing with this combined 1969 studio-concert meeting. The music isn't particularly praiseworthy, with the scions formal and obeisant, the elders steady but seldom inspired, and the excitement of the day—this confirmation of the new generation—long passed. (65:16/Reissue)

Robben Ford

Talk to Your Daughter (Warner Bros.) ★★

Trying to capture a mainstream audience, the talented San Francisco–based guitarist squeezes out stylized rock guitar runs *and* Albert King–inspired riffs that point to his blues training under Charlie Musslewhite, etc. The blend is mildly interesting. Alas, Ford's singing is wan, devoid of any appeal at all, and his old comrades from the pop-jazz Yellowjackets don't share his feel for the twelve-bar genre. (41:55/1988)

Jimmy Forrest

Night Train (Delmark) ★★★

The early 1950s found Forrest, a big-toned tenor saxophonist recently departed from the Duke Ellington Orchestra, waxing sides for a pop market clamoring after robust and sensual sounds. Melding two Ellington songs, he came up with the jukebox staple "Night Train," included here with sixteen more R&B tunes that pleasingly evidence his affinity for blues and jazz. (49:12/Reissue)

T. J. Fowler

T. J. Fowler and His Rockin' Jump Band (Savoy Jazz) ★★

Little-known Detroit pianist and his aptly named group don't have the precision and bounce of the best postwar merrymakers, though "Little Baby Child" and "Got Nobody to Tell My Troubles To" are worth hearing for Calvin Frazier's stirring guitar and vocals. (41:09/Reissue)

Carol Fran and Clarence Hollimon
Soul Sensation (Black Top) ★★★

The polished, professional duo of Gulf Coast vocalist Fran and guitarist Hollimon perform a soulful, simmering brand of contemporary blues/R&B with a strong dash of gospel. This first feature album also features a couple of searing vocals by the late James "Thunderbird" Davis. (J.T.) (56:02/1992)

Denny Freeman
Blues Cruise (Amazing) ★★★★

Austin guitarist Freeman exhibits considerable poise and intimacy playing the twenty songs that make up this disc, the entirety of two mostly instrumental late-1980s albums titled *Blues Cruise* and *Out of the Blue*. Never sounding one-dimensional, Freeman maintains a fundamental quality of spontaneity even when his lines and arrangements have been carefully thought out beforehand. He has a firm grip on Texas, Delta, and Chess blues, pre-pomp rock 'n' roll, country, and jazz à la West Montgomery. Jimmie Vaughan on steel guitar and bass and singer Angela Strehli are among his spirited accompanists. (72:34/Reissue)

Frank Frost
Midnight Prowler (Earwig)   ★★★⯪

Recording in 1986 and 1988, the Helena singer/harpist bur-
rows into assorted song rhythms with a combination of slyness
and suspicious urgency, transfixing original and cover songs
alike. His fellow Jelly Roll Kings and other roughhouse Sunflower State musicians are with him all the way. (52:03/1989)

Blind Boy Fuller
East Coast Piedmont Style (Columbia/Legacy)   ★★★★

Rollicking 1935–39 sides from one of the leading guitarists in
the prewar Piedmont style. Some tracks feature Blind Gary
Davis on second guitar and Bull City Red on clattering washboard, others are solo, and 1939's "I'm a Stranger Here" finds
the young Sonny Terry on harp. All twenty songs possess an
engaging sense of swing. (B.D.)   (61:55/1991)

Truckin' My Blues Away (Yazoo)   ★★★⯪

Fuller's hallmark double-entendres and protestations concerning bothersome women—the gist of this collection of late-
1930s songs—ring with unremitting warmth. Although a
popular entertainer, the accomplished guitarist and singer
doesn't swathe the true feelings of the blues in the soft cotton
of sentimentality. This Yazoo set duplicates part of the Columbia disc's program and has rougher sound.   (40:37/Reissue)

Jesse Fuller
Frisco Bound (Arhoolie)   ★★★★

An impassioned guitarist and confident if self-styled vocalist,
Jesse Fuller's acoustic blues provided a musical bridge from
the earliest Southern traditions to the folk blues revival of the

1960s. This collection, including his famed "San Francisco Bay Blues," is drawn from sessions in 1955 and 1962. (J.T.) (65:24/1991)

Jesse Fuller's Favorites (Fantasy)   ★★★✦

Part of Fantasy's reissue of the Prestige catalog, this 1963 album is a studio set of Fuller performing his one-man-band folk blues. Most of the songs are familiar, and all are performed in Fuller's inimitably sparse style. (J.T.) (38:40/Reissue)

Lowell Fulson
Hung Down Head (MCA/Chess)   ★★★✦

Fulson is a lodestar of the postwar Texas/West Coast school whose stinging guitar and measuredly urgent singing over polite swinging rhythms make up this 1970 collection of Chess/Checker sides from 1955–61. "Reconsider Baby" is a slow blues classic, and nine more songs ingratiate themselves quite nicely too . . . but not "Tollin' Bells," a nine-minute-plus monstrosity of outtake after outtake. (37:37/Reissue)

It's a Good Day (Rounder)   ★★★★

One of the most influential of postwar blues artists—B. B. King's guitar was heavily influenced by him, as was Johnny Adams's singing style—Lowell Fulson enjoyed a string of hits of his own in the 1950s and 1960s. His guitar is sophisticated and fluid, bordering on jazz, with vocals to match. This "comeback" album shows no signs of slipping from past standards. (J.T.) (38:17/1988)

Anson Funderburgh
She Knocks Me Out! (Black Top) ★★

In 1982, mesmerized by Otis Rush, Magic Sam, and other idols, Funderburgh was sharpening his guitar skills leading the Dallas bar band known as the Rockets. Their second recording is *almost* worth the price for his playing.

(38:09/Reissue)

Sins (Black Top) ★★★✦

Funderburgh's guitar tone has become so steady and his single-string manner of expression so natural, easeful, and economical that it's, ahem, sinful. Myers knowingly grips good material from Earl King, Percy Mayfield, and himself as if it were forbidden fruit. Clear-witted to various tempos, three more Rockets are virtuous reprobates too. (42:04/1988)

Rack 'em Up (Black Top) ★★★✦

The Rockets solidify their reputation as one of the most dependable and unassuming Texas blues band in existence. Myers's guttural vocalizing has lost some of its solidity, but otherwise everyone's on top of the game. Songs on loan from Earl King, Otis Rush, and others, plus the occasional original, scud or traipse along invitingly. For revelatory and progressive blues, however, the Rockets aren't the ticket.

(38:18/1989)

Tell Me What I Want to Hear (Black Top) ★★★✦

Funderburgh again fits the templates of creative intelligence and order over his lines and chords, while Myers, as always, evidences his conscientious craftsmanship. There's new emphasis on the songwriting, with only four nonoriginals among the fourteen selections. The title track, written by the Rockets for the movie *China Moon*, and the group composition "I'm Innocent" rumble with the most appeal. New faces on drums and bass, sorry to say, don't lend themselves to the ensemble sound as well as their predecessors. (50:25/1991)

Anson Funderburgh and Sam Myers
My Love Is Here to Stay (Black Top) ★★✦

The pairing of Funderburgh with Sam Myers in a Dallas studio in 1984 is advantageous for both men. The young blood is stirred emotionally by the experienced and diversely talented bluesman, who had been playing drums behind Robert Jr. Lockwood. Myers, singing and blowing harp, reciprocates by feeding off the vitality of his new friend. While they're not always comfortable with each other, Chuck Berry's "Wee Wee Hours" and a few more numbers find them in synch like a quarterback and his favorite center. (43:06/Reissue)

Grady Gaines
Full Gain (Black Top) ★★✦

Gaines used to rip it up in the 1950s throttling the tenor saxophone for Little Richard. These days he fronts an exciting Houston-based outfit of longtime R&B campaigners who sing and play their hearts out—not always to an attractive result. Joe Medwick is the most capable of Gaines's five vocalists. (40:41/1988)

Black Top Blues-a-Rama, Volume Four (Black Top) ★★★

The Black Top down 'n' dirty blowout at New Orleans's Tipitina's in 1989 featured Gaines and the Texas Upsetters Revue, complete with guitarist Joe Hughes and a horn section. The soul-time revivalists, once inciters to Otis Redding and James Brown, work hard to provide quality entertainment behind unremarkable singers Big Robert Smith, Paul David Roberts, and Joe Medwick. (52:00/1990)

Paul Gayten
Chess King of New Orleans: The Chess Years ★★★★ (MCA/Chess)

Singer/pianist Gayten was chief producer for Chess in New Orleans during the 1950s, recording some fine R&B for the firm himself. Saxophonist Lee Allen and his vaunted session partners (including drummer Earl Palmer) blast behind Gayten on "You Better Believe It," "Down Boy," and the irrepressible "Music Goes Round and Round," all dating from 1954–56. Take special note of his eccentric piano style throughout the brief set. (B.D./F.J.H.) (28:50/1989)

Jimmie Gordon
Jimmie Gordon (1934–1941) (Story of Blues) ★★★

In the seven years leading up to World War II singer Jimmie Gordon kept busy recording in jazz- and blues-rich Chicago. Whether singing of suffering or "feelin' high," he maintains emotional equilibrium with his unruffled, steady voice. He's accompanied on these twenty decent-sounding sides by respected musicians such as guitarist Lonnie Johnson and trumpeter Frankie Newton. (59:01/Reissue)

Gospel Hummingbirds
Steppin' Out (Blind Pig) ★★★

The Oakland church quintet doesn't lose sight of its religious calling even as several Robert Cray band members and the production team of Cray/Hummingbird keyboardist Jimmy Pugh and rocker Bonnie Hayes give the ensemble sound temporality. The solidly planted backbeat anchoring traditional hymns and new spirituals contrasts engagingly with the uplift of the singers. (48:00/1991)

Stefan Grossman

Yazoo Basin Boogie (Shanachie) ★★↲

In 1967 folk bluesman Grossman packed his guitar and left New York for Europe, where in the ensuing years he recorded these twenty-two songs. The onetime student of Reverend Gary Davis and Son House has mastered the techniques of those two and other heroes he knows from old shellac records, coalescing his ideas with borrowed ones in pleasant fretboard commentaries. (53:20/Reissue)

Love, Devils and the Blues (Shanachie) ★★★★

As time passes, Grossman's guitar playing gains greater personality. He uses styles and techniques from all over the blues map as springboards for drawing from his own fertile imagination. Just don't expect any of the poignant majesty of his elders, though his stunning bottleneck comes close.
(41:09/Reissue)

How to Play Blues Guitar (Shanachie) ★★★★

This primer on fingerpicking blues guitar is at once educational and entertaining, covering a panoply of down-home styles and techniques, from Lonnie Johnson's to Charlie Patton's to Blind Boy Fuller's. No-talk instructor Grossman wisely involved the late British folk blues singer Jo Ann Kelly, guitar expert Mickey Baker, and Deltaman Son House in the project. The package includes sheet music and detailed notes on the songs. (71:13/Reissue)

The Groundhogs
Split (BGO import) ★★★★

Few young Britons made the transition from 1960s straight blues to 1970s head-smashing blues rock as successfully as Tony McPhee, leader/vocalist/guitarist of the Groundhogs. Several years before this monster album stormed the 1971 English charts McPhee had been instructed in blues expression by a visiting baron he befriended and backed on stage, namely John Lee Hooker. The mandarin is given direct tribute here by McPhee's superb country blues rendering of "Groundhog." (39:53/Reissue)

Gigi Gryce
The Rat Race Blues (Prestige) ★★★★

A superior composer and a good alto saxophonist, Gryce directs his early-1960s jazz quintet through a blues program. His moods—ebullient, wistful, wary—are the equal of more renowned musicians'. (40:11/Reissue)

Guitar Slim
Sufferin' Mind (Specialty) ★★★★✦

Eddie "Guitar Slim" Jones's Specialty collection starts off with the ultrasensuous R&B chart-topper "Things that I Used to Do" and keeps the pressure on our pleasure points for the next twenty-five songs, all waxed between 1953 and 1955. His voice is at once cavernous and infectious, at all times permeated with true feeling. His spiky guitar phrases, emulated by a legion of players, rock between torment and eroticism. Pianist/arranger Ray Charles lends his handiwork to the four songs done in New Orleans, and Slim's trusty Crescent City/Chicago/Hollywood adjutants include bass player Lloyd Lambert and drummer Oscar Moore. (71:23/Reissue)

Buddy Guy

The Complete Chess Studio Recordings (MCA/Chess) ★★★★

Barely restrained fervency is the hallmark of headlining artist Buddy Guy's music on Chess in the years 1960–67. Forty-seven songs arrayed over two discs take in the twentysomething West Side singer and guitarist's dramatic and colloquial blues utterances; try the single "Ten Years Ago" and about twenty more, a great number of them rare. Also here, in bounteous quantity, are chart wannabes of do-the-frug pop/R&B orientation that have moguls Phil and Leonard Chess in bed with P. T. Barnum proposing "The bigger the humbug, the better the people will like it." (2:19:16/1992)

I Was Walking Through the Woods (MCA/Chess) ★★★★♪

Chess sessions player Buddy Guy cried from the heart on this 1970 gathering of ten tracks recorded between 1960 and 1964 as *featured* guitarist and singer. His axe moves from out of the shadow of B. B. King's, mercilessly cleaving the material, and his vocals dangle as dangerously as exposed live wires. Future partner Junior Wells (on three selections) and a top-drawer rhythm section of Jack Myers, Otis Spann, and Fred Below pack a surprising eventfulness into their ancillary contributions; the three saxophonists are an unappealing window dressing. (37:41/Reissue)

Left My Blues in San Francisco (MCA/Chess) ★★★

Leonard Chess didn't appreciate Guy's studio raucousness, and the guitarist only recorded sparingly as sessions leader during his last years at the record company, 1965–67. Most of the eleven songs on his first long-player, issued in 1967, belong stylistically to the era's soul boom; Guy fervidly muscles out of hot, busy orchestrations designed by Chess men Gene Barge (most recently a singer with the Mellow Fellows) and

Charlie Stepney (Earth, Wind and Fire's producer in the 1970s). Too often attitude replaces conviction, although "I Suffer with the Blues" and "Leave My Girl Alone" seem fraught with ardor. (32:53/Reissue)

This Is Buddy Guy! (Vanguard) ★★✦

In the upside-down, psychedelic San Francisco of 1967 the lily-white Steve Miller Band was playing replicas of Chicago blues at the Avalon Ballroom in Haight-Ashbury, while Guy was across the bay in Berkeley energetically performing soul and R&B with only scant attention to twelve-bar truths. Captured on tape in a club, Guy doesn't have the star power of James Brown nor his band the driving sound of the J.B.'s, and covers of material belonging to Guitar Slim, Little Willie John, and Eddie Floyd are earnest but lacking. His blues-inflected guitar lines do now and then supply thrilling suspense. (39:43/Reissue)

A Man and the Blues (Vanguard) ★★★✦

On this 1968 album thirty-one-year-old Guy's minor-key vocals are decisive, his guitar shudders and shakes with a judicious sort of vehemence, and his songs please to no end. It should be noted that pianist Otis Spann turns in an impressive performance. The music disappoints only when the horns bleat in a dated R&B fashion. (38:40/Reissue)

Hold That Plane! (Vanguard) ★★

This 1972 release has not aged well—not that it was anything superior to begin with. Guy's flashy guitar clashes with a plodding rhythm team and dragging saxophones, and of seven songs on the bill only "Come See About Me" (recorded at a different session from the rest) is worth hearing. (38:29/Reissue)

Stone Crazy! (Alligator) ★★↗

The headachy speed-jumble guitar in the opening track, "I Smell a Rat," scared blues purists away from Guy's 1979 French session when it surfaced stateside on Alligator in the early 1980s. Too bad. If they'd hung on through the Jimi Hendrix simulacra and magnific postures they'd have found the album closer, "When I Left Home," utterly riveting for its raw, sincere bloodletting. (42:38/Reissue)

Damn Right, I've Got the Blues (Silvertone) ★★★★

An apropos title. Back in the studio after a decade's absence, Guy cauterizes emotional sores with his stronger-than-ever vocals and his slyly accented guitar. Every time he threatens to fly into hysteria, he draws back and toughens up, steeling himself for more purging pain—the method of a master. Variety is welcome, but he's roused to do his best on blues originals and covers (from Eddie Boyd and Willie Dixon) rather than R&B numbers (compliments of John Hiatt and Wilson Pickett). Also, all he needs is his alert coterie of American and British sidemen, not horns, not backup chanteuses, not "names" Eric Clapton and Jeff Beck. (54:01/1991)

Buddy Guy and Junior Wells
Drinkin' TNT 'n' Smokin' Dynamite (Blind Pig) ★★★

In 1974 the tensely persuasive firm of Guy & Wells enfiladed a Montreux Jazz Festival audience with deadly, understated Chicago blues. The two alone, in effect, since Muddy Waters confidant Pinetop Perkins was defused by an inexpressive electric piano and rockers Bill Wyman (bass) and Dallas Taylor (drums) never rose above the functional. (41:28/Reissue)

Alone & Acoustic (Alligator)

Originally recorded and released in France in 1981 by Isabel Records, this recent reissue features contemporary blues stars Guy and Wells accompanying each other with unamplified instruments (guitar and harmonica, respectively) and shared vocals. The concept works best on the traditional covers and originals; the results are far less satisfying on acoustic covers of songs by John Lee Hooker and Jimmy Reed. The sense of informality and improvisation running throughout, though, makes this a very rewarding disc. (J.T.)   (59:38/Reissue)

Travis Haddix
Winners Never Quit (Ichiban)   ★★★

Backed by a yeoman rhythm section and horns, Cleveland singer Haddix favors a contemporary blues approach that finds him walking the fence between sleek artificiality and believable feeling. The gospel modulations in his voice pull his shuffles, ballads, funky blues, and a Latin-spiced original in the right direction. He's more a self-assured "winner" here than on the marginal victory that was his first Ichiban release, *Wrong Side Out.*   (51:53/1991)

John Hammond
The Best of John Hammond (Vanguard)   ★★★✦

Hammond has been a respected standard-bearer of the country blues tradition since acquitting himself at the 1962 Newport Folk Festival. Yet the most rewarding tracks on this compilation of his Vanguard work from the 1960s aren't the personalized solo adaptations of down-home blues, represented by eight songs, but rather the fourteen electric ensemble workouts. There Hammond's fervent directness is equaled by, among others, Charlie Musslewhite, Mike

Bloomfield, and Jimmy Spruill, the guitarist immortalized on Wilbert Harrison's "Kansas City." In recent years Hammond has recorded with less individuality for Rounder.

(70:59/Reissue)

Got Love If You Want It (Pointblank/Charisma)　★★★★

In the 1990s, Hammond's voice, guitar, and harp are those rarest of all instruments: the mediums of African-American expression managed absolutely by a white blues performer. Using producer J. J. Cale's band, Lil' Charlie and the Nightcats, and John Lee Hooker to prime advantage, he sends a steady charge of subtle fervency through backwoods or citified tunes from the likes of Charles Brown, Tom Waits, Chuck Berry, and Son House (whose "Preachin' the Blues" finds interpreter Hammond almost speaking in tongues).

(42:32/1992)

James Harman
Strictly Live . . . in '85! Volume One (Rivera)　★★★↗

If you strolled into your neighborhood blues bar and encountered a set as pleasurable and sensible as the one provided by the James Harman Band at the Belly Up Tavern in California you'd hoist a few tankards in honor of your good fortune. The Alabama-born leader's back-alley harp and sly-dog vocals have bite. The late Michael "Hollywood Fats" Mann on guitar has intelligent and decisive ideas. Plus there's a certain spirit to the shuffling ensemble textures beyond commonplace Chicago/West Coast blues revivalism.　(45:47/1990)

Do Not Disturb (Black Top)　★★★

The friendliness of Harman's music—his low-tension vocals, his light lyrics on motel life and relationships, and his songs' graceful, deceptively unassuming rhythms—can lull one into forgetting how gritty a musician he is. Temporarily, anyway. Before too long he raises harmonica to lips and talks straight. Sharing room service with the Harman band are Los Lobos's Dave Hidalgo on accordion and storied R&B saxophonist Lee Allen. (51:38/1991)

Harmonica Fats and the Bernie Pearl Blues Band
I Had to Get Nasty (Bee Bump) ★★★

Los Angeles–based Harvey "Harmonica Fats" Blackstone sounds right out of the 1950s on this R&B-influenced contemporary blues outing. Guitarist Bernie Pearl and tenor saxophonist Hollis Gilmore strongly support Fats's gruff vocals and exuberant harp work. (B.D.) (47:25/1991)

The Harper Brothers
You Can Hide Inside the Music (Verve) ★★★⌐

This sextet of young hard-bop proponents is moved by the sway of blues, and its fourth recording (the first with three new faces on tenor saxophone, piano, and bass) does the slow burn. The superfine arrangements of Jimmy Heath, the quietly intense work of singer Ernie Andrews, melody-adoring muted trumpeter Harry "Sweets" Edison, and organist Jimmy McGriff—all seasoned hands—lend part of the program's music an especially nice blues design. (59:25/1992)

Slim Harpo
The Best of Slim Harpo (Rhino) ★★★★

Harmonica player and singer James "Slim Harpo" Moore patrolled the Louisiana swamplands for the Excello Label from 1957 to 1966, recording slinky, lubricious numbers such as "Baby Scratch My Back" and "I'm a King Bee" (note Fats Perrodin's supernatural bass), which found favor with the Rolling Stones and other young white shapers of blues-dripping rock 'n' roll. This collection has the aforementioned and sixteen more of the grinning iconoclast's wettest and spongiest grooves, including three 1967–70 tunes outside the Excello fold. (47:26/1989)

Bill Harris
The Fabulous Bill Harris (V.S.O.P.) ★★♪

Count B. B. King, Kenny Burrell, and Andrés Segovia among the admirers of the ex-Clovers guitarist who played blues, jazz, and classical music with equal aplomb. Here we have club and concert hall performances captured on tape between 1957 and 1986. (61:47/1988)

Wynonie Harris
Mr. Blues Is Coming to Town (Route 66 import) ★★★★

Harris's big tenor voice, full of fun, jumps out of the locomotivelike shuffle rhythms of his pop/jazz/R&B band in these wonderful if obscure tracks from 1946–54. (His hits aren't included.) The racial mores of the time wouldn't allow Harris free travel, but his rock 'n' roll scions have come to everyone's town. (42:35/Reissue)

Screamin' Jay Hawkins
Voodoo Jive: The Best of Screamin' Jay Hawkins (Rhino) ★★★♪

In 1956, Hawkins's "I Put a Spell on You" was banned from the airwaves. Why? Glorious R&B dementia—even without the open-coffin visual shockeroo of his performances—wasn't

deemed fit for civilized tastes. Sixteen other lunatic fringe numbers, including a hearing-is-believing rendition of Cole Porter's "I Love Paris," track his unpredictable career up to 1969. Some of the fine blues players contributing to the mayhem are guitarist Kenny Burrell and saxophonist Al Sears.
(46:41/1990)

Johnny Heartsman
The Touch (Alligator)   ★★★✦

Heartsman cut to the very heart of the blues, providing guitar to sessions in Oakland through the 1950s and 1960s, which won him renown among history-minded musicians and fans in the ensuing years. His early-1990s Alligator debut makes a favorable impression for the inventive cast of his songwriting and the intelligent language of his guitar, keyboards, and flute. Minor drawbacks: Heartsman struggles a little as a singer, and his idea of funk (e.g., "Endless" and "Oops") relies on musty 1970s formulae.   (56:53/1991)

The Jimi Hendrix Experience
Radio One (Rykodisc)   ★★★★✦

Jimi Hendrix was a supreme bluesman, early on in his Greenwich Village days and right to the end, and this treasury of live BBC radio tracks from 1967 may be the most representative of his flatted-fifths affinity. The guitarist staggers listeners with ingeniously conceived sound effects that are integrated into his resounding playing on, among others, reinvented eruptions of Howlin' Wolf's "Killing Floor," Muddy Waters's "Catfish Blues," and Willie Dixon's "Hoochie Coochie Man" (the last with British blues dean Alexis Korner on bottleneck guitar). By the bye Hendrix's concert blues staple "Red House" arguably receives its most exciting treatment on CD on the remarkable *Live at Winterland* (Rykodisc), a memorable late-1960s San Francisco performance not cheapened by facile crowd pleasing. (59:39/1988)

Chuck Higgins
Pachuko Hop (Specialty) ★★★★

Storming 1954–56 Los Angeles R&B, with over half of the twenty tracks previously unissued. Higgins's skills on tenor saxophone were comparatively primitive, but there's no denying the primal energy and good humor of "Broke" and "Eye Balling," which feature vocals by Higgins's brother Fred (billed as "Daddy Cleanhead"), and the rollicking "Oh Yeah." (B.D.) (48:42/Reissue)

Z. Z. Hill
Greatest Hits (Malaco) ★★★★✓

After twenty-odd years of undervalued singing, soul bluesmaster Hill hit it big on the 1982–83 black charts with his four-star *Down Home* album—only to pass away months later, at age forty-four. His breakthrough label, Malaco, of Jackson, Mississippi, does his memory proud with this eleven-song salute, just chock-full of his stray-beyond-the-marriage-bed compunction. Forget about his voice lacking firmness and emotional sway à la Bobby Bland; its earthiness is dignified by one excellent song after another from on-call Malaco scribes and by soul-stirring arrangements. (43:26/1990)

Eddie Hinton
Cry and Moan (Bullseye Blues) ★★★★

Put simply, Southern soul bluesman Eddie Hinton is one of the most rousing singers of the past twenty-five years. Resurfacing of late after abject times, he bears down on a dozen good-to-fine originals with all the stark immediacy and subjective certainty his crying, moaning, rasping, pleading, and testifying can muster. Loads. Furthermore, his guitar playing still has the intrinsic merit it had when he was an acclaimed Muscle Shoals studio musician in the late 1960s. Hinton and Ron Levy are responsible for the triumphant cry of the production. One hopes Capricorn reissues his 1978 album *Very Extremely Dangerous.* (41:24/1991)

Billie Holiday
The Legacy (1933–1958) (Columbia/Legacy) ★★★★★

Holiday's voice, small yet supple and always unswervingly faultless in diction and phrasing, recomposed Tin Pan Alley songs as blues-tinged jazz poetry. This three-disc boxed set offers seventy tracks (including ten rarities), the vast majority coming from the 1930s, when she flamed with an all-knowing intensity well beyond the ken of other young singers. Saxophonist Lester Young, to single out her most sympathetic studiomate, brings out all the rational, shaded meanings of the melodies; Lady Day and Pres together on "I Must Have That Man" and several more capture the essence of sublimity. Boasting excellent digital sound, the retrospective includes a sixty-page booklet that contains rare photographs, session information, and Michael Brooks's interesting musings. (3:30:49/1991)

Lady in Autumn: The Best of the Verve Years (Verve) ★★★★♪

Worn down by a life scarred with tragedy and heartache, Holiday struggles with her voice during her last epoch, 1946–59. Still, her willpower and musical intelligence remain unconquered throughout the thirty-five studio and concert tracks filling two discs; the results are a great deal more

artistic than certain caviling arbiters of taste would have one believe. The four January 1957 songs with saxophonist Ben Webster and trumpeter Harry "Sweets" Edison are prima facie evidence of why she's this century's preeminent vocalist.
(2:07:42/1991)

Groove Holmes
Blues All Day Long (Muse) ★★★

Richard "Groove" Holmes saturated his every utterance on the Hammond B-3 organ with tremendous feeling. This typically swinging session, recorded in 1988, profits from the urgencies contributed by jazz/blues experts Jimmy Ponder, on guitar, and Houston Person, on tenor saxophone. (40:29/1989)

The Holmes Brothers
In the Spirit (Rounder) ★★★★

After almost ten years of New York barroom anonymity, siblings Wendell and Sherman and close friend Popsy Dixon suddenly sprang onto the national stage with one of the outstanding releases of the early 1990s. They have empathy for gospel, blues, soul, R&B, and country music and freshly reconceiving ideas about how the musical traditions should define their ensemble sound. Lead vocals and three-part harmonies reach for the sky, with Dixon's falsetto in the lead, while drums, guitar, bass, and horns burrow grooves that abound with enthusiasm and wisdom. Originals and standards from Jimmy Reed, Sam and Dave, the Falcons, and others all please immensely. (47:08/1990)

Where It's At (Rounder) ★★★★

The threesome apparently view the singing and playing of blues as a moral activity. There's a stately, sanctified quality to the ascents and slides of their vocals, the subtle but sure drive of their music, and their interpretation of lyrics. One senses a spiritual purification in progress during, for example, Brother Wendell's "The Love You Save" and Ray Charles's "Drown in My Own Tears." (47:48/1991)

Homesick James
Blues on the South Side (Prestige) ★★★

Homesick James Williamson's approach to his bottleneck guitar—scurrilous, gruff, severely emotional—was an extension of his second cousin's, Elmore James. The Tennessean's lines are the perfect complement for his raggedy vocals on this electrified 1964 date with pianist Lafayette Leake, bassist Eddie Taylor, and drummer Clifton James. (37:00/Reissue)

Miki Honeycutt
Soul Deep (Rounder) ★↙

It's strange that the so-called wailingest white woman singer in the Louisiana-Texas area should have to travel to Boston and record her first album with breezy Rhode Islanders the Blue Tones—certainly not the Southern soul undercurrent her husky, tough voice requires. Her studio-song selection consists of ersatz soul tunes, an unflattering Junior Wells song, and wearisome pop numbers. Indifferent sound engineering to boot. (35:38/1989)

Earl Hooker
Two Bugs and a Roach (Arhoolie) ★★★↙

Taught slide guitar by Robert Nighthawk, Delta-born Earl Hooker earned his reputation as a stalwart of amplified blues in the 1950s and 1960s. This collection shows sufficient grounds for his place in the sun: Hooker's guitar speaks volumes on both early 1950s recordings and country- and soul-mannered numbers cut shortly before his death in 1970. The stunner is "Sweet Black Angel," in which the young man's suspended-in-air notes—Azrael hovering—delineate a sepulchral, frightful mood. As a singer Hooker always had a tough time depicting any particular state of feeling at all.

(61:52/Reissue)

John Lee Hooker
The Ultimate Collection: 1948–1990 (Rhino)　　★★★★♩

Hooker's retentive salacity binds the thirty-one songs spread over the two discs of this intelligently assembled collection. Famous singles "Boogie Chillun," "I'm in the Mood," and "Boom Boom" are present, along with expected and surprising choices from his affiliations with labels such as Modern, Vee-Jay, Chess, Blues Way, and Liberty. Nearly all of the selections are timeless for his minatory monotone and his fibrillating rhythm, though the claim in the accompanying forty-five-page booklet about this being the "definitive" survey of his recording career incites protest. (1:44:19/1991)

House of the Blues (MCA/Chess)　　★★★★

In 1951 Delta émigré John Lee Hooker was a Detroit resident enjoying the raging success of recent singles and gearing up to wax his urgent folk blues for a host of record companies under various *noms de blooze*. Chess was one of the firms, and twelve sides cut between 1951 and 1954 eventually turned up on this 1959 long-player. Hooker's singing, lubricious and steely, inveighs against annoying women; his rudimental guitar is exciting; and his stamping the plywood floor in ruttish insistence makes for exemplary blues rhythm. Most of the tracks have him solo. Caveat emptor: Two songs have atrocious sound. (35:51/Reissue)

John Lee Hooker Plays and Sings the Blues (MCA/Chess) ★★★★

By himself, Hooker brings home the bacon performing eleven songs originally recorded for Gone or Chess in 1951–52; a twelfth, "Just Me and My Telephone," has Eddie Kirkland adding bass guitar. All convey strength of purpose, including adaptations of Big Joe Williams's "Baby Please Don't Go" and Big Maceo Merriweather's "Worried Life Blues."

(36:38/Reissue)

Sad and Lonesome (Muse) ★✦

Ponderous and forgettable late-1950s date, interesting only for how the unidentified second guitarist (Eddie Burns?), bassist, and drummer adapt to Hooker's eccentric musicality.

(45:33/Reissue)

The Country Blues of John Lee Hooker (Riverside/Fantasy) ★★★✦

Never one to stand on formality, Hooker sings and agitates his acoustic guitar according to his own errant musical logic. Deeply passionate song subjects include Delta floods, sexual misadventure, wanderlust, Mississippi justice, and tilling the fields. These thirteen songs were made for Vee-Jay in Detroit in 1959. (43:00/Reissue)

Boogie Chillun (Fantasy) ★★★★

Hooker's old *Live at Sugar Hill* and *Boogie Chillun* albums, both documents of November 1962 solo performances, are back-to-back with only one track missing (thanks to CD time constraints). His music is defiantly elemental—mood, tempo, chord sequences (almost none), and jagged rhythms vary little. Due to his individual touch and naked feeling, all nineteen selections escape tediousness and preserve the rural blues' aura of foreboding mystery in an amplified setting.

(76:07/Reissue)

The Real Folk Blues (MCA/Chess) ★★★★

A darling of mid-1960s rockers, electric boogiemeister Hooker savaged his soul essaying nine songs in the company of second guitarist Eddie Burns and unknown Chess players. "One Bourbon, One Scotch, One Beer" is his famous last call for alcohol, and "The Waterfront" exists as an especially affecting solo rumination.

(37:42/Reissue)

More Real Folk Blues: The Missing Album (MCA/Chess) ★★★★

After languishing in the Chess vaults for almost fifteen years, the follow-up to *The Real Folk Blues* finally sees the light of day, amid the early-1990s upswing in Hooker's long and cyclical career. The revelatory track is "Nobody Knows," where his voice crawls, moans, and maunders in cogent explanation of why he sings the blues. Elsewhere, seasoned hands Eddie Burns, Fred Below, and Lafayette Leake help him menace 1966 updates of 1950s material.

(43:03/1991)

Never Get Out of These Blues Alive (MCA) ★★★♪

Song title "Boogie with the Hook" fairly well sums up this 1971 San Francisco studio affair that included harmonica player Charlie Musslewhite, guitarists Elvin Bishop and Mel Brown, and rock singer Van Morrison. Take several deep breaths before hearing the Hooker requiem "T.B. Sheets."

(39:56/Reissue)

Alone (Tomato)   ★

Suffering from insomnia? Here's a guaranteed cure—two
discs' worth of soporific latter-day Delta John in a 1970s concert at a New York college. Hooker's "Boogie Chillun" was
once urgent personal testimony; here it's a rugged endurance
test. The preponderance of sloppily played slow blues is a
literal drag. (B.D.)   (1:22:54/Reissue)

The Best of John Lee Hooker: 1965 to 1974 (MCA)   ★★★

Governed by integrity, Hooker brings a brooding lyricism to
his vocal and guitar phrases in most of these eighteen selections recorded for Chess, ABC, Bluesway, and Impulse during
a nine-year period when he won the cachet of white listeners.
The digitally remastered material, though, is often soggy, and
he isn't provided much spark by at least seven of nine studio
groups; the Bob Thiele–produced sides in 1965 with drummer
Panama Francis and string bassist Milt Hinton are more prof-
itable than the later offerings.   (72:36/1992)

The Cream (Tomato)   ★★✦

Hooker rises to the top on performances at the Keystone in
Palo Alto, California, in mid 1977. Not hard at all, really, since
his nondescript backup band had all it could handle precari-
ously following his quirky musical strategies. Hooker dedi-
cates "Tupelo" to the recently departed Elvis Presley, who he
claims in stage chatter was a "really good friend."
                                                   (73:43/Reissue)

The Healer (Chameleon)   ★★★

Hooker crosses over successfully into the pop market with
assistance from progeny Bonnie Raitt, Carlos Santana, Robert
Cray, Los Lobos, George Thorogood, Charlie Musslewhite,

and fifth- or sixth-generation Canned Heat. The most fetching encounters are with Raitt ("I'm in the Mood") and Santana (the title track). On his own, the Hook cuts right to the bone with three typically sensual affirmations. (41:44/1989)

Mr. Lucky (Charisma/Pointblank) ★★★↗

John Lee, he of the mojo hand and wearing voice, says, "Bad luck can't do me no harm." Certainly not with attendants named Robert Cray, Albert Collins, John Hammond, Van Morrison, Keith Richards, Carlos Santana, Johnny Winter, and Ry Cooder on hand to make him feel better. The highlight is "I Cover the Waterfront," wherein true believers Hooker and Morrison go deep into the mystic. (47:23/1991)

• See also **Canned Heat and John Lee Hooker**

Lightnin' Hopkins
The Complete Aladdin Recordings (EMI) ★★★★↗

The prolific Texas guitarist Sam "Lightnin' " Hopkins began his career with Aladdin in 1946 and recorded for the label into early 1948, and this excellent two-disc collection contains everything he cut for Eddie Mesner's firm—forty-three titles in all. Hopkins's first two Aladdin sessions paired him with driving pianist Thunder Smith, who contributes vocals on four cuts. Lightnin' is at his dark, threatening best on the thirty solo tracks that follow. Sound is rough in spots, but certainly acceptable. (B.D.) (1:55:46/1991)

The Gold Star Sessions: Volume One (Arhoolie) ★★★★✦
The Gold Star Sessions: Volume Two (Arhoolie) ★★★★✦

One of the great men of Texas blues, Hopkins recorded innumerable 78s in the years following the Second World War. Forty-eight of his seminal country blues sides for Gold Star, a Houston label, have been stacked evenly on two volumes sporting excellent sound. Throughout both the tone of his voice is wholly convincing and his smoothly delivered guitar commentaries, ever so eloquent, elucidate the dark and bright facets of a pained soul. The same melodies and chords over and over don't tire the listener because he endlessly creates fresh, witty lyrics. (Vol. One 66:38/Reissue)
(Vol. Two 67:50/Reissue)

The Herald Recordings: 1954 (Collectables) ★★★★✦

If you're looking for Lightnin' Hopkins at his most exciting, search no further. These electrifying 1954 efforts for Herald find the prolific Texas guitar legend wielding a wildly amplified axe, with blistering results—his boogies positively smoke, and the astonishing up-tempo instrumental "Hopkins' Sky Hop" is one of the most torrid blues performances ever laid to wax. Sound quality isn't first generation, but in this case it's entirely forgivable. (B.D.) (44:23/Reissue)

Lightnin' Hopkins (Smithsonian/Folkways) ★★★

Producer Sam Charters recorded this solo acoustic album in 1959 with a hand-held microphone in the Texas guitarist's living room, and it served as Hopkins's introduction to the folk audience. Much of the album is downbeat, although there are a few intricate boogies such as "She's Mine" and "Fan It." Considering the circumstances, the sound is surprisingly decent. (B.D.) (32:15/Reissue)

The Complete Prestige/Bluesville Recordings ★★★★★
(Prestige/Bluesville)

Detailing an idiosyncratic world of bad luck and smiling anxiousness, Hopkins sings and skillfully picks his guitar on 112 songs fit onto the seven discs of this boxed set. Eleven albums from his Prestige-Bluesville period (1960–64) are present in their entirety, joined by thirteen previously unreleased tracks from a 1963 suburban Philadelphia college concert. One gets solo recitals, small group boogies (sidemen include Sonny Terry and Billy Bizor), and spoken reminiscences—nearly everything rewarding to hear in short spells. The thirty-two-page booklet includes an alphabetical listing of song titles, sessions information, photographs, and Sam Charters's knowledgeable writings on the Texan and his music.

(7:05:00/1991)

Double Blues (Fantasy) ★★★★

Anyone who finds the mammoth Hopkins box too overwhelming is advised to turn to this single-disc compression of two May 1964 recordings, *Down Home Blues* and *Soul Blues*. Assisted at times by a metronomic drummer and bassist, Hopkins is the antithesis of rusty relics fawned over by folkies of the time. He sings of autobiographical concerns in a steady, low-key manner, and his guitar is continuously lucent and alert. (76:01/Reissue)

• See also **Otis Spann/Lightnin' Hopkins**

Shirley Horn
You Won't Forget Me (Verve) ★★★★✦

Jazz singer/pianist Shirley Horn, based in Washington, D.C., puts her romantic material across easefully with the dramatic timing and commanding inflections of a quietly eloquent blues poetess. On her third stellar Verve recording she carries listeners through the mystery and melancholy of "It Had to Be You," "If You Go," and other American songbook riches, sometimes prying for meaning with harmonica master Toots Thielemans or trumpet savants Wynton Marsalis and Miles Davis. (71:11/1991)

Walter Horton
Fine Cuts (Blind Pig) ★★

In 1977 harmonica senior Big Walter Horton's approach to rhythm and pitch is no longer the wonderment of yesterday, and he only provides a few scintillas of creative animation on standards and marginalia. Sharing the studio with six young musicians, including saxophonist Mark "Kaz" Kazanoff and pianist Ron Levy, he cuts even a worse figure singing.
(36:44/Reissue)

Joe Houston
Cornbread and Cabbage Greens (Specialty) ★★★★

The mighty tenor saxophonist, a premier 1950s R&B honker, recorded prolifically for a slew of Los Angeles firms. This twenty-five-song compilation contains Houston's early to mid 1950s output for John Dolphin's labels, including a savage version of his trademark "All Night Long," two vicious takes of the saxophone national anthem "Flying Home," and sixteen unissued blowouts. (B.D.) (68:09/Reissue)

Howlin' Wolf
The Chess Box (MCA/Chess)

MCA's three-disc-set celebration of Howlin' Wolf (Chester Burnett) offers seventy-one tracks, including all his famous songs and nineteen obscurities. Sequenced chronologically, the first disc is given over mostly to his nastily ominous Memphis years (1951–54); the second covers the more controlled devilry of his storied Chess sessions in Chicago (1956–63); the last grouping of Chess singles and hitherto unreleased tunes takes us close to the end of his mortal reign (1964–73). Nary a lame lupine song anywhere. The enclosed thirty-two-page booklet, with its two essays, splendid photographs, and more, is as carefully assembled as the material. Another feather in the plume of MCA producer Andy McKaie.   (3:34:07/1991)

Cadillac Daddy: Memphis Recordings, 1952 (Rounder) ★★★★★

Once heard, Howlin' Wolf is never forgotten. Recording for an astonished Sam Phillips of Sun Records, the physically imposing singer/harpist from the Delta fields filled the studio with primordial enunciations of feverish sexual desire, unholy dread, spiteful rage, and leering jubilation, mixing his ingenious country blues with the amplified tones of his rough-and-tumble band, notably Willie Johnson on guitar. The twelve slow blues or boogies in this Colin Escott compilation have never before been available in North America.   (31:57/1989)

Howlin' Wolf/Moanin' in the Moonlight (MCA/Chess) ★★★★★

The feral 1950s and savage (early) 1960s. On two classic Chess LPs now combined on a single CD the catastrophic voice shakes "Red Rooster," "Spoonful," "Wang Dang Doodle," "Smokestack Lightnin'," "Evil," "How Many More Years?" and eighteen more songs that together exist at or near the pinnacle of electric blues.   (65:55/Reissue)

Change My Way (MCA/Chess) ★★★

Only Wolf fanatics truly need to hear this lesser grab bag of Chess singles that first saw the light of day between 1958 and 1966. "I Ain't Superstitious" and "Love Me Darlin'" (for Hubert Sumlin's anguished guitar) are the keepers—and they're both on the boxed set. (42:33/Reissue)

The Real Folk Blues (MCA/Chess) ★★★★✦

Blue ribbon material and performances point up the mighty Wolf's strong challenge to the Chicago blues hegemony of Muddy Waters in the 1950s and 1960s. Each of the dozen tracks anthologized here (in 1966), among them "Sittin' on Top of the World" and "Three Hundred Pounds of Joy" (Wolf: 6'6", 300 lbs.), is a declaration of purpose and sensual appetite. Wolf's Chess box has everything but "Poor Boy" and "Nature." (32:41/Reissue)

More Real Folk Blues (MCA/Chess) ★★★★★

With a voice full of volcanic soot the back door man terrorizes the lyrics to twelve songs from the Chess 1950s (eight duplicate the big box's program). The material may not be well known, but from start (the paint-peeling "Just My Kind") to finish (the salacious "I Have a Little Girl") this is rewarding listening. Factotums include Hubert Sumlin, Henry Gray, Otis Spann, and Willie Dixon. (34:24/Reissue)

The London Howlin' Wolf Sessions (MCA/Chess) ★★★★

The Wolf is more crotchety than frightening on this 1970 session with English gamins Eric Clapton, Bill Wyman, Charlie Watts, Steve Winwood, and his right-hand man Hubert Sumlin. But he still makes them shudder as they help him send forth worlds of dusky emotion with "Rockin' Daddy" and other lair favorites. (41:30/Reissue)

• See also **Muddy Waters and Howlin' Wolf**

Joe Hughes
If You Want to See the Blues (Black Top) ★★★

Veteran Joe "Guitar" Hughes is an undervalued Texas blues-man given a new lease on life by New Orleans' Black Top label. His first album ever is a classy R&B/blues affair, enabling him to bring to bear the full resources of his talent. Hughes writes decent songs, sings fairly well, and plays guitar as if back in 1950s Houston clubs locking horns with compatriot Johnny Copeland. Splendid sessions support from either Gulf Coast friends or Anson Funderburgh's Rockets.
(37:59/1989)

Mississippi John Hurt
1928 Sessions (Yazoo) ★★★★★

This ordering of thirteen blues, ballads, rags, and spirituals features the gentlest of Delta performers. Sharecropper/songster Hurt sings confidently in a throaty but quiet voice and picks guitar patterns that tell of his inner delight. His winsome music—from the John Henry tale "Spike Driver Blues" to the smilingly off-color "Candy Man Blues"—is essential listening. Bear with the surface noise of the 78s. (38:17/Reissue)

Avalon Blues 1963 (Rounder) ★★★✦

Hurt's recordings after his celebrated 1963 "rediscovery" by the folk music crowd and the national press are possessed by a characteristic genteelness. Delicate charm wins out over preciousness in "Casey Jones" and eleven more reflections on life or love in the Mississippi Valley, albeit few are technically compelling performances. Equally recommended is Rounder's *Worried Blues*, a 1963 long-player recorded in concert that is also finally out on small disc. (34:11/Reissue)

Last Sessions (Vanguard) ★★★

Only a few months away from a fatal heart attack, the elder statesman has some trouble getting the fingers and voice box to do his bidding on this 1966 session. But his inner flame burns bright. (46:25/Reissue)

J. B. Hutto
Slidewinder (Delmark) ★★★★

Fire in his eye, Joseph Benjamin "J. B." Hutto specialized in wringing from his slide guitar tones of such acidity and rough-hewn vividness that he went a long way toward making the distinctions between rural and urban blues—and blues rock—meaningless. He and his three 1972 studio revelers ravage the songs here as if boogie were a devastating force of nature. (36:10/Reissue)

Illinois Jacquet
The Blues; That's Me! (Prestige) ★★★✦

Texas tenor saxophonists, according to jazz mythos, have the blues stamped on their souls. Houston's Jean-Baptiste "Illinois" Jacquet plays glowingly all through this rewarding 1969 blowing session, even hauling out his bassoon for one number. What's especially interesting for blues fans are his and four-string guitarist Tiny Grimes's choruses on the slow twelve-bar gait that identifies the man and the album. (40:28/Reissue)

Elmore James
Let's Cut It (Virgin/Flair) ★★★★✦

Seminal work by the most imitated slide guitarist of his generation. These are James's earliest attempts at cracking the R&B market, circa 1953–56, before he began endlessly rehashing his well-known theme, "Dust My Broom" (present in a classic early incarnation). There are some intriguing departures: the rhumba-beat "No Love in My Heart," the doo-wop-influenced "Goodbye Baby," and the crashing instrumental "Hawaiian Boogie (No. 2)." (B.D.)

(52:07/Reissue)

Dust My Broom (Tomato)   ★★★

Solid cross section of the slide guitar great's early-1960s output for Harlem entrepreneur Bobby Robinson's Fire label, including the blistering "Shake Your Moneymaker," his grinding classic "The Sky Is Crying," and another remake of the title track. Sound quality isn't first generation, but it's adequate. (B.D.)   (41:37/Reissue)

Street Talkin' (Muse)   ★★★★

Eddie Taylor, a well-respected guitarist and singer, should rightfully share feature billing with bottleneck guitar nonpareil James on this amplified Chicago blues collection. Taylor and a truculent outfit are heard on his signature song "Big Town Playboy" and on six more good tracks from 1955 to 1956. Jimmy Reed plays wobbly harmonica on five songs; George Mayweather takes over for him on two. On the other half of the program James and his Broomdusters (including Taylor) wrestle emotion from every blue note of "It Hurts Me Too," the instrumental "Elmore's Contribution to Jazz," and five more 1957 tracks, making them musical hand grenades that could explode at any instant.   (40:11/Reissue)

Rollin' & Tumblin'—The Best (Relic)   ★★★★♪

Taken from the original masters, this twenty-two-track collection of the slide guitar wizard's early-1960s work for Fire proves that James's last sides were as combustible as his first.

Three fine unissued titles share space with scalding revivals of "Dust My Broom," "Sunnyland," and "It Hurts Me Too" on the best CD reissue by far of James's Fire output. (B.D.)
(67:01/Reissue)

Elmore James and John Brim
Whose Muddy Shoes (MCA/Chess) ★★★↗

Fifties Chicago blues brethren James and Brim share the spotlight on the return of a long-unavailable 1969 Chess album. James's rousing vocals perfectly suit the racy mood defined by the Broomdusters on nine songs, from the famous "Dust My Broom" to the little-known "Tool Box Blues." His guitar, of course, plays a big role, showcasing the intense drama and portentous technique of a postwar twelve-bar blues paladin. Singer/guitarist Brim's six sides, made in 1953 and 1956, tell of his honesty and modest skill, with only "Tough Times," elbowed along by Snooky Prior's harmonica and Eddie Taylor's guitar, leaving a lasting impression for its edgy music and timelessly pertinent lyrics.   (43:04/Reissue)

Etta James
R&B Dynamite (Virgin/Flair) ★★↗

British collection of middling R&B tracks that singer Etta James made for Modern during her flirtatious teenage years in the 1950s. In the New Orleans and Los Angeles studios she turns a phrase with a precocious sense of self-possession, but her emotional believability is that of a callow artist. While James's 1955 hit "Good Rockin' Daddy" and "Roll with Me Henry," written with her mentor Johnny Otis, are good fun, a great many songs have been outfitted with emetic melodies, puerile lyrics, and showy but worthless arrangements.
(56:55/Reissue)

The Second Time Around (MCA/Chess) ★★

After James's initial R&B hits in the mid 1950s, which reveal a spirited ingenue, the singer chalked up a string of chart successes for Chess. Pop material such as "One for My Baby" and the 1961 hit "Don't Cry Baby" feature her tougher but not necessarily wiser alto. (28:12/Reissue)

The Sweetest Peaches: Part One (1960–1966) (MCA/Chess) ★★
The Sweetest Peaches: Part Two (1967–1975) (MCA/Chess) ★★★

In her early Chess years James was spurned by Harvey Fuqua of Moonglows fame, and that apparently gave a deeper shading to the melancholy in her singing. Yet beyond infrequent signs of a growing emotional maturation, there isn't much else to recommend the saccharine collection *Part One (1960–1966)*. The years covered on *Part Two (1967–1975)* offer a more compelling vocalist and a few splendid Muscle Shoals grooves (i.e., "Tell Mama," "I'd Rather Go Blind") but also a fair amount of Los Angeles studio dross. It's unfortunate that two Chess vinyl compilations with stronger programs, *Peaches* and *Her Greatest Sides, Volume One*, aren't available on CD. (Part One 35:49/1988)
(Part Two 36:41/1988)

Tell Mama (MCA/Chess) ★★★★✔

Southern soul outpost Fame Studios in Muscle Shoals, Alabama, was where the California singer, then plagued with personal demons, went to record her best 1960s work. Accompanied by the same house bluesmen who'd roweled Aretha Franklin just months earlier, James unleashes "Tell Mama" (a Top Forty hit in 1967), "I'd Rather Go Blind" (her magnum opus), and ten pearls of slightly lower luster. Her vocals throughout are paragons of female virility. (30:10/Reissue)

Seven Year Itch (Island) ★★★★

Twenty years on, James records an unplanned companion album to *Tell Mama*, with the organist at that storied session, Barry Beckett, now acting as producer. With her texturally rich voice she commandingly seizes hold of fine ballads and up-tempo numbers, making discretionary use of firiness and giving sure thought to interpretations of lyrics. Gone is the screaming and shouting of the 1970s and 1980s. She sings sassily and guardedly, full of shrewd insight and pent-up anger—hear, in particular, her rendering of Ann Peebles's "Breakin' Up Somebody's Home." Guitarist Steve Cropper and other Nashville cats tap a soul blues vein also plentiful in rock and R&B components. (35:58/1988)

Stickin' to My Guns (Island) ★★

One supposes *Seven Year Itch* didn't sell enough units and the Island brain trust made a bottom-line decision. Los Angeles shlock rock and funk flourishes have been grafted onto Barry Beckett–produced soul blues tracks, and tough cookie Etta James has all the credibility of those toy pistols she brandishes in the cover photograph. Special guest: Def Jam, of rap notoriety. (40:06/1990)

Etta James and Eddie "Cleanhead" Vinson
The Late Show (Fantasy) ★★

Neither Mister Cleanhead nor Miss James makes a particularly good impression performing evergreens at—where else?—Marla's Memory Lane Supper Club in Los Angeles in 1986. Companion volume *The Early Show* (Fantasy CD) groans beneath an even greater load of nostalgia. (43:59/1987)

Skip James
Today! (Vanguard) ★★★★★

The tone, spirit, and feeling of Nehemiah "Skip" James's country blues evokes an aura of haunting augustness. After decades of self-willed obscurity, the Mississippian resurfaced for the 1964 Newport Folk Festival and a few recording sessions, the most invocatory of which were done for Vanguard. The songs on the marvelous *Today!* find a self-respecting and sensitive black American being completely true to himself, using a feyly tuned guitar and a heart-stopping high tenor to give emotional cogency to his lyrics on life in an unforgiving, merciless prewar Mississippi. Two numbers have him spiritedly playing a piano with characteristic eccentricity.

(46:46/1988)

Devil Got My Woman (Vanguard) ★★★★★

The 1968 Vanguard follow-up to *Today!* has another dozen semiautobiographical or entirely personalized traditional songs that attest to his almost unparalleled artistry. As is his wont, women figure prominently in his poetic piques. More mandatory listening: *50 Years: Mississippi Blues in Bentonia, 1931–1981* (Wolf import CD), James's eighteen existing sides from 1931 along with five songs by kindred spirit Jack Owens in 1981.

(49:41/Reissue)

Blind Lemon Jefferson
King of the Country Blues (Yazoo) ★★★★★

Some of the monumentally important 1920s Texas blues guitarist's best work, taken from 78s. These twenty-three sides, including Jefferson's often-covered "Matchbox Blues," offer an in-depth examination of his complex guitar playing and powerful vocal style—an overriding influence on the enduring

Lone Star blues legacy that developed after Jefferson's death in 1929. (B.D.) (66:01/Reissue)

Big Jack Johnson
Daddy, When Is Mama Comin' Home? (Earwig) ★★★★

Clarksdale, Mississippi, part-time musician Jack Johnson has a blues sensibility that is bold and contemporary, unsentimental and direct. Taking a respite from his duties with the local Jelly Roll Kings band, he traveled to New York and Chicago in the late 1980s and recorded as featured artist with exceptionally able ensembles led by trombonist Bill McFarland. Subsequently, Johnson, with more droll tricks to turn than Helen of Troy had ships to launch, fills his songs with an electric guitar indebted to no one but his own idiosyncratic self *and* guileless, strong vocals that handle his lyrics on subjects like domestic violence, sex, a favorite airline, China, and AIDS. (64:07/1988)

Blind Willie Johnson
Praise God I'm Satisfied (Yazoo) ★★★★★

Treating a hymnal of sorts, Johnson expertly moves a penknife over his guitar strings to second the haunting modulations of his contrived bass voice. The title track and thirteen more songs from the late 1920s, some without the benefit of his celestial blade, are the folk music equivalent of Jonathan Edwards's written entreaties on the choice of hellfire or salvation. Johnson's wife sometimes sings responses to his melodies, further heightening the end-of-the-world moods. The sound is that of fairly clear 78s. (43:58/Reissue)

Sweeter as the Years Go By (Yazoo) ★★↗

Johnson's guitar picking, not half the emotional tour de force of his slide work, prods most of the spirituals rounding out his recording legacy. Late-1920s slide supplications "You'll Need Somebody on Your Bond" and "Lord, I Just Can't Keep from Crying" make the best case for purchasing this disc.

(50:40/Reissue)

Jimmy Johnson
Johnson's Whacks (Delmark) ★★

Although a leading modern bluesman, Chicago's Jimmy Johnson is poorly represented on six-inch disc. This fairish, newly remixed 1979 set—a farrago of good songs and throwaways—features his high, sharp voice taking an anguished turn while his guitar slashes mercilessly in grief. Johnson's band is no better than acceptable, with pianist Carl Snyder faring poorly for the fresh sound manipulation. (40:52/Reissue)

Johnnie Johnson
Johnnie B. Bad (Elektra Nonesuch) ★★↗

Take Johnson's piano out of those timeless Chuck Berry hits and you wouldn't have rock 'n' roll. Remove his hard-pressed-to-be-the-featured-player contributions from his first headlining album and you'd have a set reminding one of a decent little NRBQ album circa 1968, only with Eric Clapton and Keith Richards thrown into the bargain. As it is, nothing too exciting. (44:50/1991)

Johnnie Johnson/Clayton Love/Jimmy Vaughn
Rockin' Eighty-Eights (Modern Blues) ★★

Three skilled St. Louis–based pianists conversant with boogie 'n' blues (Johnson played with Chuck Berry, Vaughn served Albert King, Love recorded for several 1950s labels) take four turns apiece at the Steinway on a recent date. Pleasing enough, but the sessions' jump blues guitarists, horn players, and rhythm sections carry on like toadying, loud-mouthed neighborhood brats. (49:35/1991)

Lil Johnson
Hottest Gal in Town (1936–1937) (Story of Blues) ★★★

Bawdy double-entendre material from the prewar Chicago vocalist, who recorded the likes of "Get 'em from the Peanut Man" and "Let's Get Drunk and Truck" with an all-star array behind her that variously included pianist Black Bob and guitarist Big Bill Broonzy. Very acceptable 78 transfers utilized here. (B.D.) (54:12/Reissue)

Lonnie Johnson
Steppin' on the Blues (Columbia/Legacy) ★★★★★

Lonnie Johnson's linear invention and chordal solidity on guitar was of such a magnitude that he attained Olympian status in jazz and blues. This grouping of nineteen Okeh sides (four previously unreleased) from a seven-year period (1925–32) offers long looks at his duple wizardry. Also, Victoria Spivey shares lead vocals on two songs, Texas Alexander sings lead twice, and fellow single-string guitar expert Eddie Lang duets with Johnson on the wonders "Guitar Blues" and "How to Change Keys." Fine liner notes by Pete Welding and state of the art sound reproduction. (58:29/1990)

Losing Game (Prestige/Bluesville) ★★★★

At the tail end of 1960 the ageless soloist recorded this attractive assortment of blues and ballads. His vocals are as rich as Godiva chocolate, and his guitar phrases glide through tempos with the ease, sophistication, and intense feeling that won him the admiration of comrades Duke Ellington, Louis Armstrong, and Victoria Spivey decades earlier.   (36:18/Reissue)

Luther "Guitar Junior" Johnson
I Want to Groove with You (Bullseye Blues) ★★★

High chief of the Boston blues scene and onetime Muddy Waters sideman, Johnson packs a red-hot pistol of a guitar and sings acceptably on a Chicago-style session. He takes his boastful "I'm from Mississippi" right back home, though his workaday Magic Rockers are only along for the ride. Refreshingly, Johnson grooves to enjoyable originals and lesser-known standards, not predictable material.   (46:58/1990)

Luther "Houserocker" Johnson
Houserockin' Daddy (Ichiban) ★★★

Unrelated to either of the Luther Johnsons that backed Muddy Waters, this Atlanta guitarist's low-down sound would have pleased the Chicago legend. Now if Johnson could only locate some decent original material to match his talent (eight of ten tracks are covers). (B.D.)   (41:47/1991)

Robert Johnson
The Complete Recordings (Columbia/Legacy) ★★★★★

The forty-one tracks Robert Johnson recorded in Dallas and San Antonio in 1936–37—his entire *known* recorded legacy collected by Columbia on two discs—provide the astonishment of seeing the Taj Mahal float by on a purple cloud. His tenor and falsetto tell you of the complicated emotions harbored by an acutely perceptive blues musician in the denigratory South; so does his guitar playing, which amazingly often mixes leads with chords. Johnson's thematic lyrics—further bespeaking his restlessness, fatalism, and defiance—are stately in their imagery. Twelve alternate takes are as stunning as the originals. The music, somehow, further benefits from the digital restoration and engineering of one Frank Abbey. Incidentally, the value of the forty-two-page accompanying booklet is subject to debate. (1:46:44/1990)

Louis Jordan
The Best of Louis Jordan (MCA) ★★★★★

Jordan and the Tympany Five's delicious jump blues and novelty numbers sold millions of 78s throughout the 1940s. The good-natured bandleader was a marvelous blues singer, especially on ballads, and as a saxophone-playing veteran of the Chick Webb Orchestra he brought intelligent jazz motives to his repertoire. "Choo Choo Ch'Boogie" and "Caldonia," shuffle boogies deluxe, stand tall with the other eighteen tunes as some of the most pleasurable music ever committed to wax. Originally a two-record set issued in 1975. Fans with an insatiable appetite need the eight-CDs-and-one-LP collection, *Let the Good Times Roll: The Complete Decca Recordings* (Bear Family import). (63:28/Reissue)

Five Guys Named Moe (MCA/Decca) ★★★★

Swaggering, bouncing, or vaulting into joyful moods, Jordan animates eighteen little-known singles from the Decca 1940s and early 1950s that have been collected for this follow-up volume to *The Best of Louis Jordan* (and tie-in to Broadway's Jordan celebration, *Five Guys Named Moe*). His alto is liquid and dashing, his singing is full of charm, and concentrated arrangements by Wild Bill Davis or Bill Doggett magnify the well-drilled Tympany Five's sauciness. Louis Armstrong contributes to the clownishness of "Life Is So Peculiar."

(51:11/1992)

Willie Kent
Ain't It Nice (Delmark)   ★★★

Kent is a seasoned Chicago singer and bass player who comes by his restless feeling honestly. The modern bluesman writes durable songs, and he employs a talented harmonica squabbler in "Mad Dog" Lester Davenport. The change-of-pace "Feels So Good" is a jazzy philter that works admirably.

(56:38/1991)

Albert King
Let's Have a Natural Ball (Modern Blues)   ★★★★

Guitarist Albert King, a Mississippi native, settled into a recognizable mode of expression while fronting a jump blues band in St. Louis during the 1950s. This compilation of Bobbin and King sides from 1959 to 1963—including the 1961 R&B hit "Don't Throw Your Love on Me So Strong"—has him condensing B. B. King expositions into dagger-sharp phrases that carry more pained feeling than does his church-trained singing. Refined St. Louis combos, often with Ike Turner or Johnnie Johnson on piano, pilot his displays of technique and conviction. Exciting mono sound.   (39:49/1989)

Live Wire/Blues Power (Stax)   ★★★

King signed with Stax in 1966 and soon began winning over young white listeners. Six songs wrung out onstage two nights at the Fillmore West in June 1968—his first headlining shows for San Franciscan longhairs—pack this album dating from the same year. He paces his attack, building levels and levels of excitement, while his sidemen do their best to hide their unfamiliarity with most of the material. His serrate vocals and homey chats are superfluous. (38:17/Reissue)

Wednesday Night in San Francisco (Stax) ★★★★
Thursday Night in San Francisco (Stax) ★★★✦

More archetypal King "blues power" from his 1968 Fillmore performances, unreleased on album until 1990. *Wednesday* has revamps of material he'd recorded in the studio just recently (e.g., "Born Under a Bad Sign") or several years earlier (e.g., "Got to Be Some Changes Made"). *Thursday* offers, for the great part, standards that are identified with luminaries such as B. B. King, Louis Jordan, and Charles Brown. Everywhere, Albert's guitar stings and clings like a spiteful horn fly.
(Wed. 43:21/1990)
(Thurs. 51:43/1990)

Blues for Elvis (Stax) ★★

Albert King from Indianola smiles on the more famous "King" from Tupelo, putting his soul blues cachet on "Heartbreak Hotel," "Jailhouse Rock," and seven more. Originally released in 1969. (37:15/Reissue)

Lovejoy (Stax) ★★✦

Finding himself in early-1970s Hollywood and Muscle Shoals studios with good studio players, King lends his rugged baritone voice and ever-ready guitar to material from the Rolling Stones, Taj Mahal, producer Don Nix, and his own funky self. The highlight is King's uplifting slow blues "Everybody Wants to Go to Heaven." (36:40/Reissue)

I'll Play the Blues for You (Stax)   ★★★★

Near-definitive blues with soul, first heard in 1972. King's
piercing notes and vitriol-soaked phrases respond tellingly to
his warm, reassuring vocals—his title declaration of intent
and "Breakin' Up Somebody's Home" are extremely compelling. The Bar-Kays truckle to his will with stirring groove, but
one can't help pining for the rhythm magic of first-call Stax
backups the M.G.s.   (40:14/Reissue)

I Wanna Get Funky (Stax)   ★★★

This 1973 release has King using his upside-down Flying V to
slash a blues path through the Memphis Horns, the Memphis
Symphony Orchestra, and the dawn-of-disco funk rhythm
players. He half-sings with one eye on B. B. King and Bobby
Bland and the other fixed on hot-buttered soul crooner Isaac
Hayes. "Crosscut Saw" best captures the album title, with the
leader and astounding drummer, Al Jackson, charbroiling a
song the two had soul basted back in the mid 1960s with
Booker T. Jones.   (44:22/Reissue)

The Best of Albert King (Stax)   ★★★

Accept the title of this Stax collection with wariness. You
won't find anything at all from his splendid 1966–67 period of
"Laundromat Blues," "Crosscut Saw," and "Born Under a
Bad Sign." What you do get are eleven album tracks and two
singles from his 1968–73 years—the majority enjoyable.
                                                      (62:36/Reissue)

Blues at Sunrise (Stax)   ★★★♪

The songs King performed at the Montreux Jazz Festival in
1973, ranging from an ominous version of Ray Charles's "I

Believe to My Soul" to several up-tempo string-benders, are readily accessible. One of his better concert documentations.

(45:49/1988)

New Orleans Heat (Tomato)

Recording for Tomato in 1979, King luxuriates in the Vieux Carré soul production of Allen Toussaint. The guitarist and singer takes to the local climate well—not that he and the funkmeisters about town (including rhythm guitarist Leo Nocentelli and drummer Charles Williams) break a sweat kindly or are above sometimes coasting on clichés.

(41:39/Reissue)

The Lost Sessions (Stax) ★

We should be so lucky. In 1986 a Fantasy Records executive wondered why the master tapes on a King studio jam that he'd stumbled upon in the vault had been allowed to go unheard for fifteen years. Simple: Aside from some good rapier single-note thrusts by King, this jazz-blues fusion is a sloppy mess. Producer John Mayall was oblivious, but you can bet bored participants Ernie Watts, Clifford Solomon, and the late Blue Mitchell knew from the start this was a shaky affair.

(47:51/Reissue)

Albert King and Otis Rush
Door to Door (MCA/Chess) ★★★★♪

Esquires King and Rush pushed themselves further toward interpretative wisdom and individuality with the 1960–61 recordings found in this blue-ribbon collection. The tone in King's low-down voice shifts between sternness and leniency while his rhythmically staggering guitar distills drama. (Three 1953 Parrot singles, his earliest work, have been included, and they're notable for his up-high singing.) Rush, with "So Many Roads," "All Your Love," and four more gems, is also in fine form, his singing agonizingly pitched, his choking of the guitar neck beseeching and peremptory. (39:37/Reissue)

B. B. King

The Best of B. B. King, Volume One (Flair/Virgin) ★★✦

Something of an unintentional botch job. The CD's original compilers at Ace in Great Britain mistakenly used copies of several of Riley "B. B." King's mid-1950s hits that had later been overdubbed with big band brass, electric bass, and louder drums, and Flair perpetuates the inexcusable gaffe. Still, that leaves fourteen unaltered tracks from the young guitarist's massive RPM and Kent catalog, including "Sweet Sixteen" (both parts, in stereo), the stomping "Early Every Morning," and the touching "Please Accept My Love." (B.D.) (57:13/Reissue)

Live at the Regal (Mobile Fidelity) ★★★★★

Midway through the show at Chicago's Regal Theatre on November 21, 1964, the foremost blues guitarist articulates a series of patented licks with all the conviction of a hellfire preacher espousing the word. Someone in the audience cries out, "That's B. B. all right!" Damn straight. That November evening belonged to the former Memphis disc jockey all the way, for his masterfully nuanced singing, for his warm, sparkling guitar tones, and for those galloping single-note runs; for his refashioning of old hits and standards; for his exhilarated sextet. Note: Mobile Fidelity Sound Lab's digital mastering technique provides better sound than what's encountered on MCA's Live at the Regal. (34:47/Reissue)

Great Moments with B. B. King (MCA)   ★★★♪

Twenty-three concert or studio tracks originally issued on
ABC Bluesway between 1965 and 1967. What has solid claim
on the lofty title are his rip-my-heart-out vocals during the
club performances, where his trusty guitar and the backup
players are struggling to establish "good" let alone "great"
moments.   (70:38/Reissue)

Blues Is King (MCA)   ★★★★

At the time of this Chicago performance in late 1966, King's
popularity among blacks had ebbed and white rock 'n' roll
fans were beginning to notice him. Still, his long-faithful fans
in the club spur him on, even during a few tunes not worth his
examination (notably "Tired of Your Jive" and "Night Life").
The house sound system and mid-1960s engineering let him
down.   (40:34/Reissue)

Back in the Alley (MCA)   ★★★♪

Five of the nine selections also appear on either *Live at the
Regal* or *The Electric B. B. King*. The remainder are a pleasing assortment: "Watch Yourself" and "Lucille" (the endearing story of his guitar) were recorded in 1967 with a tight
combo (the organist is Maxwell Davis, who arranged his mid-
1950s RPM sides), while "Paying the Cost to Be the Boss" and
"I'm Gonna Do What They Do to Me" probably derive from
a different session the same year.   (42:23/Reissue)

The Electric B. B. King—His Best (MCA)   ★★♪

The title fibs. The flotsam filling this 1968 release includes
singles, tracks from earlier ABC albums, a live cut, and
Quincy Jones–produced soundtrack numbers from a minor
Sidney Poitier film. None of it is especially good, and the
soundtrack music is bad.   (33:19/Reissue)

Live and Well (MCA)   ★★★★

Five late-1960s studio tracks and as many recent concert takes add up to a solid outing. "Why I Sing the Blues," utilizing contemporary studio players who spare no energy, was a R&B hit in edited form in 1969. This was the first of several King albums produced solicitously by Bill Szymczyk. (47:55/Reissue)

Completely Well (MCA)   ★★★★

King's exciting vocals and guitar are provided a sympathetic sounding board by respectful but not fawning young sessionsmen. Points of interest include "The Thrill Is Gone," a Top Twenty hit, and the open-ended jam "Cryin' Won't Help You Now/You're Mean," which has his lordship stirring it up with uncredited guitarist Hugh McCracken. Lucky for everyone King steers clear of the Age of Aquarius funk then debasing the music of T-Bone Walker and other bluesmen cutting pop-slanted records in the late 1960s. (50:08/Reissue)

Indianola Mississippi Seeds (MCA)   ★★★♪

Not once during his immersion in the pop waters here does Riley B.'s commitment to blues flag. Never far from his mind are the hometown "seeds": church choirs, plantation work, prized recordings of Charlie Christian and Lonnie Johnson, the enduring virtues of humility, inner strength, and generosity of spirit. Leon Russell and Carole King are among several musicians skillfully helping out on this absorbing set of originals and Russell's "Hummingbird." Initially released in 1970. (39:34/Reissue)

Live in Cook County Jail (MCA)   ★★★★♪

The stockade show opener "Every Day I Have the Blues" is tossed off so quickly that King gives the impression he wants to be elsewhere (can't blame him). But on this summer day in 1971 his heart goes out to 2,000 inmates, and he takes his time offering the sublimated "How Blues Can You Get," the ever-forceful "The Thrill Is Gone," a medley combining his first hit, "Three O'Clock Blues," "Darlin' You Know I Love You," and three more effusions of hopefulness. He bends vibrato-drenched notes out of Lucille with all the attention to rhythm and melody expected of a master.   (38:50/Reissue)

Guess Who (MCA)   ★★★♪

Soul arrangements dressed up with subcutaneous fat of sing-ers, strings, and horns impede King's attempts to pierce to the core of the material. Yet he succeeds, even if on occasion the song isn't worth the perspiration—to wit, the Lovin' Spoon-ful's "Summer in the City" and Eddie Boyd's played-to-death "Five Long Years." A 1972 release.   (43:41/Reissue)

The Best of B. B. King (MCA)   ★★★★

This "best" package has seven acceptable songs (plus the idiotically engineered "Nobody Loves Me but My Mother" and a Cook County Jail bagatelle) that King recorded for ABC between 1969 and 1971. Completely Well gets short shrift, but two good numbers on the unavailable-on-CD B. B. King in London turn up (though one's truncated).   (40:33/Reissue)

Midnight Believer (MCA)   ★★★♪

The patriarch, just a fellow who plays the blues, pairs up with the Crusaders—keyboards specialist Joe Sample, bassist Wil-ton Felder, drummer Stix Hooper—and greases the skillet with classy late-1970s funk. Sample feeds King's palatable songs that don't unduly tax his wearying voice; only Hooper's "Never Make a Move Too Soon," not coincidentally the most thrilling selection, challenges him. Lucille gets plenty of bed rest.   (33:27/Reissue)

Live "Now Appearing" at Ole Miss (MCA) ★

King and the University of Mississippi audience rise above their troubles for a spell in the late 1970s—purportedly captured on this two-disc package. The main man sings evenly and sprays blue tones with typical onstage intensity, handling repertoire mainstays and tunes recently recorded with the Crusaders. Fine if you were there; no one at the show was subjected to extra horns, a string section, Brazilian percussion, and other execrable "sweetenings" added later in the New York recording studio. (1:25:03/Reissue)

There Must Be a Better World Somewhere (MCA) ★★★★

Someone had the good sense to invite Hank Crawford and Fathead Newman to a B. B. King session. The two grizzled saxophonists speak the blues language as knowingly as the guitarist, no idle claim, and they help Dr. John and others set relaxed, evocative moods that give insight into the title of this 1981 album. Smart, too, having the good Doctor and friend Doc Pomus supply almost all the material. (36:02/Reissue)

Love Me Tender (MCA) ★

Ouch. King traveled to Nashville in the early 1980s and recorded overproduced pop ballads written by the likes of honky tonk angels Conway Twitty, Willie Nelson, and Mickey Newbury. King plays guitar about as often as Perry Como and Tom Jones would have. (44:23/Reissue)

Blues 'n' Jazz (MCA) ★★★

The leader's voice and guitar, the former a tad worn in spots, converge with riffs from spruce New York jazz musicians in sharp arrangements. This program, with several old songs changed into new clothes, first appeared in 1983. (36:59/Reissue)

Six Silver Strings (MCA)   ★◢

King's fiftieth album, a 1985 release. Instead of an effort worthy of the occasion, MCA parades one of the most unctuous albums of his long recording career. Producer Dave Crawford, responsible for a couple more blots on his escutcheon in the mid 1970's, is back again, reducing the gilt-edged voice and sterling strings to plethoric product on a part with gewgaw synthesizers. Crawford also ignobly shares songwriting credits with veteran Luther Dixon.   (33:55/Reissue)

King of the Blues: 1989 (MCA)   ★

Another King-size contretemps. King is so accommodating that he doesn't blanch at singing invidious pop-pap songs with emotion. He acquiesces in the production decisions of four Hollywood types. Rodney Kelly programs one mean computer.   (51:28/1988)

Live at San Quentin (MCA)   ★★★★

In concert, beneath guard towers or not, King's string-bent prose is always thick with inventive wit, uncanny declarations of pain and pleasure, and gritty *beaux gestes*. The baritone voice packs a wallop; surprisingly so if you thought his studio albums in recent years evidenced declining power. "Into the Night" and "Peace to the World"—cotton candy for the ears—drag down the concert just a little.   (64:13/1990)

Live at the Apollo (GRP)   ★★★★◢

One night in the winter of 1990 the SRO audience in Harlem's Apollo Theatre rocked in ecstasy to the blessed tones offered them by the master musician and the swinging eighteen-piece Philip Morris Superband, conducted by pianist Gene Harris. Salutes to Percy Mayfield, Ivory Joe Hunter, and Jesse Belvin (along with repertoire staples and the wondrous slow blues "All Over Again") have no problem at all going over with the demanding African-American audience. (44:33/1991)

There Is Always One More Time (MCA) ★★★★

This recent adult blues session's shortcoming lies in its pedestrian material (guitarist Arthur Adams, pianist Joe Sample, and Will Jennings shoulder all of the blame), but die-hard King's solo breaks and riffing on the nine tunes fairly well burst with grand rhythmic articulateness. His non-Lucille singing is also augustly steady and resolved, especially when he sheds a proud man's tear for the late Doc Pomus in the songwriter's eight-minutes-plus title track. (46:12/1991)

B. B. King and Bobby Bland
Together for the First Time . . . Live (MCA) ★↗

What a bust. Bland and King sharing the make-believe 1974 studio nightclub proves as interesting as watching two top prizefighters cinch, sleepwalk, and smile hollowly at each other for ten lousy rounds. Bland shows the most vigor and acumen, winning on points. Meanwhile the men in their corners—twenty-one different musicians—strike attitudes for effect. (68:41/Reissue)

Together Again . . . Live (MCA) ★★↗

In an authentic club, Los Angeles's Coconut Grove, King is in better form. Yet the material is shopworn ("Let the Good Times Roll," "Stormy Monday Blues," etc.) and the strut-then-rest headliners force exaggerated gestures of gaiety rather than allow pleasures to arise naturally and flow—assuming they might. Johnny Pate's arrangements for an excellent horn section provide the longest-lasting tingles. (44:23/Reissue)

Bobby King and Terry Evans
Live and Let Live! (Rounder)   ★★

King and Evans have served Ry Cooder well as backup singers, and the slide guitarist reciprocates by producing their feature debut. Cooder, however, doesn't know how to reconcile King's gospel leanings with Evans's R&B touches or how to improve the flat material written by the two headliners.
(44:17/1988)

Earl King
Sexual Telepathy (Black Top)   ★★★★

A sensual and felicitous Crescent City spirit is at the heart of everything King sings, plays on guitar, and scrolls on staff paper. That carefree élan flows all through the disc's eleven songs—no matter if his voice grapples with problems of timbre and timing. First-call musicians from Boston, Austin, and his home city make it obvious they're delighted to be in his company.   (41:00/1990)

Earl King and Roomful of Blues
Glazed (Black Top)   ★★★

New Orleans music in the two decades following World War II owes a great deal of its stirring mettle to King—prominent exhibits include his two-chord blues classic "Those Lonely Lonely Nights" and his Imperial sides. Active again as an artist in the mid 1980s, after a long spell writing songs and handling production work for others, he sings unevenly amidst Roomful of Blues, but his Stratocaster cuts through the five horns to good, idiosyncratic effect. His songs? Enjoyable. Roomful? Ditto.   (39:28/Reissue)

Freddie King

The Best of Freddie King (Shelter/DCC) ★★✦

Championed by white rock fans and musicians, King waxed three albums for Leon Russell's Shelter Records between 1970 and 1973. This pick-of-the-litter collection—six Russell compositions and another half dozen—wobbles between King's demonstrations of showmanship and his expressions of unaffected emotion. Compact disc engineering has done wonders for the flat music heard on vinyl. Consumer aside: Unless you're a completist, this set obviates the need to purchase King's *Getting Ready,* a spotty 1971 effort recently issued on small disc by DCC. (44:41/Reissue)

Texas Cannonball (Shelter/DCC) ★★

King continued to hold sway over a crowd of hip-to-the-gills blues rock guitarists with this uneven 1972 album, whose release in the CD configuration adds seven formerly lost tracks from three different sessions. When not engaged in idle muscle-flexing, he uncorks incisive guitar leads that put his spotty vocals to shame. Thanks but no thanks: King and his 1970–71 accompanists taking to Elmore James's "Dust My Broom" and Jimmy Rogers's "That's All Right" like ducks treading molasses. (76:45/Reissue)

Freddie (Freddy) King

Freddy King Sings (Modern Blues) ★★★★✦

King Records was home to the hottest young modern blues artist of the early 1960s—Freddie King. The Texan's first album for the Cincinnati label made famous by Bill Doggett and James Brown contains "Have You Ever Loved a Woman?" and other perdurable tunes that show a self-assured and sincere singer in his late twenties who delivered lyrics on love trouble without presumption. King's electric guitar spoke even more clearly, achingly poised between hard-core Chicago blues and Texas swing. While the CD sports impressive digitally mastered "true stereo" sound, two numbers have vocals seemingly phoned in from the bottom of an oil well. (33:43/Reissue)

Just Pickin' (Modern Blues) ★★★★

The combining of the two long-lost albums *Dance with Freddie King* (1961) and *Freddy King Gives You a Bonanza of Instrumentals* (1965) is a godsend to anyone interested in modern guitar. Genuine blues feeling pervades his virtuosic guitar bends and slurs throughout twenty-four all-pickin' selections, including hall of fame member "Hide Away." (72:02/1989)

Little Jimmy King

Little Jimmy King and the Memphis Soul Survivors (Bullseye Blues) ★★↓

Busting out of Memphis, this former Albert King band guitarist shoots from the hip à la Stevie Ray Vaughan and takes orbit on a Jimi Hendrix trajectory. More personal is his smoky voice, whose subtleties of timbre and phrasing make it smart beyond his twenty-odd years. The material is virile, entertaining club fare, with strong rock and soul touches, the latter provided in part by neighborhood semilegends Teenie Hodges, on rhythm guitar, and Andrew Love, on tenor saxophone. The most appealing track is the deceptively lazy "Born Again." (48:46/1991)

The Kinsey Report
Edge of the City (Alligator) ★★★

The three Kinsey brothers, offspring of noted Mississippi blues musician Lester Kinsey, and their fast friend Ron Prince immediately established solid footing on contemporary blues ground with this promising debut in 1987. Unyielding and self-confident, they work sweatily at balancing references to Chicago blues, hard rock, funk, and soul. "Come to Me" is downright infectious. (40:31/Reissue)

Midnight Drive (Alligator) ★★↗

Lead guitarist Donald Kinsey has technique to spare, and here it's used more for look-at-me turgidness than real expression. As songwriter his lyrics are just too simplistic and his melodies moribund. Still, fifteen years after he and brother Ralph first tried their hand at "white lightning" blues rock, Donald fronts an outfit that has completely settled into an interesting, explosive hybrid music. (40:50/1989)

Powerhouse (Pointblank/Charisma) ★★★↗

Donald's guitar still has a wild rock 'n' slam thrust, yet this time he reins it in some and offers a tighter blues focus. Indeed, a certain spirit gleaned from the music of his singer/guitarist father Lester (present on the country blues "Good Mornin' Mississippi"), Jimmy Reed, Muddy Waters, and B. B. King informs the ordering of his vocals, playing, and songwriting—the melodies and lyrics are often better than passable. The other Kinseys bluster their thickly textured patterns with clear logic and relentlessness. (42:15/1990)

Smokin' Joe Kubek
Steppin' Out Texas Style (Bullseye Blues) ★★✦

Dallas guitar stylist Kubek and his band marshal their forces to show that the confidently expansive mood of Stevie Ray Vaughan endures. Kubek and vocalist/guitarist B'nois King discipline their interplay, with the latter's singing warmer than a sip of middle-shelf scotch, and bassist Greg Wright and drummer Phil Campbell know how to push the beat in that special sagebrush fashion. Only together a year at the time of this session, in mid 1991, they display a pentatonic stylishness that bodes well for the future. (41:05/1991)

Latimore
The Only Way Is Up (Malaco) ★★★★

In the 1970s, Latimore (aka Benny Latimore) stirred up attention as a respectable contemporary soul singer who had firm control over down-home blues feeling. Finding his niche at Malaco in the last decade, this progenitor of Robert Cray imparts a smooth conviction to high-quality happy or sad love songs on a typical set. The topnotch accompaniment by the Muscle Shoals players, including stalwarts Roger Hawkins and David Hood, accentuates his husky sexiness. (45:01/1991)

Lazy Lester
Harp and Soul (Alligator) ★★★✦

In the late 1950s and the first six years of the 1960s, multi-instrumentalist Leslie "Lazy Lester" Johnson helped define the Louisiana "swamp blues" sound of Jay Miller's Excello label. Lester recorded again in the late 1980s, and this set of originals and cover material (hooray for Slim Harpo and James Carr, nix on Bo Diddley and Eddie Boyd) captures all of his distinctiveness: an indolently swinging voice whose tonality belongs to country and western and Cajun music rather than blues, and a plaintive-happy harmonica that suggests Jimmy Reed's without any mimicry. Lester's King Snake sessionsmen are ham-handed in their attempts at conjuring peat bog ambience. (35:24/1988)

Leadbelly

King of the 12-String Guitar (Columbia) ★★★★⌐

Huddie "Leadbelly" Ledbetter, the storied folk bluesman, recorded these eighteen blues, ballads, and prison worksongs for commercial purposes in 1935—not long after folklorists Alan and John Lomax helped him earn release from a Louisiana prison. (Only three sides have been issued before.) Although unnerved some by the tape recorder, the middle-aged Louisianian sings or hollers robustly and gives credence to his claim of sovereignty over the guitar. Also recommended unconditionally is Columbia's *Leadbelly*, with sixteen more early recordings. (55:32/1991)

Midnight Special (Rounder) ★★★★⌐

This is a trove of fifteen Leadbelly blues and ragtime songs recorded primitively in the 1930s by folklorists John and Alan Lomax for the Library of Congress. Included are two rawboned performances of "Irene," the voice and slide guitar tableau "Matchbox Blues," and an Angola prison entreaty for parole to the Louisiana Governor (it fell on receptive ears). Bravura is on full display everywhere. Before Rounder had the good sense to issue *Midnight Special* and two other impressive volumes of Lomax-sponsored Leadbelly material— *Gwine Dig a Hole to Put the Devil In* and *Let It Shine on Me*—this music was unavailable stateside for almost twenty years. (59:34/Reissue)

Alabama Bound (RCA)   ★★★┩

Two equally attractive 1940 sessions designed for popular acceptance. One has Leadbelly and the Golden Gate Jubilee Quartet offering church affirmations on "Rock Island Line" (a hit for the Weavers ten years later) and seven secular songs. The other is Leadbelly alone, engaging the intellect and emotions with "Easy Rider," "Good Morning Blues," and six others. (49:03/1989)

Frankie Lee
The Ladies and the Babies (Hightone)   ★★┩

Lee is a soul blues singer of moderate talent whose "Part Time Love" and "Taxi Blues" on Peacock made the R&B charts in the 1960s. The Texas native's long overdue debut album from 1984 is decent enough, but his voice lacks suppleness and the musicians often make stylized gestures. (35:40/Reissue)

The Legendary Blues Band
Keepin' the Blues Alive (Ichiban)   ★★┩

The Legendary Blues Band has existed in one form or another since 1980, when four Muddy Waters bandmembers set out on their own. With only two founding members still aboard in the 1990s, this recording becomes something more than just another Chicago blues exercise when one concentrates on Willie Smith and Calvin Jones, eternal keepers of the incantatory heartbeat. (40:53/1990)

Kari Leigh and the Blue Devils
Blue Devil Blues (Amazing) ★★

This Austin band, fronted by singer Kari Leigh and guitarist Mark Lyon, conceives of the blues as a tradition, and it favors historical material from Robert Johnson, John Lee Hooker, Muddy Waters, Son House, etc. But there's no explication (let alone interpretation), nor any sensibility evident, and the competently performed music just sits there, unexceptional and short-lived. (42:23/1991)

J. B. Lenoir
Natural Man (MCA/Chess) ★★★

Fourteen J. B. Lenoir originals from the Chess 1950s have the little-known Chicagoan's poignant high voice and elementary guitar amid the unperturbable boogie settings of perfunctory sidemen. His politicizing, rare for the time in Windy City blues, is conveyed through the caustic, unforgiving lyrics of, say, "Eisenhower Blues" and "I'm in Korea." An acquired taste. (37:57/1990)

Ron Levy
Ron Levy's Wild Kingdom (Black Top) ★★

Levy isn't worth crossing the street to hear sing, but he's one fine organist and pianist. The constancy of friends named Kim Wilson, Jimmie Vaughan, Wayne Bennett, and Ronnie Earl pleases modestly. This 1986 release was followed by the similarly tame *Safari to New Orleans*, also on Black Top. (38:35/Reissue)

Furry Lewis
In His Prime 1927–28 (Yazoo)   ★★★★⁄

Walter "Furry" Lewis, the avuncular dean of the Memphis scene who enjoyed belated fame in the 1960s and 1970s, makes a solid case for consideration among the country blues *corps d'elite* with these fourteen tunes, all but one solo performances. Coddling his ardor, he pleases with musing vocals and versatile bottleneck and fingerpicking guitar work. As an interpreter of pre-blues folk material, his refashioning of the lyrics to the two-part folk ballad "Casey Jones" is particularly memorable. The unclean sound of the 78s detracts nothing from the music's value.   (41:43/Reissue)

Jimmy Liggins
Jimmy Liggins and His Drops of Joy (Specialty)   ★★★★

Guitarist Jimmy Liggins's brand of jump blues swung considerably harder than his more sophisticated older brother Joe's, and his 1947–53 Specialty yield includes the driving rockers "Cadillac Boogie," "Saturday Night Boogie Woogie Man," and the convincingly loopy "Drunk." Harold Land, Charles "Little Jazz" Ferguson, and Maxwell Davis provide sizzling saxophone work on this twenty-five-song disc. (B.D.)
(65:16/Reissue)

Joe Liggins
Joe Liggins and the Honeydrippers (Specialty)   ★★★★

Los Angeles–based pianist Joe Liggins led one of the hottest black dance bands during the postwar years, and his 1950–54 Specialty stint included the classic booze ode "Pink Champagne." Liggins's slower material sounds somewhat dated now, but saxophone-based jumpers, including a remake of his signature "The Honeydripper," predominate this fine-sounding twenty-five-track collection. (B.D.)   (72:13/Reissue)

Lil' Ed and the Blues Imperials
Roughhousin' (Alligator)   ★★★✦

Lil' Ed Williams's Chicago slide guitar is the dirtiest fun to be had since the passing of Hound Dog Taylor and his uncle, J. B. Hutto. Williams and his band learned the ropes in West Side dives, and their three hours in the studio one night in 1986 resulted in first takes that mirror their club wildness. The *Roughhousin'* session came about when label head Bruce Iglauer was floored by the band's wild one-song contribution to the Alligator anthology titled *The New Bluebloods*.
(44:13/Reissue)

Chicken, Gravy & Biscuits (Alligator)   ★★

For whatever reason—probably a combination of personnel changes, personal problems, road weariness, and formulaic new material—the Imperials seem to have lost some of their edge, their flattering coarseness. The counters in their favorite greasy spoon are just *too* clean.   (47:41/1989)

What You See Is What You Get (Alligator)   ★★★✦

The Blues Imperials' latest album marks a new level of strident indecency in their slash-and-burn approach to performing. The group, expanded two years back by the addition of a crowd-pleasing tenor saxophonist, now takes periodic breaks from the clamor with affective slow blues that steam for Lil' Ed's desperate, measured singing and guitar wringing. There are fourteen enjoyable songs, all from the pen of the head Imperial except J. B. Hutto's "Please Help" and group bassist Pookie Young's "Upset Man."   (62:17/1992)

Mance Lipscomb
Texas Songster (Arhoolie) ★★★♪

On a disc compressing most of two old Arhoolie records, the sexagenarian Lone Star State sharecropper is more sure of himself singing and fingerpicking his guitar for Chris Strachwitz's tape recorder in his home in 1960 than he is performing for Berkeley coffeehouse hangers-on four years later. Not surprisingly, emotion best governs those performances of blues, ballads, and popular songs in his parlor.   (61:20/1989)

Little Charlie and the Nightcats
All the Way Crazy (Alligator) ★★♪

Northern California harmonica players Charlie Baty and Rick Estrin joined forces in 1976, the former switching over to guitar as they fine-tuned an ensemble sound indebted to Chicago and jump blues styles, swing-bebop jazz, country and western, and rockabilly. At long last, in 1987, the quartet broke out on the national scene with this entertaining, intelligent, and promising debut. On the debit side, Estrin's affected singing on witty and frisky originals takes getting used to, and the studio inhibits all four Nightcats.   (40:19/Reissue)

Disturbing the Peace (Alligator) ★★★♪

One is caught between smiling over songwriter/singer/harpist Estrin's keen wit and nodding in appreciation at guitarist Baty's easeful way with gutbucket blues and jazz à la Kenny Burrell and Charlie Christian. Drummer Dobie Strange and bassist Jay Peterson please by swinging their tails off with personality. The studio, however, still constrains the full release of their felicities.   (40:28/1988)

The Big Break! (Alligator)   ★★★★

The fun and seriousness flow easier now because they're
pulled along by Nightcats finally at ease with the recording
process. Estrin's vocals have become entirely passionate, and
his Chicago harp now displays a wider spectrum of emotions.
Baty knows exactly where the beat is and his phrases swing,
swing, swing. Boredom is also kept at bay by splendent material that never lacks for savvy rhythms and dynamic variety.
                                          (42:43/1989)

Captured Live (Alligator)   ★★★♪

More dependable than a Swiss train, the band regales club
audiences back home in Sacramento and San Francisco with
old favorites and new titles. The shows catch fire when Baty
refashions countrified Jimmy Bryant licks on his showcase
"Wildcattin'" and pays homage to blues-jazzman Tiny
Grimes here and there. Yet things drag considerably when the
band tries to transport the audience to Chicago with a long
version of Buddy Guy's "Ten Years Ago." Further, Estrin's
vocals are full of unintentional affectation, the new bass
player's fingers lack the surety of the man he replaced, and
Baty bores with his Guy mannerisms.   (57:07/1991)

Little Milton

We're Gonna Make It/Little Milton Sings Big Blues   ★★★★
   (MCA/Chess)

Little Milton Campbell's bold and brawling voice, belonging
to the secular church attended by Bobby Bland, stomped
through the two Chess albums that have been set side by side
on this disc, *We're Gonna Make It* (1965) and *Little Milton
Sings Big Blues* (1966) (minus one track off the latter). Classic
sides "Blind Man," "Who's Cheating Who," and "We're

Gonna Make It" belong to the first half of the program, marred somewhat by meretricious horn arrangements. *Sings* pleases to no end for the urgency the vocalist/guitarist expends upon his interpretations of standards such as "Reconsider Baby" and "Sweet Sixteen."   (72:20/Reissue)

If Walls Could Talk (MCA/Chess)   ★★★★

By dint of his ironbound larynx and his total involvement with lyrics, Milton pins to the wall a soul blues program from 1969 that includes appraisals of Guitar Slim's "The Things that I Used to Do" and Cash McCall's "Let's Get Together." The Chicago studio horns punch and recoil, efficiently so, as the rhythm players funkily underscore Milton's heaven-sent verve.   (32:30/Reissue)

Grits Ain't Groceries (Stax)   ★★★★

Showtime at Los Angeles's Summit Club in 1972. Milton's intensity level hits summits where only the most emotionally involved testifier can breathe the air, and his B. B. King–style guitar jabs the listener like a recently sharpened darning needle, especially during Otis Rush's "I Can't Quit You Baby." Milton's band slouches only during the anticlimatic show closer, "Walking the Back Streets and Crying." (38:49/Reissue)

Waiting for Little Milton (Stax)   ★★

Milton's blues spirit is so possessed that he may not have noticed the early-1970s overkill of the Soul Children backing singers, the Memphis Symphony Orchestra, and the Memphis Horns. Or the questionable material. Such a thought is belied by studying the album credits: "Produced by Milton Campbell."   (37:56/Reissue)

Walkin' the Back Streets (Stax) ★★★★

Milton's guitar and voice capture shadings of emotional pain in nine good songs recorded in 1972 and 1974. The Stax sessionsmen revive his spirit whenever he teeters on the brink of despair, though the horn section sometimes oversteps its bounds.   (39:19/Reissue)

What It Was (Stax) ★★

What it is isn't much. Milton's 1973 Montreux Jazz Festival appearance, tapes of which sat on the shelf for fifteen years, is recommended only to his most staunch supporters. Overall his singing gets by, but his guitar repellently capers or repines. Five slopmakers share the Swiss stage.   (47:28/Reissue)

Blues 'n' Soul (Stax) ★★★★

Worth his salt, Little Milton can make bittersweet love pleas and assents seem spontaneous and formal at once. That's often true on this 1974 set, where he bores into good material (from B. B. King, Betty Everett, and himself) as Memphis rhythm shamans put a funky soul spell on the blues. The strings and horns, thankfully, don't draw undue attention to themselves.   (36:05/Reissue)

Reality (Malaco) ★★★★

As he has for years, Milton sings in the present decade with just the right blend of sensitivity and inner anguish; he also continues to shade textures and explore the grottos of his range. Two originals concerning illicit love and its accompanying discomposure, "A Right to Sing the Blues" and "I'm Jealous of Her Husband," best live up to the disc title—not to say that songs from Bobby Womack, George Jackson, and others aren't involving too. It need be noted his guitar still satisfies and the Malaco production is classy yet gritty.   (46:39/1991)

Little Richard

The Formative Years: 1951–1953 (Bear Family import)

Excellent twenty-two-track compilation of the rock pioneer's early days, featuring everything he waxed prior to his hitmaking run on Specialty. The influence of shouters Roy Brown and Billy Wright is quite obvious on the earliest 1951–52 RCA material, and a few items from his pair of 1953 Peacock dates already exhibit definite rock tendencies. Loaded with unissued alternate takes and boasting pristine sound, this is a disc worth searching for. (B.D.)   (58:39/1989)

The Specialty Sessions (Specialty) ★★★★★

If Chuck Berry didn't invent rock 'n' roll, Little Richard Penniman must have. At least that's the way you'll feel after listening to this indispensable, beautifully annotated three-disc boxed set that contains all seventy-three titles the piano pounder cut for Specialty during his seminal 1955–57 period and in his brief 1964 return. The hits are digitally breathtaking, but the obscurities are revelatory—an alternate "Keep A-Knockin' " with an even more incendiary saxophone solo by Grady Gaines, early workouts on "Slippin' and Slidin' " that document the development of Richard's version, and hilarious radio spots for Royal Crown Hair Dressing. (B.D.)
(2:58:42/1989)

The Georgia Peach (Specialty) ★★★★↓

This generous single disc gathers most of the unquestionably essential rockers the pianist/singer waxed for Specialty. Whether backed by the nonpareil New Orleans studio band or his own wild road combo, the Upsetters (hear "Keep A-Knockin' "), Richard's brief 1955–57 stint on Specialty marked him as a true rock visionary, and the galvanic energy level of "Tutti Frutti," "Long Tall Sally," and "Good Golly Miss Molly" is unmatched in R&B history. For the full effect, turn to *The Specialty Sessions*. (B.D.)   (58:37/Reissue)

Little Walter
The Best of Little Walter (MCA/Chess)   ★★★★★

Little Walter Jacobs's amplified harmonica embodied the sound of postwar Chicago blues: supple-toned wails indicating subtle renderings of emotional intent. Melodic sophistication and phrasing similar to a modern-minded jazz saxophonist's were key components of his astonishing style. Moreover, his singing was more than adequate, his repertoire outstanding, and he benefited from fine arrangements that accented the considerable worth of accompanists Robert Jr. Lockwood, Louis Myers, Fred Below, and others. This collection, first in record stores in 1958, has twelve uniformly excellent songs from his 1952–55 Chess trove.   (35:24/Reissue)

The Best of Little Walter, Volume Two (MCA/Chess)   ★★★★★

More blues with a feeling from the august personage. "Key to the Highway," "Oh Baby," and "Mellow Down Easy" are among the twelve songs compiled late last decade by MCA's Andy McKaie and *Billboard*'s Chris Morris under the only slightly arbitrary "best" rubric. Blues gourmands will salivate over three obscurities: the early-1950s instrumental "Boogie," the 1960 Willie Dixon composition "I Don't Play," and a song released as a Muddy Waters single, "Evans Shuffle."
(32:05/1989)

Hate to See You Go (MCA/Chess)   ★★★★⧳

Originally issued in 1969, this worthwhile assemblage has
fifteen Walter selections from 1952 to 1960. "Blue and Lonesome" is one of the most harrowing songs in all of blues, and
a number more are classics, though "As Long as I Have You"
and a few others do huff and puff, going nowhere in particular. Three tracks overlap with *The Best of Little Walter*,
Volume Two.   (39:44/Reissue)

Lynyrd Skynyrd
Second Helping (Mobile Fidelity/MCA)   ★★★★

When these Jacksonville hard rockers took a softer approach
(as on this 1974 album's "I Need You"), an unsentimental
melancholy pervaded their music that Delta blues players
would have understood. When vocalist Ronnie Van Zant and
the three guitarists lead fiery rebel charges, their jubilation—
intertwined with sad-hearted impulses or not—is built of
bluesy voicings.   (37:22/Reissue)

Willie Mabon
Chicago Blues Session! (Optimism)   ★★

Journeyman singer/pianist Willie Mabon turns in a satisfactory performance, while guitarists Hubert Sumlin and Eddie
Taylor, bassist Aaron Burton, and drummer Casey Jones build
on the three basic diatonic chords. Recorded mid 1979.
                                                 (43:39/Reissue)

Jerry McCain
Blues 'n' Stuff (Ichiban)   ★★★

Swamp blues advocate Jerry McCain wields a good Little
Walter–influenced harmonica, sings tolerably well, writes at-

tractive shuffles, has a sense of humor, and fronts a decent Atlanta group called the Bluse Guys. "A Rose for My Lady," a mix of city and marshland sounds, deserves return visits.

(38:48/1989)

Cash McCall
No More Doggin' (Optimism)   ★★

On a 1983 date, singer Cash McCall theatricalizes ho-hum lyrics that the former Chess soul songwriter has set to funky R&B rhythms. He plays a decent guitar, especially on the oddly attractive fourteen-minutes-plus "Hurry Sundown."

(44:39/1990)

Mighty Sam McClain
Live in Japan (Orleans)   ★★★

Soul singer McClain had his fifteen minutes of fame in 1966 with a cover of Patsy Cline's "Sweet Dreams." In the mid 1980s, back in action after years of anonymity, the rejuvenated soul-bluesman embarked on a successful Japanese tour that produced this moderately agreeable concert document. His strong baritone evinces his need for love, hope, and honesty. What annoys are a few maudlin songs and the over-playing of Tokyo backup robots. The marvelous ex–Bobby Bland guitarist Wayne Bennett is underutilized.   (71:13/1988)

Delbert McClinton
Live from Austin (Alligator)   ★★

Augmented by three horns, the Texas singer/harpist and his band pound out their late-1980s show, which includes several unctuous originals and McClinton's 1980 pop hit "Givin' It Up for Your Love." His shellacked smooth-and-easy combination of country and western, R&B, blues, and soul gives no sign of his roadhouse tutelage under Sonny Boy Williamson and Howlin' Wolf way back when.   (41:42/1989)

Jimmy McCracklin
My Story (Bullseye Blues)   ★★★★

McCracklin's recording career has encompassed nearly a half century, taking in the 1958 pop smash "The Walk" and a great deal of other fine work (whether well remembered or lamentably obscure). Without sacrificing any of his enduring charm his early-1990s Bullseye Blues debut has a resolutely contemporary blues quality that places the Bay Area singer/pianist/songwriter (he wrote B. B. King's "The Thrill Is Gone," for one) in the limelight again. Refashioned jump blues alternate with funky R&B items and two songs cofeature New Orleans soul chanteuse Irma Thomas—every last one a good-natured exposition. (B.D./F.J.H.)   (45:15/1991)

Larry McCray
Ambition (Charisma)   ★★

This former Detroit autoworker's approach to the blues is admirable, fusing it with rock and pop influences, but his debut is largely uninspiring. The songs are sub-par, McCray's guitar playing seems overly dependent on rock clichés, and he attempts a crossover that pales in comparison to that of Chris Thomas or the Kinsey Report. (J.G.)   (46:05/1990)

Country Joe McDonald
Superstitious Blues (Rykodisc)   ★★★

McDonald, the nominal leader of the 1960s politico-psychedelic band the Fish, has always fancied himself a folk and blues connoisseur. Recording solo in the 1990s, he sings attractively and switches between well-played guitar and harmonica on original songs ideal for present-day coffeehouse listening. If only his lyrics and music were more inventive.

(37:16/1991)

Fred McDowell
Mississippi Delta Blues (Arhoolie) ★★★★★

McDowell first recorded in 1959, when folklorist Alan Lomax discovered him during a field trip. Five years later the sixty-year-old northern Mississippian was taped performing in his living room by Arhoolie's Chris Strachwitz. The results are outstanding: McDowell's commanding singing and slide guitar commentaries, tied to clear thinking and acute feeling, refashion traditional fare into entirely personal folk music. Added to the original program are six stunning tracks, including "You Gotta Move" (covered by the Rolling Stones) and two 1965 field recordings cofeaturing history book guitarist Eli Green. (64:04/Reissue)

Shake 'em on Down (Tomato) ★★

Eight months before his final passage, McDowell was recorded at Greenwich Village's The Gaslight in November 1971. Accompanied by an acolyte on electric bass or second guitar, the faltering rural bluesman nevertheless gets the job done singing and working his slider over his strings. "I'm Crazy About You, Baby" is the one spellbinder.

(44:01/Reissue)

Jack McDuff
The Reentry (Muse) ★★↗

The griddle sizzles quietly with the soul-seasoned jazz and blues prepared by agile organist Brother Jack McDuff and five friends at a conservative little feast last decade. Finger snapping is encouraged. (35:32/1988)

Brownie McGhee and Sonny Terry
Brownie McGhee & Sonny Terry Sing ★★★★ (Smithsonian/Folkways)

A reissue of a 1958 Folkways album, this CD captures the duo during their prime, performing traditional blues songs with spartan instrumentation (joined only by drummer Gene Moore). Terry's spirited harp work and McGhee's rhythmic guitar combined with their sweet vocal harmonies to make them among the most popular artists of their day. (J.T.) (39:15/1990)

• See also **Sonny Terry and Brownie McGhee**

Jimmy McGriff
Blue to the 'Bone (Milestone) ★★★

Despite unimaginative song selection, organist Jimmy McGriff's studio encounter with ex–Count Basie blues trombonist Al Grey is a success. McGriff's walking bass pedals, Grey's struttin' work, and limpid, unforced blues grooves defined by guitarist Melvin Sparks and drummer Bernard Purdie converge in a swell of enthusiasm. (44:21/1988)

In a Blue Mood (Headfirst) ★

Veteran Jimmy McGriff is one fine blues organist, but he needs direction in the 1990s. Ex-Prince keyboardist Dr. Fink takes him down a junk-strewn funk path. The rendition of Albert King's "Born Under a Bad Sign" is sublime kitsch.

(39:34/1991)

• See also **Hank Crawford and Jimmy McGriff**

Lonnie Mack

Strike Like Lightning (Alligator) ★★★★

Anyone who thought Lonnie Mack was only a rock-guitar history book name—thanks to his seminal country-and-blues instrumental version of Chuck Berry's "Memphis"—got slapped upside the head by his 1958 Gibson Flying V guitar when this Stevie Ray Vaughan co-produced album appeared in 1985. On both fast and slow songs his fluid leads fulgurate like bolts from the blue, with additional illumination provided by his heavy, worn-and-torn singing voice. A gang of Mack's old Cincinnati cronies contribute glowingly as if at a road-house torching, while Vaughan supplies still more sizzle to the shuffle with "If You Have to Know" and four more.

(42:14/Reissue)

Live!: Attack of the Killer V (Alligator) ★★★★

After two uneven efforts (*Second Sight* and *Roadhouses and Dancehalls*, on Alligator and Epic respectively) Mack got back on track with a recorded performance at a Lincoln State road-house in 1989. Guitar is aplenty, loud, acutely controlled, and of convictive emotional pull. The absolute high point arrives when he makes it cry, remonstrate, and plead in the original slow-blues "Stop." He's not a half bad singer, either.

(50:18/1990)

Jackie McLean
Bluesnik (Blue Note)   ★★★★

Alto saxophonist Jackie McLean appreciates how blues is the
bone marrow of jazz. On a blues date in 1961 he exhibits
creative spontaneity and wisdom beyond the ken of most
twenty-eight-year-old improvisers. Trumpeter Freddie Hubbard, six years younger, is a rhythmic turbine of down-home
inflections. Two alternate takes have been added for the CD.
(53:43/Reissue)

Doug MacLeod
Ain't the Blues Evil (Volt)   ★★★

Based in Los Angeles, MacLeod is best known for writing
intelligent songs covered by Son Seals, Albert Collins, and
Albert King. He's also a capable if blanched singer/guitarist
who employs subtle shifts in tone to get across a reserved
warmth or uneasiness. His band's remembrance of Stevie Ray
Vaughan, "SRV," is touchingly sincere.   (58:27/1991)

Blind Willie McTell
1927–1933: The Early Years (Yazoo)   ★★★★★

An outstanding country-bluesman hailing from Georgia,
McTell transformed downcast melodies into songs of silvery
vibrancy. His distinct tenor *Sprechstimme* bores directly to
the heart of his poetry of love and family concerns. The "ear-
sighted" diviner's twelve-string guitar playing, either finger-
picked or done with a slider, is nothing short of marvelous,
showing his delicate control of pitch shadings, rhythm, and
dynamics. Well-known songs "Statesboro Blues" and "Broke
Down Engine Blues" are among the fourteen stellar examples
of his vast talent.   (42:56/Reissue)

Magic Sam
1957–66 (Paula) ★★★★

Eschewing any emotional distance, Sam Maghett poured his heart into his melodic music while singing and playing guitar on twenty-one tracks from his abbreviated career as a vastly gifted Chicago modern blues artist. Sam's uncle, James "Shakey Jake" Harris, sings to good purpose on four numbers, and West Side notables such as Little Brother Montgomery, Willie Dixon, and Otis Spann also lend a hand. Calling card "All Your Love" appears in a variety of forms. Only a very few sides, notably 1960 pop misfire "Mr. Charlie" for Chief Records, are regrettable. (56:43/Reissue)

The Late Great Magic Sam (Optimism) ★★★♪

This album, first designated for West German consumers in 1980, positions ten tightly arranged recordings from 1963 to 1964 next to concert tracks recorded just before Sam's passing in late 1969. On the early work, songs fade prematurely and an unidentified organist tends to be obtrusive; no matter, Sam still triumphs, his power and exuberance imploding listeners' skulls without losing anything in nuance. (33:37/Reissue)

Magic Sam Live (Delmark) ★★★★

Incorporating ideas gleaned from B. B. King and Bobby Bland's Clarence Hollimon into his guitar style, Sam creates a great commotion at Chicago's Alex Club in 1963–64 and at the 1969 Ann Arbor Blues Festival. The recording equipment is inferior both places, yet one keenly senses the eloquence of his string bends and his predatory voice. This jewel box also holds an informative sixteen-page booklet. (73:09/Reissue)

West Side Soul (Delmark) ★★★★★

Magic Sam's 1967 recording *West Side Soul* belongs to the highest heaven. He ravages his fretboard with boldness, sometimes playing lead, rhythm, and bass simultaneously, keeping his tone clear and focused, his runs inventive and searching. He also lends true feeling to his dithyrambic singing of every syllable in "My Love Will Never Die," "Sweet Home Chicago," and nine more stellar numbers. A twelfth, "Looking Good," is a boogie-locomotive instrumental, another slice of bliss. Fellow travelers to the realm of light include rhythm guitarist Mighty Joe Young and eponymous father-and-son drummers Odie Payne. (45:54/Reissue)

Give Me Time (Delmark) ★★★★

In a casual 1968 recording made at his West Side residence, Sam gives it his all on a variety of solo blues and soul tunes (including a few he never cut anywhere else). Triumph and pain go hand in hand in his performing. Eddie Boyd drops by and sings "I Can't Quit You Baby." Sound quality isn't the best, but considering the value of the contents one shouldn't carp. (B.D./F.J.H.) (38:14/1991)

Magic Slim and the Teardrops
Raw Magic (Alligator) ★★★☆

Mississippi-born guitarist Morris "Magic Slim" Holt, an occasional accompanist to Magic Sam Maghett in the 1960s, paints Chicago blues in flat, broad colors that complement the coarse-grained intensity of his performances. This 1982 Alligator release, one of the sleepers in the label's catalog, gathers seven studio tracks from two French albums. (39:46/Reissue)

Taj Mahal

Giant Step/De Ole Folks at Home (Columbia) ★★★★

Taj Mahal (Henry Sainte Claire Fredericks)—singer, multi-instrumentalist, and ethnomusicologist—has described blues as "a very sensual, down-into-the-body music." Now twenty-odd albums into his recording career, his most convincing argument for that definition was back in 1969 with the release of this set (originally a two-record package). Bridging the chasm between country blues and rock, Mahal and three friends created a worldly wise charm on the *De Ole Folks* half of the program. The other part, *Giant Step*, has Mahal alone, undertaking a warmhearted study of Leadbelly, Reverend Gary Davis, and the African-American ethos. Indifferent engineering at the original session. (74:00/Reissue)

Mule Bone (Gramavision) ★★

An aural souvenir for admirers of the Broadway play that was based on a Zora Neale Hurston short story. The poetry of Langston Hughes graces nearly all of Mahal's specially written country blues songs, which really do need the visuals and a narrative context. Guitarist Kenny Neal, who took to his lead stage role well, is not on the soundtrack. (33:45/1991)

Big Joe Maher

Good Rockin' Daddy (Powerhouse) ★★

Singer and drummer Big Joe Maher, usually found in the Washington, D.C., area, plays his swinging or slow blues with care and understanding. Guitarist Tom Principato and pianist Deanna Bogart are among his Dynaflows. Fans of Mitch Woods and Roomful of Blues will especially enjoy this offering. (37:17/1989)

Bob Margolin
Chicago Blues (Powerhouse) ★★★

Margolin is one of those pilgrims who makes the symbolic holy journey to Muddy Waters's Chicago by holing up in the recording studio for a "tribute" session. The former Waters band guitarist (1973–80) has enlisted fellow alumni Pinetop Perkins, Jimmy Rogers, Calvin Jones, and Willie Smith for half the program. On the remaining songs he performs solo or with his competent North Carolina band. By the way, they don't call Margolin "Steady Rollin' " for his singing.

(52:58/1991)

Wynton Marsalis
Thick in the South (Columbia) ★★★★

Marsalis knows the blues is the crucial substructure of jazz, and with typical self-assurance he heralds the fact exhaustively over the course of a three-CD blues triptych entitled *Soul Gestures in Southern Blue* (probably recorded in the late 1980s). The first volume, *Thick in the South,* has the well-known jazz trumpeter at the helm of a combo that improvises superbly and handles the intricate demands of his compositions with consummate skill. They could stand to loosen up some, though—get from beneath the Damoclean sword.

(56:07/1991)

Uptown Ruler (Columbia) ★★★♪

On the second album the moods and tones of the blues take an abstract turn in which Marsalis introspectively examines the emotional/musical makeup of New Orleans's folkloric figure, Uptown Ruler. The trumpeter's refined expressions of joy, when perceivable, have a puritanical cast.   (53:04/1991)

Levee Low Moan (Columbia) ★★★★

The beauty of rhythm and the swinging connotations of the blues according to Marsalis and his five no-nonsense musicians. They gladly sweat in their expensive suits, probing the music's whispered and clarion disclosures on this last installment of the cycle. (48:50/1991)

John Mayall

Bluesbreakers with Eric Clapton (London)

John Mayall, a British blues minister of state, enlisted former Yardbirds guitarist Eric Clapton for two stints with his ever-changing Bluesbreakers in 1965–66. On the puristic group's debut recording, Clapton's succession of spontaneous runs within a blues harmonic framework add up to immensely pleasing performances. Every nuance of "Slowhand's" rational playing, from bent tones of flaming immediacy in Otis Rush's "All Your Love" to fresh utterances in Robert Johnson's "Ramblin' on My Mind" (where he also sings well), make their deep-felt point without emotional manipulation. (37:45/Reissue)

The Turning Point (Polydor) ★★

Mayall's 1969 Fillmore East performance, acoustic with a guitarist and reed player, is on the drowsy side despite the "chicka-chicka" fun of "Room to Move." Just goes to show that singer/multi-instrumentalist Mayall had little to say once away from the wide-awake guitarists Eric Clapton and Peter Green (the latter was the star of 1967's starring *A Hard Road*, a London CD reissue). (43:23/Reissue)

Chicago Line (Island)   ★★♪

After about fifteen years' worth of derailments, the graying
Bluesbreaker gets on track with a recording worth more than
a single pained listen. Coco Montoya, who's sharper than
many a better-known guitarist, gives vocalist Mayall the kick
in the trousers he needs. The highlight is a respectful rework-
ing of Blind Boy Fuller's "Evil Hearted Woman" called "Cold
Blooded Mama."   (53:04/1988)

A Sense of Place (Island)   ★★♪

How true is Mayall's titular claim? He sings of Vicksburg,
New Orleans's Congo Square, the road out of Fort Worth, and
so forth as a visitor who truly cares about such places. Yet he's
written just one of the eleven songs, a brief piano romp.
Guitarist Coco Montoya still heats up the band.   (40:28/1990)

Percy Mayfield
Live (Winner)   ★★★

In these 1981–83 California club performances broadcast over
ex–Paul Butterfield pianist Mark Naftalin's blues radio program, Mayfield (who died in 1984) maintains an unconquer-
able spirit while making the best of a weatherbeaten voice.
Given moral and musical support by Naftalin, guitarist Pee
Wee Crayton, and a throng of other local players (some of
whom move as if in concrete shoes), the versemaker sends
shivers down the backbone of admirers with "Please Send Me
Someone to Love" but not with the eleven other reinvented
originals. Mandatory listening: his pithily titled *Poet of the
Blues* (Specialty CD), with tunes cut in the early 1950s com-
passing city Blues–style romantic melancholia.   (52:21/1992)

"Earring" George Mayweather
Whup It! Whup It! (Tone-Cool) ★★★↓

This native of Alabama used to front his own band and engage in after-hours bandstand tussles with Elmore James and Muddy Waters in Chicago taverns in the golden age. A member of Boston's blues codfish aristocracy in recent years, Mayweather flies quite high while playing harmonica on his very first feature album, egged on by keyboardist Ron Levy, guitarist Chris Brown, and three of Luther "Guitar Junior" Johnson's regulars. No harm at all if his singing—splintery, wayward, cantankerously individualistic—doesn't take wing in any of the relumed classics that dominate the set.

(47:16/1992)

Loren Mazzacane
Rooms (St. Joan) ★★★★

The New Haven electric guitarist spontaneously creates spare, enigmatic, plangent solo "blues," his sounds appropriate to a midnight graveyard stroll in a hill fog. Pixilated singer Suzanne Langille adds to the Karloffesque atmospherics of one of the seventeen pieces. Their artistry demands rapt attention and a vivid imagination. (48:10/1990)

The Mellow Fellows
Street Party (Alligator) ★★★★

After the death of group leader Larry "Big Twist" Nolan, the Chicago-based Mellow Fellows could easily have become another running-on-empty R&B horn band. Instead, vocalists Martin Allbritton and Gene Barge, graying local legends, fill the breach with dazzling spirit and immoderate confidence, and the six other Fellows heat up a start-to-finish delightful program with their fresh, surprising approximations of the

Stax/Volt sound, Chicago soul, and Leiber and Stoller–style R&B. (46:22/1990)

Memphis Jug Band
Memphis Jug Band (Yazoo) ★★★★

Singer/guitarist/harmonica player Will Shade (Son Brimmer) and his colleagues on kazoos, empty containers, banjos, etc., lifted country blues, rags, dance songs, and hokey jazz to dizzy heights of rascality. These twenty-three numbers, digitally mastered, date from 1927–34. The accompanying fourteen-page booklet has a fine essay, old photographs, and song information. (58:41/Reissue)

Memphis Minnie
Hoodoo Lady (1933–1937) (Columbia/Legacy) ★★★★✦

Minnie McCoy, aka Lizzie Douglas, was a supernova in the constellation of blues performers recording in the Chicago of the 1930s. The tonal inflections of her reliable voice were as seductive or threatening as her song lyrics on crime, hoodoo, and sex. A conduit between country and urban blues, her guitar playing is every bit as fascinatingly emotive as her singing. These eighteen selections, five rare, find her in the deferential company of mandolinist Charlie McCoy, pianist Blind John Davis, and others—but *not* guitarist (and husband) Kansas Joe McCoy, with whom she recorded most of her finest sides. (59:23/1991)

Memphis Slim
The Real Folk Blues (MCA/Chess)

Peter "Memphis Slim" Chatman's surging piano style forever dripped with the pungent flavor of the Arkansas barrelhouses and Memphis/Chicago speakeasies of the 1930s and 1940s. This 1966 grouping of twelve 1950–52 sides cut for Premium, however, find some of his zest smothered by the kudzu of commercial R&B arrangements. (33:22/Reissue)

Raining the Blues (Fantasy) ★★★★↗

Shoved into the background by rock 'n' roll, Slim's career righted itself with a Carnegie Hall appearance in 1959, and soon he was ushered into the recording studio. Throughout this union of two Prestige/Bluesville albums, *Just Blues* and *No Strain*, the imposing singer and pianist gives valuable lessons on the thesis that commitment to working through sadness pays off in transcendence. On occasion slim gets a lift from either little-known harmonica player "Harpie" Brown or a guitar-and-bass team. (76:48/Reissue)

Blue This Evening (Black Lion) ★★↗

Nineteen-track 1960 British studio set by the prolific pianist, including many of his customary standards. Guitarist Alexis Korner and drummer Stan Greig tamely follow the leader on some items, while others feature Slim in a solo setting. The CD sound becomes noticeably distorted toward the end. (B.D.) (74:30/Reissue)

All Kinds of Blues (Fantasy) ★★★★

Solo Slim from 1961, presumably just before his emigration to Paris. He sings with the clarity and easeful movement of a mountain stream, his fingers travel the piano keys insistently if not always accurately, and his sexual metaphors (notably in "Churnin' Man Blues") join his homespun insights (try "Mother Earth") in holding out pleasure to the listener—at the time collegians and the city-dwelling folk cognoscenti. (46:00/Reissue)

Steady Rolling Blues (Fantasy) ★★

Slim amuses himself rolling the organ keys in four of ten songs on yet another Prestige/Bluesville album recorded in 1961. Stick to his lusty voice-and-piano escapades, because when he pulls out the stops waves of funereal or giddy schmaltz spew forth. (39:00/Reissue)

The Legacy of the Blues, Volume Seven (GNP Crescendo) ★★★

First released in 1973, this New York studio session is at once likable and disappointing. Singer/keyboardist Slim is in fine fettle, and guitarist Billy Butler supplies him tasty chords and good solos, but erratic saxophonist Eddie Chamblee should have been shown the door. Features a strong version of slim's classic, "Everyday I Have the Blues." (32:23/Reissue)

Memphis Blues (Milan) ★★★✦

Slim sings and rattles the keyboard with untrammeled glee on a 1980 session made under the auspices of Le Hot Club de France, a coterie of Gallic supporters of expatriate and visiting blues musicians. Actually, he graciously hands over many of the songs to little-known friends Don McMinn (on vocals and guitar), Sunny Blake (on vocals and harmonica), Booker T. Laury (on vocals), and Evelyn Young (on vocals and alto saxophone). The first three, spurred by an electrified small band, have the spirit and spontaneity to surprise delightfully, while Young does little to recommend herself. (38:59/1992)

Memphis Slim and Matt Murphy/Eddie Taylor

Memphis Slim and Matt Murphy/Eddie Taylor (Antone's) ★★✦

Two albums on a single CD. One of the pleasures of Chicago blues in the 1950s was the team of pianist Memphis Slim and guitarist Matt Murphy, and three decades later the two reunited at Antone's in Austin to evidence their perseverance of integrity and technique—*Together Again One More Time.* The latter section of the disc is Eddie Taylor's *Still Not Ready for Eddie*; unfortunately the esteemed guitarist's musical powers had diminished in the 1980s, and the club performance with old friends Sunnyland Slim and Hubert Sumlin is difficult to listen to. Three stars for *Together Again* and two bighearted ones for *Still Not Ready* result in the rating above.

(65:26/1990)

The Meters
Look-Ka Py Py (Rounder)   ★★★★✔

The Meters were the most inspired of New Orleans R&B purveyors, on their own and as first-call backup for singer Lee Dorsey and many other local artists produced by Allen Toussaint in the late 1960s and 1970s. This classic album, first released in 1972, captures all of their syncopated funk hoodoo: guitarist Leo Nocentelli's jazz chords scrape against Art Neville's flavorful keyboards while the truncated cross-rhythms of bassist George Porter, Jr., and drummer Joseph "Zigaboo" Modeliste jounce a dozen relaxed "do your own thing" instrumentals. (32:35/Reissue)

Roy Milton
Roy Milton and His Solid Senders (Specialty)   ★★★★

Credited by some as the father of the backbeat in jump blues, vocalist/drummer Roy Milton's 1946 smash "R.M. Blues" established Art Rupe's fledgling operation, and Milton's swinging Specialty sides (twenty-five of which are featured here) kept him on the R&B charts through 1952. Pianist Camille Howard was also integral to the Solid Senders' sound, adding her supple boogies to the combo. (B.D.) (68:08/Reissue)

Charles Mingus
Blues and Roots (Atlantic)   ★★★★

As bassist, pianist, bandleader, composer, arranger, and modern jazz mahatma, Charles Mingus had plenary control of all the expressive devices needed to manifest blues cries from the soul. The gospel blues "Wednesday Night Prayer Meeting" and five more numbers on this famous 1959 release have his ten musicians' spontaneous phrases in perfect balance with his ingenious compositional turns.   (38:52/Reissue)

Sam Mitchell
The Art of Bottleneck/Slide Guitar (Yazoo)   ★★★

Sophomore blues guitarists looking for home instruction are sought by Mitchell, a talented English plectrist (and distressing singer) with twenty-four tracks to offer for enlightenment. Enjoyable for nonmusicians as well. Supplemented by a fourteen-page CD booklet and sheet music.   (61:36/1991)

James Montgomery Band
The Oven Is On (Tone-Cool)   ★★↲

Only an ordinary singer, the Boston R&B veteran makes his best impression on this stylistically varied set when playing his harmonica with affluent blues pleasure, namely on the instrumental title track and "Yonders Wall." His tight group is comfortable with twelve-bar patterns, funk, and rock.
(50:02/1991)

Little Brother Montgomery
At Home (Earwig) ★★★

Singer/pianist Eurreal "Little Brother" Montgomery tickled and thumped the ivories playing the blues, boogie-woogie, and stride styles for almost seventy years. His last recordings—most made in his living room between 1967 and 1982—are recommended not so much to sentimental boogie mavens as to anyone who wants to experience the autumnal glow of a keyboard giant. (47:51/1991)

John Mooney
Late Last Night (Bullseye Blues) ★⌐

John Mooney's meld of country blues and New Orleans R&B is wearisome. His mannered singing and antigroove band have all the spark you'd expect of songs with such dismal titles as "It Don't Matter," "RIP," "Late Last Night," and "Late On in the Evening." The Crescent City guitarist's earlier albums, *Telephone King* (Ichiban CD) and *Comin' Your Way* (Blind Pig CD), are livelier but empty. (38:37/1990)

Gary Moore
After Hours (Charisma) ★★⌐

Gary Moore had time for a couple cups of tea with Irish rockers Thin Lizzy in the mid 1970s before carving out a successful solo career in Europe as a rock guitar hero. This decade he's emphasizing his long-festering love for blues, first with Charisma's best-selling *Still Got the Blues* and then this equally pleasing album. While his singing has little depth or personality, his guitar plumbs slow blues like Duster Bennett's "Jumpin' at Shadows" with concern and caprioles effectively next to Albert Collins's in a busy arrangement of Little Milton's "The Blues Is Alright." (48:16/1992)

Mike Morgan and the Crawl
Raw and Ready (Black Top) ★★✦

The Dallas-based band known as the Crawl, fronted by guitarist Mike Morgan and singer/harpist Lee McBee, makes an
impression on its first disc. Morgan is working toward a passionate syntax and McBee's assertions show that he already
has character. (39:27/1990)

Mighty Fine Dancin' (Black Top) ★★★

Influenced by Stevie Ray Vaughan, young turk Morgan mar-
shals his considerable technique into runs fraught with dance
floor–filling excitement. McBee sings and plays harp as if a
gang hook were caught on his leg, and the band's new, gar-
den-variety rhythm section shuffles, sways, and whiplashes
tempi on call. And what's a Black Top session without tren-
chantly soulful horns? (48:07/1991)

Van Morrison
T.B. Sheets (Columbia) ★★★

Van Morrison, weaned on blues records while growing up in
Belfast, concentrates pungent feeling in his voice on this mid-
1960s singles session for Bang Records. Breaking loose from
Eric Gale's blues-rooted guitar, the twenty-one-year-old
blends sensuality, despair, and courage facing a dying woman
friend in "T.B. Sheets" and at the same time creates an
emotional-mythic bond with John Lee Hooker that's solidified
by Morrison's appearances on the elder statesman's *Never
Get Out of These Blues Alive* (MCA CD) and *Mr. Lucky*
(Pointblank/Charisma CD). See also Morrison's five-star 1973
concert set *It's Too Late to Stop Now* (Warner Brothers, two
CDs) for his deeply personal incantations of Bobby Bland,
John Lee Hooker, Sonny Boy Williamson, Ray Charles, and
Muddy Waters. (42:52/Reissue)

Bill Morrissey
Inside (Rounder) ★★★★

Morrissey is one of the most eloquent and intelligent singer/songwriters working the national folk circuit, and his "Robert Johnson" is a wonderful, poetic statement of fealty to the storied blues traveler. His latticelike guitar playing here and there shows his devotion to country blues gentleman Mississippi John Hurt. (41:51/1992)

Jelly Roll Morton
Mr. Jelly Lord (Tomato) ★★★★

The braggart New Orleans pianist claimed to have invented jazz (pure balderdash) and touted himself as a musical genius (true indeed). Sixteen small band recordings, dating from his classic Red Hot Peppers session in 1926 to a Wingy Manone date eight years later, show off his expert theme-and-variations soloing style and his great skill at songwriting and arranging. Shown too is his music's dual nature as "classic jazz" and blues. For further reference look to *The Jelly Roll Morton Centennial* (Bluebird, five CDs). (50:59/Reissue)

Matt "Guitar" Murphy
Way Down South (Antone's) ★★★

Murphy's feature debut is packed with the same lucid excitement the guitarist has accorded Memphis Slim, James Cotton, the Blues Brothers, and many more. His clean tone and surety of inflection are on display, and his guitar-toting brother Floyd—a former Sun Records sessionsman—is on hand to give the shuffles and down-home originals even more appeal. Matt's singing, though, tries one's patience and sometimes the two guitarists heat up predictably—or, worse yet, stumble. (47:25/1990)

• See also **Memphis Slim and Matt Murphy/Eddie Taylor**

Charlie Musslewhite
Stand Back! (Vanguard) ★★★★✦

Chip away at the patina of time encrusting those many records made in the 1960s by young white musicians spreading the Chicago blues word and you'll find only a scant few that are still fresh, colorful, and inviting. This 1967 issue is one such gem. Singing and blowing harp in twelve songs, Little Walter's aide-de-camp Charlie Musslewhite sounds wise enough at age twenty-two to give pause. Contemporaries Harvey Mandel on electric guitar and Barry Goldberg on organ can't equal his relaxed freedom of expression, but their contributions have aged fairly attractively.   (45:48/Reissue)

Memphis, Tennessee (Mobile Fidelity) ★★

As an impressionable teenager Musslewhite studied blues at the knee of venerable Memphis jug musicians before heading to Chicago in the early 1960s. The phrases that spill out of his harp and vocal cords during this 1970 homecoming session tell of his love of tradition—southwestern Tennessee, the Delta, Maxwell Street—while sounding indisputably full of life. Unfortunately the songs are a mixed lot and his trying accompanists and sound engineer don't deserve the time of day.
(38:23/Reissue)

Memphis Charlie (Arhoolie) ★★★★✦

Two early-1970s albums compressed on a six-inch disc, *Takin' My Time* and *Goin' Back Down South*, are a sheaf of benchmark harmonica solos, heartfelt vocals, and fine electric ensemble work trussed up in uncluttered songs. As one title affirms explicitly, Musslewhite favors a slow and steady attack that provides the adrenaline rush of a half-speed roller coaster ride. Celebrated pianist Lafayette Leake contributes his vibrant blues intelligence to several numbers, notably Little Walter's "Take Me Back" and the feel-it-in-the-spine "This Old Nightlife."   (65:06/1989)

Ace of Harps (Alligator)   ★★★↯

Twenty-seven years and fourteen albums since taking up the Chicago blues torch, Musslewhite's rich instrumental tone has the emotional specificity of a spectrographic analysis and his low voice saturates lyrics with unfeigned feeling. Today, too, his working band—three firebrands conversant with funk and rock as well as blues changes—keeps him alert, though it should have butted out on this set's wistful chestnut, "Yesterdays." On ten songs, including a country blues featuring his acoustic guitar, Musslewhite is compelling more often than entertaining.   (44:19/1990)

Signature (Alligator)   ★★★↯

Musslewhite's harp playing is always crisply purposeful while his singing is usually intense in a phlegmatic son-of-the-South manner. The three Silent Partners again speak eloquently, with a bit more blues direction than on *Ace of Harps*. The new wrinkles, nothing worth crowing over, are a horn section on two songs and longtime pal John Lee Hooker hanging loose in "Cheatin' on Me."   (46:59/1991)

Louis Myers
Tell My Story Movin' (Earwig)   ★★★

It's astonishing that this multitalented Chicago legend hasn't recorded more frequently as a leader. Unfortunately a slight stroke left Myers temporarily unable to accompany himself on guitar when this disc was cut. But he always was better than average on harp anyway, and he proves it anew with help from some of the circuit's top session players. (B.D.)

(61:38/1992)

Nathan and the Zydeco Cha Chas
Steady Rock (Rounder) ★★★ɟ

On their exhilarating studio debut the Zydeco Cha Chas keep an attractively tense balance between the formal structures of the material and their flashes of zydeco ebullience. They're traditionalists keen to funk and rock rhythms, eager to put new spins on propriety. Leader Nathan Williams, an accordion-slinging protégé of Buckwheat Dural, who also sings, has brought some fine originals to the session, notably the bump-and-shake "If You Got a Problem" and Paul Kelly's sunny title tune. (46:21/1989)

Your Mama Don't Know (Rounder) ★★ɟ

The Louisianians keep dancers' aortas pumping excitedly, but now when Williams tries to get the song over rather than the beat he flounders; his new boogaloos and covers (British Invasion pop chestnut "Keep On Running," for one) aren't in the creative thick, and the studio as never before points out the limitations of his voice. To the music's detriment also, only one Cha Cha from the debut outing remains in the fold, washboard agitator Mark Williams. (44:01/1991)

Kenny Neal
Walking on Fire (Alligator) ★★★★

Neal's nastily sharp guitar first scythed a path across blues America upon the release of *Big News from Baton Rouge* in 1987. That release and 1989's *Devil Child*, equally enjoyable items in the Alligator catalog, demonstrated however that bluesman Raful Neal's eldest had more in mind than the same old reheated riffs. *Walking on Fire* has his hefty, mature vocals and alert guitar radiating earthy moods rather than flamboyant dispassion on strong material flattered (like the two earlier albums) by the soul blues production of Bob Greenlee—only this time the horns are inspired by two ex–James Brown zealots. In sharp relief are two country blues that Neal has built around poems by Langston Hughes, whose work he had embraced as a cast member of Broadway's *Mule Bone*. (45:11/1991)

Raful Neal
Louisiana Legend (Alligator)   ★★✦

Baton Rouge's Raful Neal is a decent vocalist and a talented, terse harp player whose debut album, in 1987, relies too heavily on full-bodied Bob Greenlee production and Alligator's remastering to get him over. Neal's son Kenny contributes lead guitar to material that careens from swamp and Chicago blues to *faux* Muscle Shoals soul. A Louisianian club recording would capture the "legend" more honestly.
(33:50/Reissue)

Oliver Nelson
Blues and the Abstract Truth (MCA/Impulse)   ★★★★★

Oliver Nelson was a jazz arranger, composer, and saxophonist of considerable imagination and skill. With this 1961 recording session, he built on the letter and the spirit of simple unadulterated blues to create timelessly memorable hard bop. Key players Eric Dolphy (flute, alto saxophone), Freddie Hubbard (trumpet), Bill Evans (piano), Roy Haynes (drums), and Paul Chambers (bass) provide lyricism and propulsion.
(36:45/Reissue)

Aaron Neville

The Classic Aaron Neville: My Greatest Gift (Rounder) ★★★✦

This is a strong collection taken from the New Orleans vocalist's late-1960s through early-1970s singles. The material may seem unfamiliar, even obscure, but Neville is in top form here. The formidable Allen Toussaint produced these sides. (J.T.) (44:24/1990)

The Neville Brothers

Treacherous: A History of the Neville Brothers ★★★★
(1955–1985) (Rhino)

Rhino's two-CD survey of the Nevilles' endeavors over thirty years is an invitation from the first family of New Orleans R&B to attend a grand Carnival Ball. Included in the generous twenty-eight-track program are singles credited to Aaron, Cyril, or Art, samplings off three family albums, and odds and ends featuring their fiery rhythm consanguinity. Aaron's radio hit "Tell It Like It Is" appears in the form of a 1984 concert track. (102:51/1988)

New Black Eagle Jazz Band

1971–1981 (Black Eagle) ★★★✦

New Black Eagle Jazz Band is a world-class traditional jazz ensemble whose members present more than enough individuality to rebuff any thoughts of embalming them for the wax museum on Bourbon Street. This fourteen-song sampler, culled from a decade's worth of long-players, contains rousing twelve-bar blues from the songbooks of Louis Armstrong, Ma Rainey, and Duke Ellington. Neoconservatives you can trust. (75:23/Reissue)

The New York Rock and Soul Revue
Live at the Beacon (Giant) ★↦

Insipid Manhattan concert extravaganza with Steely Dan's Donald Fagen as the ringmaster, Phoebe Snow as the fake Etta James, Michael McDonald as a pretend Jackie Wilson, and Charlie Brown as Charles Brown—all twenty performers involved should have prostrated themselves at his piano when the stylish bluesman and his guitarist Danny Caron deigned to perform "Driftin' Blues."   (66:46/1991)

Robert Nighthawk
Live on Maxwell Street (Rounder) ★★★★↦

Live on Maxwell Street is as good an impromptu album as one is likely to come upon, with all the exciting, loose esprit de corps among singer/slide guitarist Robert Nighthawk (Robert Lee McCollum) and his Flames of Rhythm that made their Sunday street performances so agreeable to Chicagoans. Captured on fan Norman Dayron's tape recorder in 1964, the Helena-born patriarch of city blues rough-hews Little Junior Parker's "I Need Love So Bad," Big Joe Turner's "Honey Hush," and seven others, cutting single-note runs from the same bolt of cloth as B. B. King without compromising his own amplified guitar poetics. Also heard are thirteen minutes of an interview with the underappreciated musician (encompassing a reluctantly delivered song) that was conducted by a respectful Mike Bloomfield.   (49:00/Reissue)

The Nighthawks
Trouble (Powerhouse/Ichiban) ★★★

Twenty-plus years the cornerstone of Washington, D.C.–area contemporary blues, singer/harpist Mark Wenner and his revived Nighthawks indulge their concern for Chicago twelve-bar music and other "roots" forms with surprising effectiveness. New faces on guitar and keyboards are refreshing. So are soar-and-attack compositions "Treat a Dog" and "99 Pounds." Probably their best album since 1977's *Jacks and Kings*, now available as a Genes CD. (42:25/1991)

Darrell Nulisch and Texas Heat
Business as Usual (Black Top)   ★↗

Inspirational title, eh? Singer Nulisch, formerly with Anson Funderburgh and Ronnie Earl, fronts his own band at long last, essaying a soul blues revival with smartly performed covers and originals that were apparently suppressed by his ex-employers. If his limited, dank-basement voice had sufficient grace, sensuality, humor, pain, *anything*, he might qualify as a second-tier soul man. The absolute horrors: James Carr songs rendered as emotional ciphers. (43:45/1991)

St. Louis Jimmy Oden
St. Louis Jimmy Oden (1932–1948) (Story of Blues)   ★★★

Only a middling singer and pianist, James "St. Louis Jimmy" Oden is worth knowing about for the dramatic sense of his music and the clever nature of his often metaphorical lyrics. The sixteen-track program has him in the company of pianist Roosevelt Sykes eleven times and alongside the postwar Chicago combo of Muddy Waters twice. Oden's famous "Goin' Down Slow," a favorite of postwar urban musicians, isn't here. The sound quality of the 78s varies from impressive to bothersome. (50:07/Reissue)

Omar
Blues Bag (Bullseye Blues)   ★★★✦

Singer and guitarist Omar proffers a feature album consisting of solo performances (harp player Fingers Taylor joins him a few times) followed by just a couple of jousts with his regular rhythm section. His singing—a hoarse, intelligible glossolalia—and tradition-bound picking on Robert Johnson's "Gotta Good Friend," Hound Dog Taylor's "Give Me Back My Wig," and the many *lupus* originals aren't for everybody, but one can do much worse than confront the Texan's sinewy suggestiveness.   (48:02/1992)

Omar and the Howlers
Monkey Land (Antone's)   ★★★

Wiser for his two-disc fling with a major label, Kent "Omar" Dykes signs up with the local Austin blues label and unleashes his rabid Howlin' Wolf growls in a stripped-down blues rock mix he and his threesome can live with. We too, if all the dybbuk's Wolfisms and other high-energy mannerisms don't weary.   (41:50/1990)

Larry O'Neill
You Got Me Runnin' (Muse)   ★★★★

Surprising set from an unheralded middle-aged singer whose deep-chested tones and warmth of gesture restyle material from Jimmy Reed, Roy Brown, Ivory Joe Hunter, Willie Dixon, Chuck Willis, and Broadway. Aided and abetted by saxophonist Houston Person and a well-bred rhythm section, he has a rare savoir faire and gallantry. A real find, especially for fans of Roy Brown and Jimmy Witherspoon.   (48:03/1992)

Johnny Otis
Be Bop Baby Blues (Night Train)　　　　★★★✦

The prolific Los Angeles bandleader is relegated to the background on these late-1940s and early-1950s jump blues sides from the Exclusive, Swing Time, and Supreme vaults. Obscure vocalists Joe Swift, Earl Jackson, Johnny Crawford, and Clifford Blivens are front and center, and the Otis orchestra is spotlighted on a few instrumentals. (B.D.)　　　(38:39/Reissue)

The New Johnny Otis Show (Alligator)　　　　★★★

The R&B revue Johnny Otis organized in 1981 for this studio effort isn't on a par with his rocking powerhouses of the early 1950s (with Etta James, Little Esther Phillips, etc.) or late 1960s (Phillips with many more), but it supplies modest pleasure. "New discoveries" Linda Dorsey and Charles Williams, neither of whom went on to wide acclaim, are among the five pleasing singers, and old hands such as Johnny's son Shuggie on guitar and Earl Palmer on drums help shape the flow of the clear-headed fun.　　　(36:39/Reissue)

The Paladins
Years Since Yesterday (Alligator)　　　　★★✦

Dave Gonzales is a brute of a guitarist, roughing up rockabilly, bare-bones blues rock, and swamp blues with roily leads and chords. He and electric or upright bass player Thomas Yearsley are singers in name only, and their phrasing is sludgy and labored. The production fails to simulate the kick-in-the-butt frenzy of the San Diego–based trio in concert.　　　(32:02/1988)

Let's Buzz! (Alligator)   ★★★★

With the important assistance of dial-and-knob specialist
Mark Linett, the three Paladins transform the studio into a
beer-reeking dive full of carousers, applying electric shocks to
strong originals plus material from Chuck Willis, Otis Rush,
Ray Charles, and others. The singing may waver at times, but
the playing bowls over listeners like tenpins.   (40:15/1990)

Junior Parker
"Little" Junior Parker (LRC)   ★★★

At the end of the 1960s, Parker entered the studio to record
this breezy pop blues set, one of his last. Backed by Jimmy
McGriff (on organ and electric piano) and a functional small
band, his vocals and harmonica are graceful and stirring on
the minor hits "Drownin' on Dry Land" and "Sweet Home
Chicago," and on seventeen others.   (64:02/Reissue)

Junior Parker/James Cotton/Pat Hare
Mystery Train (Rounder)   ★★★★♪

The years 1953 and 1954, like the previous few and many
more to come, were artistically prosperous ones for Parker, an
excellent singer and harp player then recording with his Blues
Flames on Sam Phillips's famous Sun label. The nine Parker
songs assembled here are a veritable feast for the ears, from
the disarmingly gloomy title track (later appropriated by Elvis
Presley) to the prototypical boogie "Feelin' Good" (a big R&B
hit) to enthralling blues numbers only here released stateside.
This disc also has three interesting if raggedy songs recorded
by Sun artist James Cotton (he sings, no harp) in 1953–54 and
two obscurities credited to inventive guitarist Pat Hare, including his eerily prophetic and previously unissued "I'm
Gonna Murder My Baby."   (37:49/1990)

Maceo Parker

Roots Revisited (Verve)   ★★♪

Parker earned his reputation among R&B insiders playing alto saxophone with James Brown off and on for twenty years, and almost no one figured the sideman deluxe would one day enjoy mainstream acclaim as a bandleader in his own right. This best-selling album produces pleasure with its funk-sauce and soul-stew grooves, but Parker is not low-down or burly enough to be the new King Curtis (as if that were possible), and his "soul" doesn't run as deep as that of, say, lesser-known saxophonists Hank Crawford, Arnold Sterling, or Houston Person. Replace Don Pullen's Hammond organ with some studio hack's electric piano and already marginal songs "Over the Rainbow" and "Children's World" would be excruciatingly cloying.   (50:54/1990)

Mo' Roots (Verve)   ★★

Mo' safe fun. Young sensation Larry Goldings on the Hammond B-3 ups the pleasure quotient. Parker and Kym Mazelle's vocals on Otis Redding's "Fa Fa Fa (Sad Song)" take it back down. Renditions of songs from Ray Charles, Marvin Gaye, and jazzbos Horace Silver and Lionel Hampton are kindergarten handicraft compared to the originals.   (64:11/1991)

Joe Pass

Appassionato (Pablo)   ★★★★

Joe Pass epitomizes impassioned guitar artistry, and he most always refashions jazz standards into personal expressions of blues poetry. His melodic sense is sound, his understanding of harmony thorough, and the uninterrupted momentum of his rhythmic patterns is the crux of swinging. Pass is a prolific

recording artist, and his recent quartet session is representative of his ability to communicate through electric or acoustic means, from the roseate blues of "Gee, Baby Ain't I Good to You" to the unremitting ardor of "You're Driving Me Crazy."
(56:45/1991)

Charley Patton
Founder of the Delta Blues (Yazoo) ★★★★★

Patton was the key figure in the transition between traditional folk and what came to be known as the Mississippi Delta blues. A flamboyant, popular performer, he recorded a satchelful of titles between 1929 and 1934, two dozen of which appear in this collection. He sang tales of hardship, freedom, topical events, and other matters in a rough voice that stormed with turmoil. His guitar picking was of a piece: skillfully nuanced in expression and, above all, rhythmically imperative. Yazoo's typically conscientious mastering makes the sound of primitively recorded 78s acceptable.   (74:22/Reissue)

Pinetop Perkins
After Hours (Blind Pig) ★★★

Granted his own session at long last, the former Muddy Waters and Legendary Blues Band pianist rehashes staples from the repertoires of Waters, Memphis Slim, and Robert Nighthawk with ebullient naturalness that is paramount to his charm. He never *feels* his keyboard boogie dances or functional singing as clichés, even when New Yorkers Little Mike and the Tornadoes systematically grind out the platitudes. Consumer advice: Avoid Little Mike's *Heart Attack* (Blind Pig CD) at all costs.   (45:24/1989)

Pinetop's Boogie Woogie (Antone's) ★★★♪

Perkins, an honored blues mastodon, attends to our faculties of sensual delight while seated at the piano in an Austin recording studio or on Antone's' stage at various times over the past several years. His right hand darts at a full gallop while his left pounds unmercifully, heightening the excitement natural to the playing of alley cats like James Cotton, Kim Wilson, and Jimmy Rogers. The version of Eddie Vinson's "Kidney Stew" swings deep and hard. Perkins's singing is sometimes static, sometimes dynamic. (56:19/1992)

Lucky Peterson
Lucky Strikes! (Alligator) ★★

Playing organ with panache in the road bands of Bobby Bland and Little Milton, plus spicing one session or another, is no guarantee of artistic luminance for Lucky Peterson as front man. No help that he brings bad fortune onto himself by ineffectually singing and playing run-of-the-mill lead guitar while freighted with formulaic arrangements. (35:56/1989)

Triple Play (Alligator) ★★

Journeymen's musical ideas are often deficient in clearness or purpose and thought; and when Peterson pitches bush league vocals and guitar in lackluster material he loses the game early on. One isolated cheer: All-star jazz trombonist Ray Anderson, who knows a thing or two about blues, launches a drive into the bleachers on "Funky Ray." (41:46/1991)

Rod Piazza and the Mighty Flyers
Blues in the Dark (Black Top)   ★★★♪

A fixture on Los Angeles's blues scene since 1965, Piazza's harp playing is in the spirit of Little Walter and intermittent Muddy Waters sideman George Smith—street tough, provocative, sensitive, illuminant, questing. His harp and able singing interlock perfectly with the three-men-and-one-woman Mighty Flyers's accompaniment in a twelvefold program of in-house tunes and obscure classics. They swing, they boogie, they aim to please.   (50:49/1991)

Greg Piccolo
Heavy Juice (Black Top)   ★★

Greg Piccolo, leader of Roomful of Blues, is as qualified as any baby boomer to give a primer on the R&B tenor saxophone. On his first headlining set Piccolo's huge-toned horn envelops twelve songs linked to honorees named Red Prysock, Gene Ammons, Buddy Johnson, Buddy Floyd, Jimmy Forrest. Emboldened by the klieg lights of present-day and past Roomful players, Piccolo overdraws on believable drama at times, but for the most part the results are satisfactory, in a secondhand fashion.   (41:08/1990)

Jimmy Ponder
Come on Down (Muse)   ★★★♪

Ponder is an undervalued modern jazz guitarist who has command over all the nuances and shadings of blues. This 1990 session is festooned with intelligent and decidedly bluesy contributions from saxophonist Houston Person, organist Lonnie Smith, and drummer Winard Harper. The ten-minute title track is a Vesuvius of Hammond lava, molten guitar bends, spewed tenor ash, and hot percussion magma.   (44:41/1991)

Jerry Portnoy
Poison Kisses (Modern Blues) ★★★

Ex–Muddy Waters employee Portnoy is a harmonica virtuoso whose career has drifted since he departed the Legendary Blues Band in 1986. This Kim Wilson–produced set is a giant step in the right direction, with Portnoy and his three Streamliners (now divorced) playing a variety of blues and "roots" styles with taste, efficiency, and vibrancy. Not unexpectedly, top honors go to the bandleader for his swingingly personal way with tone and rhythm. Guest Duke Robillard (of the Fabulous Thunderbirds) sings on the fetching title number, but with no more emotional depth than Portnoy or guitarist Charlie Baum elsewhere. (39:23/1991)

Lloyd Price
Lawdy! (Specialty) ★★

Twenty-five tracks recorded by Price, a New Orleans R&B singer/songwriter and rock 'n' roll pioneer, between 1952 and 1956 for Specialty make up this irregular compilation. The best songs are the chart hit "Lawdy Miss Clawdy" and six more that sport a productive little big band led by trumpeter Dave Bartholomew. (Fats Domino plays piano on four of these.) Many of the other selections are displeasing due to Price's uncertain singing and/or sloppy musicianship.
(62:06/Reissue)

Sammy Price
Barrelhouse and Blues (Black Lion) ★★★★

Texan Price, silenced just recently, was a superlative pianist whose familiarity with his instrument went as far back as the wild and woolly Kansas City of the late 1920s. This 1969 date in London has him performing solo and in a septet with young traditional jazz luminaries (including the late clarinetist Sandy Brown) who mirror his empathy for the blues. Maintaining a harmonious balance between a pliable single line and an exacting ambidexterity, this once-frequent visitor to Europe never compromises his exceptional musical intelligence during a generous program of original pieces and classics such as Leroy Carr's "How Long Blues" (on which Price also sings). It is gratifying to hear color and excitement subordinated to clarity and resolve in his playing.   (73:29/Reissue)

Gary Primich
Gary Primich (Amazing)   ★★✦

Eager and sincere, Primich is a talented mouth organ player based in Austin whose instrument points home to Chicago, even as his Midnight Creeps band and song selections (from the books of New Orleans's Dave Bartholomew, R&B centurion Louis Jordan, etc.) moor him to jumping regional blues. He sings a great deal of the time, with a thin voice.
                                                   (41:51/1991)

Tom Principato
Hot Stuff! (Powerhouse)   ★★★✦

Tom Principato, longtime linchpin of East Coast favorites Powerhouse, has slowly but surely acquired a nationwide reputation for his well-ordered, exigent blues guitar playing. This set finds the Falls Church, Virginia, resident following an intelligent commercial course, applying himself to attractive covers (from Mink DeVille, Steve Earle, and more) that usually synthesize blues, rock, and soul. "Blue Lights," an original, packs all the emotional ambiguity of the most stirring guitar blues. And his singing is quite good.   (40:41/1991)

Tom Principato/Danny Gatton
Blazing Telecasters (Powerhouse) ★↗

Neither Washington, D.C.–area guitarist lacks for technical prowess during a club performance in 1984. Both could stand self-editing, though, and blues devotees may not take kindly to Gatton's cowpoke leanings or the rinky-dink electric keyboards or gossamer sound reproduction. (51:49/1990)

Professor Longhair
Houseparty New Orleans Style (Rounder) ★↗

Shortly after a 1971 New Orleans Jazz & Heritage Festival appearance set his career right again, singer/pianist Roy Byrd, alias Professor Longhair, cut these Memphis and Baton Rouge recordings. Unreleased for sixteen years, the so-called lost sessions offer little to justify their quasilegendary status: Longhair's piano arpeggios roll unsteadily, his pitch sense is errant, and there's nothing special about his vocals or accompanists such as guitarist Snooks Eaglin. For Longhair fanatics only. (53:51/1987)

Rock 'n' Roll Gumbo (Dancing Cat) ★★★★

With top-of-the-line recording quality, songs drawn from the very fabric of New Orleans's musical history, and a tight band featuring Clarence "Gatemouth" Brown on guitar and fiddle, this set remains quintessential Longhair—and thus quintessential New Orleans boogie piano. An added horn track (the album was originally recorded sans horns in 1974) on one song ("Mardis Gras in New Orleans") is a minor quibble. (J.T.)
(33:01/Reissue)

Crawfish Fiesta (Alligator) ★★★★

Released in 1980, *Crawfish Fiesta* was the most satisfying album of the legendary New Orleans pianist's career, as well as his farewell (he died shortly before its release). Longhair's delectable rhumba-laced eighty-eights and a suitably funky band combine for spicy remakes of his classics "Bald Head" and "Big Chief," succulent covers of Fats Domino's "Whole Lotta Loving" and Solomon Burke's "Cry to Me," and some pleasing new material. (B.D.) (42:53/Reissue)

Snooky Pryor
Snooky (Blind Pig) ★★

One of the architects of modern Chicago blues, vocalist and harp player Pryor isn't heard to his best advantage on a mid-1980s studio effort with guitarist Steve Freund, bassist Bob Stroger, and drummer Willie Smith. Not bad, mind you, but nothing memorable outside a few irruptions of harmonica splendor. (40:07/Reissue)

Too Cool to Move (Antone's) ★★★↵

Seventy-year-old Pryor gingers a dozen recent compositions and the Tommy McClennan warhorse "Bottle It Up and Go" with vocals that won't quit and harp tones that swagger, brood, and provoke by turns. Grizzled hands such as Pinetop Perkins, Luther Tucker, and Ted Harvey and fresh-faced Texas disciples likewise conspire to keep Chicago blues tenable in the 1990s. (49:11/1991)

• See also **Johnny Shines and Snooky Pryor**

Bobby Radcliff
Dresses Too Short (Black Top)   ★★★★

Guitarist Radcliff escaped the anonymity of New York saloons
with this startlingly good debut album. Combining melody,
bass lines, and chords, his Fender clamors in an ecstatic way
hinting of Magic Sam's and Buddy Guy's but still all his own.
Spurred by his regular bassist and drummer, the Washington,
D.C., native also sings fascinatingly, using a questing, vulner-
able voice that's a blend of Sam's and Jimmy Johnson's. He
transfigures pabulum (e.g., "You Haven't Hurt Me") and
oldies (Otis Rush's "Keep On Loving Me Baby") into sparkling lodestones that draw the listener back again and again.
(41:43/1989)

Universal Blues (Black Top)   ★★✦

One end of the Roman candle fizzles out. Radcliff's vocals at
times overreach, and his guitar liveliness seems dissociated
from feeling. Several remakes of funk, soul, blues, and country numbers from the archives sound as if done from a sense
of duty rather than willful expression of celebratory release.
(52:23/1991)

Bonnie Raitt
Bonnie Raitt (Warner Brothers)   ★★★★

Barely old enough to legally drink in Harvard Square bars,
Bonnie Raitt journeyed from her early-1970s folk blues roost
in Cambridge to record her debut album near Minneapolis—a straightforward affair with Chicagoans Junior
Wells and A. C. Reed plus several young white musician
friends. Raitt's singing, with phrasing and intonation in order,
is grounded in spontaneous passion. She seizes the songs of
forebears Robert Johnson, Tommy Johnson, and especially

Sippie Wallace as her own, extending her laid-back rapture to contemporary material as well. (38:06/Reissue)

Moses Rascoe
Blues (Flying Fish) ★★★✦

Rascoe is a fine folk blues musician whose first recording is literally an intimate coffeehouse recital—a spring 1987 performance at Godfrey Daniels in Bethlehem, Pennsylvania. The retired truck driver sings Jimmy Reed evergreens, spirituals, and traditional songs in a steady, warmly relaxed voice that corresponds to his lissome guitar picking. Someone named Ken Werner sometimes helps out on harmonica. (43:21/Reissue)

Lou Rawls
Stormy Monday (Blue Note) ★★★✦

In 1962, when this, his first, album was made, Lou Rawls was a singer fresh off the "chitlin' circuit" who had a few years to tough out till pop stardom. Here he wraps his rich, gospel-trained baritone around jazz and blues standards, with a swinging little combo led by pianist Les McCann underpinning his relaxed cordiality. Three previously unissued tracks unearthed for the CD, notably "Blues Is a Woman," further display Rawls's concentration and his deliberation of a lyric. (46:20/Reissue)

The ReBirth Brass Band
ReBirth Kickin' It Live! (Rounder) ★★★✦

It's a wonder the festive force of this New Orleans brass band—the brothers Frazier plus fellow brash cherubs—didn't reduce local establishment The Glass House to slivers. Tremendous funk fun, with garish solos and flubs part of their appeal. ReBirth's studio recording *Feel Like Funkin' It Up* (Rounder CD, issued in 1989) also lives up to its title.

(52:45/1991)

A. C. Reed
I'm in the Wrong Business! (Alligator) ★★★♪

On his feature date well-respected Chicago saxophonist A. C. Reed invites accessibility with humorous lyrics and singing to match. Furthermore, grooves are cut expertly by drummer Calvin Jones and four different bassists, while famous friends Bonnie Raitt and Steve Ray Vaughan add bravura or buoyancy to two and three songs respectively. (38:35/1987)

Jimmy Reed
Bright Lights, Big City (Chameleon) ★★★★

Jimmy Reed, an equally impressive singer, guitarist, and harmonica player, endeared himself to a sizable audience in the 1950s and 1960s with lazily polite urban blues tinctured with backwoods dirtiness. While there are a number of retrospectives in the used record bins, Reed is not all that well represented domestically on CD, and this hard-to-find Chameleon set is one of the scant few. Eight of his famous Vee Jay recordings, including "Big Boss Man" and "Baby What You Want Me to Do," are present, along with a few previously lost songs, and we're treated to guitarist Eddie Taylor's wise interjections and running commentaries with the leader. Addendum: GNP Crescendo has a three-star collection available, *Best of Jimmy Reed*, and Mobile Fidelity offers the attractive *Jimmy Reed at Carnegie Hall*, two studio sessions originally presented as a double-record package in 1961.

(44:05/1988)

Sonny Rhodes
Disciple of the Blues (Ichiban)   ★★★

Produced by Bob Greenlee, this tough release is a solid showcase for Bay Area guitarist Rhodes (Clarence Edward Smith),
who hauls out his piercing lap steel on three songs. A solemn
"Cigarette Blues" guarantees no exposure on the blues tours
sponsored by Benson & Hedges. (B.D.)   (35:52/1991)

Livin' Too Close to the Edge (Ichiban)   ★★★

The turbaned Bay Area guitarist's strong belief in his Texas
blues heritage fuels his confident approach on this second
recording for the small Georgian label. Rhodes's lap steel
guitar is distinctive, its tone wiry and quietly forceful, while
his burly Bobby Bland–wannabe voice adamantly interprets
his unexceptional lyrics on the blues life. A few of his tunes,
notably "Sonny's Theme" and "You Don't Know," are
throwaways, and Bob Greenlee's production colors are cool
and bright rather than warm and dark.   (40:09/1992)

Charlie Rich
Pictures and Paintings (Sire/Warner Brothers/Blue   ★★★★
  Horizon)

Charlie Rich, a 1970s country-music star, has harbored blues
feeling in his singing voice since the 1950s, when he recorded
for Sam Phillips's label. On track again after a long quiet
period, Rich brings a sure sense of dramatic pacing to the
eleven attractive songs on this new recording. His wistful
nature is revealed in his selection of subtle variations in
shades of color, and he evokes glows of pleasure in the listener
while his low spirits stir the soul. As a pianist, Rich—along
with his polite jazz workmen—knows how to warm the cock-
les of one's heart without straying into precious sentimentality.   (49:58/1992)

Zachary Richard
Mardi Gras Mambo (Rounder)   ★♩

Contemporary Louisiana dance music from the accordion player and his excitable retinue that is the equivalent of bouillabaisse spiced hastily and carelessly. Blues seasonings wasted.   (35:18/1989)

Paul Rishell
Blues on a Holiday (Tone-Cool)   ★★★

Country blues stylist Rishell is too smart to affect the involved emotional urgencies of the prewar Delta bluesmen he regards with deep respect. Performing solo on nine cuts on his first recording, the Cambridge-based vocalist/guitarist addresses classic material by Tommy Johnson, Blind Blake, and others, with a sharp eye toward capturing the timelessness of themes such as anxiety in hard times and the urge to roam. Far less involving are several tracks with a Chicago-style band, where he sacrifices personality to generic partying.   (43:31/1990)

Marcus Roberts
As Serenity Approaches (RCA Novus)   ★★★★♩

New Orleans pianist Marcus Roberts plays with warmth of blues feeling, profluent ideas rooted in jazz/blues piano history, beautiful sound, and absolute instrumental mastery. He's a precocious artist who seems to perform for his own sake rather than the audience's, yet without self-consciousness, and it is a privilege to hear him employ mood, tempo, melody, and harmony en route to a state of poetic placidity. On his third RCA outing he performs solo and in duet settings with trumpeter Wynton Marsalis, pianist Ellis Marsalis, and three other searching musicians at the Big Easy's St. Joseph Cathedral.   (75:05/1992)

Duke Robillard
After Hours Swing Session (Rounder) ★★

The former Roomful of Blues guitarist (now with the Fabulous Thunderbirds) has had a void of a solo career. His Pleasure Kings are eminently forgettable (snub the 1988 Rounder CD compilation *Rockin' Blues*), and his 1986 jazz album entitled *Swing* impressed only when saxophonist Scott Hamilton took flight. Yes, Robillard is a technically gifted player with a refined taste in music, but, as in this antiquarian jazz-with-hints-of-blues session, a certain wont of iciness in his phrasing and tone always makes for monotony. Furthermore, his ever-empty singing now has the earmarks of an affected Harry Connick wannabe, and the competent jazz stylings of his *After Hours Swing Session* friends cannot resuscitate warhorses like "Sweet Georgia Brown." (40:45/1992)

Carol Joy Robins
Off Color Blues (Optimism) ★★♪

Robins is a new student of risqué material from blues days of yore. Fortunately she has the voice, grit, libido, and integrity necessary to make recasts of come-ons such as "I Know How to Do It" and "Snatch and Grab It" entertaining. Graybeard Clifford Solomon on saxophone is the best known of her Los Angeles studio players. (36:10/1990)

Fenton Robinson
Somebody Loan Me a Dime (Alligator) ★★★★

Modest, literate, sensible, searching, integrity-bound—that's Fenton Robinson, the Mississippi-born modern blues singer and guitarist who doesn't get a tenth of the attention that smoke-and-verbiage poseurs do as a matter of course. This 1974 album's eleven songs, including the famous title one (swiped by Boz Scaggs), impart a warmhearted sensibility pushed forward by his sophisticated, fluent-with-jazz guitar playing and his engagingly imperfect vocal coloratura. Robinson and his backup musicians, the best known being second guitarist Mighty Joe Young, communicate romantic yearning and resilience with equal skill—memorably so. (41:39/Reissue)

Special Road (Black Magic import) ★★★↗

As subdued and reflective as ever, the former Chicago musician is in fine shape on this recent Dutch session. Robinson draws heavily on jazz influences for inspiration during his complex guitar solos, and his rich vocals on a number of remakes of obscure 45s from earlier in his career, including "Crying the Blues" and "Find a Way," are consistently satisfying. (B.D.) (53:58/1989)

Rockin' Dopsie
Louisiana Music (Atlantic) ★★★

One of zydeco's leading spokesmen, Alton "Rockin' Dopsie" Rubin knows how to make his accordion colorful without being sensational and how to intone French and English vocals in an unaffectedly charming way. He and the Zydeco Twisters, including the wonderful ex–Clifton Chenier saxophonist John Hart, invigorate originals and covers from, among others, Guitar Slim, Jimmy Rogers, and Little Richard. (36:07/1991)

Jimmy Rogers
Chicago Blues (MCA/Chess) ★★★★★

Rogers was a key figure in the electric Chicago blues story, supplying boon companion Muddy Waters with rhythm guitar (starting in 1945) and waxing his own feature sides for

Chess Records in the 1950s. On this fourteen-song collection, first issued in 1970, the Mississippi émigré sings and plays with the effortless, understated grace of someone in complete command of his talent. The amplified Delta blues of the earliest tracks, notably the classic "That's All Right" (1950), sit well alongside fully formed urban blues on the order of "Walking by Myself" (1956). Rogers's champion coconspirators include Little Walter, Walter Horton, Muddy Waters, and Willie Dixon. (42:14/Reissue)

Ludella (Antone's) ★★★◢

In recent years Rogers and the congregation assembled here—whippets Kim Wilson and Derek O'Brien and elders Hubert Sumlin, Ted Harvey, Pinetop Perkins, and Bob Stroger—in either an Austin studio or on Antone's' stage rock the house and feign the mojo as discerningly as anyone. Here's depth, not just the illusion of depth. Here's fading technique, too. (52:27/1990)

Roy Rogers
Blues on the Range (Blind Pig) ★

Roy Rogers, recent production sidekick to John Lee Hooker, is one of the most able slide guitarists around. His precise outlay of notes, however, has a heartless, glossy feel. Worse yet, the San Franciscan's singing is inexpressive and as worthless as a paring of cheese rind. Interpretations of two Robert Johnson songs are easy-listening monstrosities. (43:04/1989)

Roy Rogers and Norton Buffalo
R&B (Blind Pig) ★★★

Norton Buffalo, a fine Bay Area harmonica player long affiliated with rocker Steve Miller, and occasional partner Rogers dispense winsome acoustic music, mostly original, that often has a pronounced blues slant. Every time Rogers's vocals begin to wear out their welcome, his lightly textured guitar or Buffalo's variegated harp sets things right. They've feelingly arranged Reverend Robert Wilkins's "Heaven Sittin' Down."

(44:05/1991)

Roomful of Blues
Hot Little Mama (Varrick)   ★★

Rhode Island's horn-powered Roomful of Blues, class of 1980, clearly loves the jump blues and jazz it swings so determinedly on its third album. But only Roomful's versions of Johnny Otis's "New Orleans Shuffle" and T-Bone Walker's "Two Bones and a Pick" encourage listeners to share the passion. Greg Piccolo defuses eight others with his washed-out singing, and two Duke Ellington numbers won't have you confusing these whippersnappers with the regal men. Truth be told, Roomful guitarist Ronnie Earl's not all that convincing a T-Bone Walker, either.   (45:03/Reissue)

Dressed Up to Get Messed Up (Varrick)   ★★★

Some changes for the better. Piccolo has emerged as a dapper little songwriter, and his earthbound vocals get a needed lift from harmonies by ensemble members and an evangelic quintet called 14 Karat Soul. The band sound is now cut from an early-day rock 'n' roll cloth, which elevates drummer John Rossi to prominence alongside the lately crackerjack horn section.   (37:18/Reissue)

Live at Lupo's Heartbreak Hotel (Varrick)   ★↗

For three spring nights in 1986, Roomful turned its favorite Providence haunt into a wild R&B conflagration. Exciting, yes, but insufferable listening for anyone attentive enough to be bothered by beastly melodramatic singing (four different culprits; only one-song guest Cesar Rosas of Los Lobos makes points) and nine-piece ensemble bombast. Haphazardly recorded, too.   (42:03/Reissue)

• See also **Earl King and Roomful of Blues; Joe Turner and Roomful of Blues; Eddie "Cleanhead" Vinson and Roomful of Blues**

Martin Jack Rosenblum
The Holy Ranger's Free Hand (Flying Fish)   ★★★

A modern-day cowboy who spurs his Harley-Davidson down America's byways. Rosenblum, alias the Holy Ranger, used to sing and play guitar in the folk blues 1960s of Lightnin' Hopkins and John Hammond. Active again musically, the Wisconsin poet fills this album (formerly found only at "biker tribal campfires") with electric and acoustic blues that is technically assured and lyrically expressive. Only rarely does his longing for the time when trigger-happy rustlers tangled with Wild West lawmen—he's serious about this—take a turn for the maudlin.   (40:26/1992)

Sparky and Rhonda Rucker
Treasures & Tears (Flying Fish)   ★★★★

Twenty-five years an unwearied folk minstrel and educator, James "Sparky" Rucker writes songs from the heart and embraces spirituals and traditional blues so masterfully it's disarming. His touch on acoustic guitar is sure and his gnarled voice taps a well of feeling where gentleness and a strong sense of social justice coexist. The maternal side of the family provides him with pleasant harmonica and an infrequent harmony.   (49:17/1991)

Otis Rush

1956–1958: Cobra Recordings (Paula)　　★★★★★

Otis Rush's first eight singles for the Cobra label, recorded between 1956 and 1958, are the aurora borealis of West Side/ South Side blues—staggeringly radiant, rare music that lodges itself permanently in the memory. Take the heart-stopping "My Love Will Never Die," where young singer/guitarist Rush sounds like he's wearing a tightening noose while phantasmic saxophones wail a dirge, or the enduring "All Your Love" with its ominous Cuban rhythms closing Rush in till he brandishes his guitar and breaks clear with a vengeance. Four alternate takes are meteors rushing through the heavens.

(59:23/Reissue)

Right Place, Wrong Time (Hightone)　　★★★★♪

This contemporary album by Otis Rush challenges the brilliance of his 1950s work for Cobra. Recorded in 1971 for Capitol but unissued until 1976, when the tiny Bullfrog label rescued the project, the album has Rush backed by a driving combo with three horns on searing revivals of "Tore Up" and "Natural Ball," a tortured "Your Turn to Cry," and the intense title track. The Chicago great's vibrato-laden guitar work is mesmerizing, his vocals impassioned, and his band combative. (B.D.)　　(40:55/Reissue)

Lost in the Blues (Alligator)　　★★★★

Recorded and issued only in Europe in 1977, *Lost in the Blues* (originally known as *Troubles, Troubles*) consists of nonoriginals that are laden with vocals of almost paralyzing pain, tension, and bereavement (the exceptions are two Jimmy Reed numbers, with Rush's anodyne singing no better than push-button entertainment). For altruistic reasons Alligator potentate Bruce Iglauer has regenerated Rush's original guitar sound in the remix, accentuating the emotional frankness of his phraseology. Furthermore, Rush's trio is augmented on this 1990 CD reissue by the harmless yet also controvertible presence of dubbed-in keyboardist Lucky Peterson.

(47:37/Reissue)

Tops (Blind Pig)　　　★★★♪

Few surprises in the Chicago southpaw's songlist for this 1985 San Francisco Blues Festival set, but the disc captures Rush's sharp guitar and distressed vocals in concert quite well. The repertoire is a mix of originals and versions of B. B. King, Earl Hooker, Chuck Willis, and classic Delta songs. (B.D./F.J.H.)

(39:16/Reissue)

• See also **Albert King and Otis Rush**

Jimmy Rushing
The Essential Jimmy Rushing (Vanguard)　　　★★★★♪

The wisest male blues singer of them all displayed his breath-taking mastery of rhythm, dynamics, inflections, and the entire spectrum of emotions for a long time after his glorious thirteen-year run with Count Basie ended in 1948. Lining up fourteen standards, this collection of recordings issued on Vanguard in the mid 1950s has his high, supple vocals glowing at ballad and medium-up tempi. Three different groups of jazz/blues players—a number of the musicians affiliated with Basie—help the blues Goliath's gentle-yet-rough music carry a kind of communal power that is forever rare and fresh.

(72:05/Reissue)

The You and Me that Used to Be (RCA/Bluebird) ★★★★★

The modest and thoughtful Jimmy Rushing considered this 1971 session, his last, to be his finest hour. Instilling eleven pop standards with sublime blues spirit, the sixty-eight-year-old vocalist is totally at ease with his working combo at the time (co-led by saxophonists Al Cohn and Zoot Sims) and with New York studio guests Budd Johnson on soprano saxophonist and multi-instrumentalist Ray Nance. Pianist Dave Frishberg's arrangements accentuate the musicians' ability to communicate total honesty in an empathic, swinging manner.
(44:01/Reissue)

Saffire—The Uppity Blues Women
Hot Flash (Alligator) ★★★★

On their second effort the three Virginians push on in the tradition of begetters Alberta Hunter and Edith Wilson. They're smart, sincere, obdurate, salty, and unapologetic about their vexatious streak—the Uppity Blues Women delight in making blues conservatives uneasy. Fine singing, musicianship, and songwriting, with a special nod to pianist and singer Ann Rabson. (54:40/1991)

Doug Sahm
Juke Box Music (Antone's) ★★

Doug Sahm, a veritable Texas music foundation, has had a sure grip on blues, R&B, Tex-Mex, and other territorial strains since the 1960s. These days he stocks his coin-operated record player with fair-to-good rehashes of vintage R&B material from Don and Juan, the Hollywood Flames, and Jesse Belvin, along with a few unprogressive shuffles and rock numbers. Best appreciated by those who remember the Eisenhower years. (42:19/1988)

Jumpin' Johnny Sansone
Mr. Good Thing (King Snake/Ichiban) ★★★

New Orleans's Sansone is a good harmonica player, singer, and tunesmith whose second album comes with Bob Green-lee's savory soul-side-of-blues production. Disregard Green-lee's hallucinatory jotting that his charge "plays the best harp in the world." (44:33/1990)

Satan and Adam
Harlem Blues (Flying Fish) ★★★★

Ecclesiastical confusion aside, Sterling "Satan" Magee and Adam Gussow are the Harlem curbside duo who spin the listener in the vortex of a most idiosyncratic and restive brand of down-home blues. Satan's pitchfork-in-the-ribs singing and simultaneous ravaging of electric guitar and percussion seemingly come direct from the fires of primeval creation. Harmonica player Adam leaves any sense of white middle-class decorum twenty blocks to the south. Fortunately the recording studio doesn't bridle the pair's raw enthusiasm any. (51:14/1991)

Little Jimmy Scott
Regal Records: Live in New Orleans (Specialty) ★★★

Neglected R&B singer Scott is heard with the 1952 Paul Gayten band in a Crescent City nightclub. Yearning beyond the moment, his ethereally high voice soars out of five songs like a beautiful dove in flight. Some may hear it as headache-inducing exhibitionism—what half the program, with hot-and-bothered saxophonists replacing Scott, undoubtedly is. (34:04/1991)

Son Seals
Midnight Son (Alligator)   ★★★★✦

The outstanding blues album of the mid 1970s was this second
recording by a thirty-three-year-old South Side guitarist who
had worked with Earl Hooker and Albert King. Seals's axe,
distorted in tone and managed superbly, rips through nine
songs with the cataclysmal surprise of a buzz saw kicking to
life outside your bedroom window at four A.M. That's not
all—his voice is brawny, clamorous, haggard, wreaking havoc
on untrustworthy lovers. One quibble: Seals and his tough
rhythm section don't need the three horns.   (38:52/Reissue)

Bad Axe (Alligator)   ★★★

Trust the title's reference to his guitar. Yet Son the singer's
snarls and groans, in the 1984 studio, have lost some of their
former testiness. Furthermore, the material is uneven, and
two different sets of support players are too willful with their
funk. His fifth Alligator recording and his last for the label for
seven years.   (42:24/Reissue)

Living in the Danger Zone (Alligator)   ★★✦

Reconciled with Alligator's Bruce Iglauer, Seals makes his
most carefully plotted album. While he's the focal point of the
songs, the mix gives unbecoming prominence to the hyperactive bass and drums, and a wispy flute undermines his
serious societal concern in "Danger Zone." There *are* fre-
quent spells of inspiration, but often Seals's long lines, as in
"My Time Now," seem lost in direction and achieve only an
anticlimax.   (52:04/1991)

Johnny Shines

Johnny Shines (Hightone) ★★★★

No less than a founding father of modern blues, James "Johnny" Shines was a valued singer/slide guitarist whose creative impulses, technical command, and expressive candor were at an extraordinarily high level in the decade or so following his mid-1960s "rediscovery." This 1970 session includes several inspired solo performances that hark back to his prewar Delta and Memphis country blues years, another elevated period in his venerable career. Of the five songs made with a tipsy West Coast ensemble, "My Love Can't Hide" drops your jaw for the ardency of his heartsick vocalization. (40:02/Reissue)

Hey Ba-Ba-Re-Bop! (Rounder) ★★★★

Peter Guralnick, who co-produced this 1971 Boston concert recording, writes in the notes that no one "displays greater vocal virtuosity than Johnny Shines." No exaggeration.

(44:26/Reissue)

Too Wet to Plow (Tomato) ★★★★⯨

On a 1975 album ten freshly composed country blues and a version of Robert Johnson's "Hot Tamale" exist as splendent rubies in the coronet of Johnny Shines. Slide guitarist/harpist Louisiana Red (on six songs), harmonica player Sugar Blue (five), and bassist Ron Rault (two) perform pithily at this studio procession, but it's Shines who's the regal personage all the way—articulate, unimpeachable, powerful, understated, innately musical, improvisatory. (48:26/Reissue)

Johnny Shines and Snooky Pryor
Back to the Country (Blind Pig)   ★★★★

By no means are Shines and Pryor dotards looking back with
teary eyes. The blues' emotional dualities—sadness leavened
with humor, warmth caught up in despair, pride alongside
disquiet—are keenly reflected by fifteen country blues the
two recorded earlier this decade. Granted their facility isn't
what it once was, yet Shines-the singer and Pryor the harp
player/vocalist, J.O.B. labelmates forty years ago in Chicago,
still employ tonal modulations, phrasing, and space with special knowledge—and *no one* has interpreted Robert Johnson
songs as knowingly as Mr. Shines (four examples here). That's
John Nicholas and Kent Du Shane ably filling in for poststroke
Shines on guitar.   (48:08/1991)

Siegel-Schwall Band
The Reunion Concert (Alligator)   ★★

The Corky Siegel–Jim Schwall outfit, enjoyable as they were,
didn't have the idiomatic understanding of Paul Butterfield's
band in Chicago's white blues subculture of the 1960s. Thirteen years after last working together, three of the four original members met up again for a single gig and roused old fans
with fun reexaminations of "Hey, Billie Jean," "Hush Hush,"
and other repertoire favorites. Addendum: Don't bother with
the Vanguard CD *The Best of Siegel-Schwall.*   (46:37/1988)

Silent Partners
If It's All Night, It's All Right (Antone's)

Mel Brown is all right any old time. The guitarist who funked
up the jazz/blues 1960s and who backed Bobby Bland for
eleven years rides a relaxed level of confidence through the
debut session of his Austin-based trio. Neither Brown nor his

rhythm team sings especially well, though, and it is his reposi-
tory of fretboard fingerings that boosts the proceedings above
the routine, with the instrumentals "Under Yonder" and
"Two Steps from the Blues" coming off best.   (42:33/1990)

Apollo Smile
Apollo Smile (DGC)   ★★★

Smile is an aging flower child with a fanciful singing voice who
turns to R&B/blues notable Johnny "Guitar" Watson for advice on futuristic Los Angeles funk. Watson always did have
a sense of humor. Strangely endearing.   (44:45/1991)

Bessie Smith
The Complete Recordings, Volume One
(Columbia/Legacy)

Bessie Smith's artistry was prodigious, and the "classic blues"
on this boxed set's two discs is beyond price. Her first thirty-
eight recordings, dating from 1923–24, are astounding pro-
nouncements of an African-American woman's life that had
her powerful contralto using clear tone and precise phrasing
to give popular songs their humanness. The Empress of the
Blues had lived the lyrics and understood all their negative
implications, and her integrity is framed fifteen times by the
quiet authority of pianist Fletcher Henderson. The digital
restoration and engineering has done wonders to the formerly
crude sound.   (2:03:44/1991)

The Complete Recordings, Volume Two   ★★★★★
(Columbia/Legacy)

This second double-disc release features material Smith recorded in 1924 and 1925. By the time these thirty-seven sides
were issued Smith was already a star, and accordingly she

found herself backed by the top musicians, including Louis Armstrong on cornet and reedman Don Redman. Smith's rising popularity when these were recorded is reflected in a heightened self-confidence and maturity of performance. These selections are not only historic, they are also very listenable, given the recording technique of the time. (J.T.)
(2:01:17/1991)

Byther Smith
Housefire (Bullseye Blues)   ★★★✦

Bullseye bigwig Ron Levy deserves a tip of the fedora for picking up this unheralded Chicagoan's 1985 album for wide release. Smith's guitar slashes and burns in an eccentric, interesting fashion, and his nothing-to-lose singing of devastatingly personal lyrics, rhyme scheme be damned, are positively gripping. One hopes these spare, dramatic expositions of trouble eased his pain. Truehearted pianist Lafayette Leake is among his Chicago and Texas backup players.   (39:46/Reissue)

Addressing the Nation with the Blues (JSP import)   ★★★

This Chicago session is another uncompromising showcase for the intense South Sider, whose Slough of Despond–gloomy lyrics and needles-up-the-spine guitar playing combine to produce perhaps the most daunting contemporary blues anywhere. (B.D./F.J.H.)   (58:12/1989)

Gregg Smith
Money Talks (Ultra)   ★★✦

Gregg Smith from Dallas is no Bobby Bland or even Z. Z. Hill, but his cozy, low, and semituneful voice gets the job when bedroom lights are down low. The session players, however, knock over the bedside table.   (43:05/1990)

Jimmy Smith
Midnight Special (Blue Note) ★★★✦

Smith's blues phrases and bebop lines on organ were the
primary instigators of the late-1950s and 1960s "soul jazz"
explosion, and of the Philadelphian's innumerable sessions
this popular 1960 chicken-shack gathering with saxophonist
Stanley Turrentine, guitarist Kenny Burrell, and drummer
Donald Bailey endures as one of his driving best.

(36:48/Reissue)

Fourmost (Milestone) ★★★✦

Reunion time. Blues heavily streaks the head-bobbing music
grooved by Smith, Burrell, Turrentine, and drummer Grady
Tate at Fat Tuesday's in New York in November 1990. Their
versions of "Summertime" and "My Funny Valentine,"
among more standards, are pleasurable, with the Burrell slow
blues "Soulful Brothers" fit for paradise.   (55:48/1991)

Tab Smith
Jump Time (Delmark) ★★★

Abounding with good cheer or teariness, saxophonist Tal-
madge "Tab" Smith recorded these twenty sides—half ballads, half jump blues—for United in the R&B 1950s. The
up-tempo numbers are more enjoyable, yet the former Lucky
Millinder sideman (who sings decently three times) has a rich
alto tone that makes the bleeding heart numbers better than
they have any right to be. Teddy Brannon plays sapid piano.

(58:38/1991)

Chris Smither
Another Way to Find You (Flying Fish)

Recording with an adoring studio crowd present, Cambridge folk bluesman Chris Smither uses his dusty baritone voice and marvelous six-string guitar to instill clever originals (especially one he gave Bonnie Raitt, "Love You like a Man") and covers (hear Blind Willie McTell's "Statesboro Blues") with a knowing sort of lyrical resonance. All's not well, though; Bob Dylan and Jerry Garcia songs have grown much moss in the twenty years since Smither first recorded them.   (56:59/1991)

Otis Spann/Lightnin' Hopkins
The Complete Candid Otis Spann/Lightnin' Hopkins Sessions (Mosaic)   ★★★★✦

Mosaic's carefully assembled boxed set consists of two discs, one featuring creative Chicago pianist Otis Spann and the other spotlighting Texas singer and guitarist Sam Hopkins. Spann's 1960 studio work for a short-lived jazz label has him walking or reeling off his notes and chords with precision, panache, and keen regard for the thirty-four songs' rhythmic structure; on vocals the moods he sets are closely observed, with the re-creation of his 1954 Checker side "It Must Have Been the Devil" an especially poignant standout. Singer "St. Louis" Jimmy Oden and guitarist Robert Lockwood, Jr., the latter performing spottily, share the dates with Spann. Hopkins's selections off his 1960 *In New York* album, along with five previously unissued pieces, evidence the country-bluesman's artistic probity and his genius for leisurely storytelling.   (3:22:13/1992)

Dave Specter and Barkin' Bill Smith
Bluebird Blues (Delmark)

Bluebird Blues succeeds by dint of a measured three-pronged attack: Chicago tavern denizen Bill Smith plows and furrows eight smart selections with the weathered textures of his voice; former Legendary Blues Band guitarist Dave Specter launches many concise solos that evidence his even temper and fairly sound judgment; and Ronnie Earl, further beyond emulation of T-Bone Walker and Otis Rush than the younger Specter, provides imperturbable bursts of guitar. Meantime, six dependable Windy City players flank them.   (48:21/1991)

Dakota Staton
Dakota Staton (Muse) ★★★♪

A late-1950s pop star, Staton is at home this decade taking a jazz approach to ballads and blues. With her candid, bold voice, she gives the lyrics of warhorses "Body and Soul" and B. B. King's "The Thrill Is Gone" an emotionalism that is completely earned. Tenor player Houston Person and a trio impress as responsive sustainers of her prideful moods.
(45:10/1991)

Frank Stokes
Creator of the Memphis Blues (Yazoo) ★★★★

A first-generation Memphis bluesman, Stokes was a stentorian singer and capable guitar strummer who recorded in the late 1920s with the more proficient, inventive fretboard surveyor Dan Shane as the Beale Street Sheiks. Fourteen sides show their staid approach and gift for emotional authenticity. The sound of the 78s isn't very good.   (42:50/Reissue)

Angela Strehli
Soul Shake (Antone's)   ★★★★

Austin's R&B pride and joy knows how to write and pick good songs from the strongboxes of Eddie Taylor, Tampa Red, Willie Dixon, and others. Miss Angela interprets her creations and discoveries with the easy air of familiarity, transforming bluesmen's plaints into sharp female manifestos. She knows, too, not to exceed the technical and emotive limitations of her lilting, sensual voice. Guess who was smart enough to keep the arrangements spare and direct and who gathered the most soul-shakin' backup players in town?   (59:33/1987)

• See also **Marcia Ball/Lou Ann Barton/Angela Strehli**

Sugar Ray
Don't Stand in My Way (Bullseye Blues)   ★★↗

Sugar Ray's confidence in his ability to sing has increased by leaps and bounds, and on his first headlining album he uses his yearning baritone to demand wider recognition. Unfortunately his voice strains when a top-flight singer's wouldn't, his inflections lack natural grace, and his and bassist Mudcat Ward's lyrics are matter-of-fact. He's an excellent harp player, one of the best in all fifty states, but his assertions on the instrument take a backseat to his vocalizations.
(47:39/1991)

Sugar Ray and the Blue Tones
Knockout (Varrick)   ★★★

This New England R&B foundation has personality and energy to spare on its debut recording. Ray Norcia's voice and harmonica are on the cusp between defiance and despair,

always under control and always understated in mood. The
other Blue Tones, including guitarist Kid Bangham (who went
on to the Fabulous Thunderbirds), also show concern for
probing the ache of the blues with restraint, not heavy-hand-
edness.   (38:29/1989)

Hubert Sumlin
Hubert Sumlin's Blues Party (Black Top)   ★★★♪

Howlin' Wolf's guitar player of twenty-odd years makes his
first stateside solo recording in the company of party planner/
guitarist Ronnie Earl, singer Sam McClain, and a Boston recording studio full of revelers. Sumlin, a diffident man, is
coaxed into singing twice and using his guitar to jolt most of
the ten songs with wild glissandi and fey chords. Still, it's Earl
and McClain who provide the bash's most enthralling moments when they tear their hearts out expounding the slow
blues "A Soul That's Been Abused," written by Earl.
                                                        (36:23/1987)

Heart and Soul (Blind Pig)   ★♪

A session from the late 1980s desperately in need of a leader.
Sumlin's voice is determined but crannied, and his guitar, no
matter how fascinatingly jagged and pained in tone, only goes
so far in the ensemble clutter of "working class" New Yorkers
Little Mike and the Tornadoes. Old friend James Cotton on
harmonica takes over on a few hand-me-down songs but falls
flat.   (37:05/Reissue)

Healing Feeling (Black Top)   ★★★♪

Sumlin is shown to best advantage with costars Ronnie Earl
and the Broadcasters at a May 1989 Tipitina's show and a
studio session just hours later. The acclaimed guitarist finds

his afflatus playing "Down the Dusty Road" in a private after-hours recital, and his energy and productive levels are high on most of the other numbers. Singer James "Thunderbird" Davis also contributes to the New Orleans club merriment.

(43:41/1990)

Sunnyland Slim
House Rent Party (Delmark) ★★★★

August 26, 1949, was an auspicious day in Chicago blues recording history. That's when pianist Albert "Sunnyland Slim" Luandrew, singer "St. Louis" Jimmy Oden, and then-unknowns Willie Mabon, on vocals, piano, and harmonica, and Jimmy Rogers, on guitar and vocals converged to cut this marathon session for Apollo. Only six of these fifteen sides were issued at the time, and the new discoveries include a pre-Chess "That's All Right" by a youthful-sounding Rogers. Sound quality is excellent considering the age of its contents. (B.D.) (41:35/1992)

Be Careful How You Vote (Earwig) ★★

The septuagenarian sovereign of Chicago blues isn't all that impressive singing and playing piano on ten songs recorded for Airway in the early 1980s. An accident kept his right hand out of action on some songs, and honorable friends Hubert Sumlin, Eddie Taylor, Bob Stroger, and Magic Slim have been enlisted to help carry the load—with patchy results.

(41:19/Reissue)

Roosevelt Sykes
Music Is My Business (Tomato) ★★★✦

Sykes had as much to do with the birth and maturation of the modern blues piano style as anyone, and almost a half century since first recording he remained a leading light. This 1977 album is agreeable because the Honeydripper's keyboards and singing retain a goodly portion of the exuberance and surety of earlier times, though he now relies on stock phrases. The ten songs having Sykes alone with his homespun truths eclipse the three duets with guitarist Louisiana Red or Johnny Shines and a triad of small group performances.

(45:54/Reissue)

The Tail Gators
Swamp Rock (Wrestler) ★★★

The three wild ones play stripped-down rock 'n' roll brimming with allusions to their Louisiana and Texas blues turf. Guitarist Don Leady's faulty, understated vocals could stand an infusion of expressivity, but not at the expense of their appeal. Originally released in 1985. Also worth hearing: *Mumbo Jumbo* and *Tore Up* (a collection of obscure material), both Wrestler CDs. (40:07/Reissue)

Tampa Red
Tampa Red (1928–1942) (Story of Blues) ★↗

Hudson "Tampa Red" Woodbridge was the inventor of sleek Chicago bottleneck guitar and a fine singer and songwriter, but you'd never know it from this Austrian compilation of eighteen sides (only two of which were recorded after 1931). The crowd pleaser "Tight like That," sung with jokey salaciousness, and the cynical "Down in Spirit Blues" are about the only selections that give cause for listening. Atrocious sound on several tracks. (55:18/Reissue)

Pam Tate
Die Happy (Left Field)   ★★★↙

Sassy, sophisticated, and urbane, Pam Tate's jazzy brand of blues/pop (or bluesy brand of jazz/pop) owes more to Ella Fitzgerald than to Koko Taylor or Big Mama Thornton. Both her vocals and composing give accessibility with tradition, but that needn't be a crime. (J.T.)   (46:33/1991)

Eddie Taylor
I Feel So Bad (Hightone)   ★★★↙

Singer/guitarist Eddie Taylor's first album in the spotlight, made in 1972 alongside mechanical Californians, shows his talent for performing originals with the proof-steel mettle and assurance suitable to a modern blues notable. Just don't expect to hear anything on a par with Taylor's golden mid-1950s singles or his benchmark sides with Jimmy Reed and Muddy Waters.   (41:14/Reissue)

• See also **Memphis Slim and Matt Murphy/Eddie Taylor**

Hound Dog Taylor
Hound Dog Taylor and the HouseRockers (Alligator)   ★★★★

Ted "Hound Dog" Taylor, a Delta slide guitarist heard regularly around Chicago after 1956, and his HouseRockers—drummer Ted Harvey and second guitarist Brewer Phillips—provide a sizzling hot poker to the synapses with their shoestring budget recording for the fledgling Alligator label in 1971.   (44:26/Reissue)

Natural Boogie (Alligator)

Taylor and his barroom patricians rock and thump the misery out of eleven tunes, giving rise to great down 'n' dirty fun in 1974. No bargain basement electric guitar and slider have evoked the spirit of Elmore James so raucously. (40:08/Reissue)

Beware of the Dog! (Alligator)

On their earlier albums the trio turned the studio into the most unmanageable Chicago joint imaginable, so their first "live" recording doesn't gain anything in grimy, sweaty boogie fun. Some of the bicentennial year's grandest fireworks are to be encountered in this posthumously released set. Revealing song title: "Let's Get Funky." (40:24/Reissue)

Johnnie Taylor
Crazy 'Bout You (Malaco) ★★★

Since 1984, Taylor has been part of the Malaco Southern soul and blues family. His singing, as it was in the Stax 1960s, is typified by an intense sensual delight asserted in bluesy terms. His limited range and lack of originality don't detract from the pleasure of ballads and up-tempo songs that have been sophisticatedly clad by producers Tommy Couch and Wolf Stephenson. (37:36/1989)

Koko Taylor
What It Takes (MCA/Chess) ★★★♪

Memphis-born Cora "Koko" Taylor was one of the few blues ladies in the 1960s with fire in her lungs. This fresh survey of her Chess recording career (1964–72) finds the tough and forceful woman working over Betty James's "I'm a Little Mixed Up," the lost-till-now trifle "Blue Prelude," and sixteen Willie Dixon compositions including singles "Wang Dang Doodle" and "I Got What It Takes." While Dixon's clever lyrics are seldom grist for her mill, his soul-cum-blues production usually provides satisfactory melodrama. Note: *What It Takes* superannuates *Koko Taylor*, a 1969 collection available on MCA/Chess CD. (56:23/1991)

I Got What It Takes (Alligator) ★★★★♪

On her Alligator debut in 1975, Taylor's gravelly burr sends frissons up listeners' spines, as it must have patrons of Chicago joints twenty years earlier when she frolicked with Elmore James and Muddy Waters. She invests Denise LaSalle's "Find a Fool" and Ruth Brown's "Mama, She Treats Your Daughter Mean," to name a few in a superb program, with a feisty, absolute frankness that finds its corollary in the directness of her mighty blues brawlers: saxophonist Abe Locke, guitarists Mighty Joe Young and Sammy Lawhorn, and three more. (39:49/Reissue)

The Earthshaker (Alligator) ★★★

Taylor's big voice moves heaven and earth when applied to material worth her hard-earned jollity or invective. On a 1978 release, however, only her Bo Diddley variant "I'm a Woman" and an updated "Wang Dang Doodle" register on the Richter scale. Unshaken are threadbare party favors such as "Let the Good Times Roll" and leaden slow blues. (36:28/Reissue)

From the Heart of a Woman (Alligator) ★★★★

Flailing her heart, Taylor gives a hortatory discourse in how to emphasize a lyric for maximum "big bad bulldog" toughness. Goaded by her fine Chicago musicians, she's fit to be tied over the blonde's hair found on her pillow in "Something

Strange Is Going On" (the highlight on this 1981 album), and she personalizes the rest of the intelligent program commandingly, from Etta James's desolate "I'd Rather Go Blind" to the knowing smile of Louis Jordan's "Sure Had a Wonderful Time Last Night." (39:15/Reissue)

Queen of the Blues (Alligator)   ★★★✦

Explosive but not strident, Taylor moves easily between emotional sublimation and entertainment, blurring the distinction. This 1985 album positions ten good songs along the plumb line to the core of her soul. Guitarists Lonnie Brooks, Albert Collins, and Son Seals heat up a song apiece, while James Cotton's harmonica stings two. (40:35/Reissue)

Live from Chicago: An Audience with the Queen (Alligator)   ★★★

Her Ladyship's court was FitzGerald's in suburban Chicago for three nights in January 1987. "Everything's gonna be all right," she boasts early on, then proceeds to back it up, even though her voice doesn't stomp as it used to. Four young, funk-savvy thoroughbreds keep her eager and alert on the usual crowd pleasers. *Live from Chicago* was followed, in 1990, by the unexciting *Jump for Joy* (Alligator CD). (52:07/Reissue)

Little Johnny Taylor
Ugly Man (Ichiban)   ★★✦

Not to be confused with *Johnnie* Taylor, this gospel-trained purveyor of the 1963 blues ballad "Part Time Love" favors a measured, conversational approach to singing the blues. What his parched voice has lost in power over twenty-five years is made up in his spirit of determination on a set with Atlanta's Bluse Guys in attendance. (36:37/1989)

Little Johnny Taylor and Ted Taylor
The Super Taylors (Paula)   ★★★↓

Soul brothers musically if not related by bloodlines, both Taylors had already enjoyed stardom separately for a decade when they momentarily teamed to wax four hot duets for Ronn in the early 1970s. The same gritty Southern soul feel reigns on the solo material that fills out the set, as Ted's fragile falsetto cries contrasts with the blues-based approach of Little Johnny. (B.D.)   (36:35/Reissue)

Ted Taylor
Taylor Made (Paula)   ★★★↓

With his soaring, vibrant falsetto pipes and a discography that takes in doo-wop, tough blues, and silky R&B, Ted Taylor recorded some blistering Southern soul during the early 1970s for Paula's Ronn subsidiary. This churning, brassy set hits on all cylinders, with Taylor effortlessly shifting between soul, blues, and even country-tinged material. (B.D.) (38:32/Reissue)

Jack Teagarden
That's a Serious Thing (RCA/Bluebird)   ★★★↓

Jack Teagarden's inventive blue-stained trombone is to be relished throughout this collection of twenty-one RCA Victor sides made between 1928 and 1957 as combo leader or sideman to corn syrup kings or fellow jazz luminaries. The invaluable "St. Louis Infirmary," with Louis Armstrong, also has Teagarden's extraordinary blues singing.   (67:10/1990)

Sonny Terry and Brownie McGhee
Just a Closer Walk with Thee (Fantasy)　　★★★★

Sonny Terry, the harmonica playing partner of guitarist Blind Boy Fuller in prewar North Carolina, and Tennessee guitarist Brownie McGhee settled in New York City in the 1940s, ultimately winning over a mainstream audience. Come the late 1950s, now singing together in addition to supplying each other instrumental support, they recorded these dozen spirituals in an Oakland concert hall. Their supplications are engrossing.　　(38:07/Reissue)

Back to New Orleans (Fantasy)　　★★★⁊

Two 1959/60 Prestige/Bluesville albums on one disc, in crisp stereo, find the prolific duo in acoustic tandem, joined only by drummer Roy Haynes on ten of twenty-one cuts. Bluesier than many of the pair's folk-oriented efforts, and quite satisfying. (B.D.)　　(76:55/Reissue)

• See also **Brownie McGhee and Sonny Terry**

Chris Thomas
Cry of the Prophets (Sire/Hightone/Reprise)　　★★★★

Chris Thomas, son of Baton Rouge bluesman Tabby Thomas, is a maverick singer/guitarist/songwriter who has spawned something close to a musical language all his own. On his second album, and first for a major label, he overreaches whenever his lyrics strive for religiomystical profundity, but his music is always a remarkably fresh blend of blues, rock, and funk.　　(42:54/1990)

Irma Thomas
Simply the Best: Live (Rounder) ★★★✦

Irma Thomas's voice is wiser and huskier than it was in the early 1960s, when she was the belle of New Orleans R&B balls. Two San Francisco nights in 1990 working Slim's had her re-dressing old hits such as "Time Is on My Side" and performing sugary contemporary tunes. Her eight-piece band, the Professionals, is what its name suggests: methodical and efficient. (65:46/1991)

Rufus Thomas
That Woman Is Poison! (Alligator) ★★★✦

Brassy back-to-the-blues comeback session for the ageless and ebullient Memphis vocalist, produced by King Snake's Bob Greenlee. There's enough greasy funk to please Thomas's Stax-era fans, and program highlights include the convincing blues workouts "Blues in the Basement" and "Somebody's Got to Go." (B.D.) (36:57/1988)

Ron Thompson
Just like a Devil (Winner) ★✦

Thompson is a West Coast singer and guitarist who, among other things, has backed John Lee Hooker on several tours. His first feature release, consisting of 1982–83 "live" radio tapings from Mark Naftalin's "Blue Monday Party" show, is earnest but forgettable. If he really must settle into the material of Robert Johnson, Jimmy Reed, and Lightnin' Hopkins, then he should be prepared to lend the senescent, hallowed songs some fresh insights. An album likely to satisfy only the easily pleased. (41:50/1990)

Big Mama Thornton
Ball 'n' Chain (Arhoolie)   ★★★

Willie Mae Thornton, full-throated and aggressive, was a gale wind of passion in the fashion of her foremothers Bessie Smith and Ma Rainey. She bears down hard on fourteen 1965–68 sides, but on several her voice pitches unsteadily and her electric blues sidemen—three different groups, including Muddy Waters's—sell her short with incongruous colors and textures. The songs that are especially long on conviction are two duets with slide guitarist Fred McDowell, "School Boy" and "My Heavy Load."   (61:52/1989)

George Thorogood and the Destroyers
Move It on Over (Rounder)   ★★✦

Delaware guitarist Thorogood's second album, from 1978, plays homage to John Lee Hooker, Elmore James, Bo Diddley, Chuck Berry, and country and western giant Hank Williams. (It was the cover of Williams's "Move It on Over" that dented the pop charts and put Rounder Records on the national stage.) Unfortunately he is a drab singer and too in thrall of the past to possess a clear-cut sensibility or creative urge. Update: Probably the most interesting of his EMI recordings in more recent years is *Bad to the Bone*, with sportive embroideries of Elmore James, Howlin' Wolf, and Chuck Berry songs.   (40:55/Reissue)

Ali Farka Toure
Ali Farka Toure (Mango)   ★★★★

In its heart of hearts this album by the Mali musician who cites John Lee Hooker as a musical kinsman is a beautiful exposition of spirituality. Each and every note he sings (in various West African languages) and plays on his bluesy guitar is imbued with a passionate artistry born of moral strength. Ten rhythmically splendent songs about love and life in the plains of his homeland run as true as his studies of the Koran. Also highly recommended are Toure's more recent *African Blues* (Shanachie CD) and *The River* (Mango CD).

(58:04/1988)

Treat Her Right
What's Good for You (Rounder)   ★★↑

This eccentric Boston foursome, after two bleak discs free from the yoke of a major record company, is worthwhile except when it tries to invoke some sort of blues sorcery—for example, the plangent treatment of Willie Dixon's "The Same Thing." They treasure rockabilly and Chicago blues equally, using atmospheric guitars, harmonica, vocals, and "cocktail drum."   (32:17/1991)

The Tri-Sax-Ual Soul Champs
Go Girl! (Black Top)   ★★↑

A fairly recent blues/R&B saxophone feast with settings for Sil Austin (a successful pre-Beatles chart artist), Grady "Fats" Jackson (formerly with Elmore James and Little Walter), and Mark "Kaz" Kazanoff (the Austin-based torchbearer). Jackson provides a few acceptable vocals and guitarists Clarence Hollimon and Snooks Eaglin are on hand to dig into the revivalistic program with gusto.   (42:55/1990)

Duke Tumatoe
I Like My Job! (Warner Brothers)   ★

Ex–Creedence Clearwater Revival leader John Fogerty recorded several nights of Indianapolis-based Duke Tumatoe's blues rock band in clubs, then spent three months splicing together choruses and bridges from various performances of Detroit Junior's "If I Hadn't Been High," until he had "songs." Dung. (39:00/1989)

Ike and Tina Turner

The Great Rhythm & Blues Sessions (Tomato) ★★

The title is nonsense. Ike Turner was too preoccupied with chasing money in the late 1960s to give these recordings better than jerry-built arrangements and production. Tina sings quite well when it's actually her; anonymous members of their popular Revue deputize on a few tracks. Her tyrannical husband plays some good blues guitar on renditions of B. B. King's "Rock Me Baby" and Bobby Bland's "I Smell Trouble," recalling his well-respected sessions work in the 1950s. (35:27/Reissue)

Joe Turner

Volume One: I've Been to Kansas City (Decca) ★★★★

Former singing bartender Joe Turner had only recently moved to New York from Kansas City when he made these sixteen sides in 1940–41. His baritone throbs with lovelorn restlessness or measured delight as it wraps around the lyrics to slow and medium blues. Turner is ennobled by the spare playing of first-class pianists (Art Tatum, Sammy Price, Willie "The Lion" Smith), guitarists (Oscar Moore, Leonard Ware), and others of similar ability. (47:00/1990)

The Boss of the Blues (Atlantic) ★★★★★

Joe Turner bellowed tales of sensual pleasure and romantic betrayal with the fiery but delicate conviction belonging to urban blues masters. He was at his very best on these two

1956 New York sessions, accompanied by stellar musicians whose ranks included Pete Johnson on piano, Lawrence Brown on trombone, and Pete Brown on alto saxophone. "Cherry Red," "How Long Blues," "Roll 'em Pete," and seven more are as valuable as the most precious stones in a lapidary's safe. (44:49/Reissue)

Singing the Blues (Mobile Fidelity) ★★✦

Turner shouts with glottal authority on new compositions and remakes of his classic songs on a 1967 BluesWay date. Of the studio players, harmonica player Buddy Lucas best asserts a feel for the rockin' blues solicited by producer Bob Thiele. (38:12/Reissue)

Flip, Flop and Fly (Pablo) ★★★✦

Despite inferior sound, this document of Turner sharing European concert stages with Count Basie's swingingly discreet orchestra in 1972 is pleasing. The lyrics and music of nine classic songs, most *owned* by the vocalist, get fresh coats of integrity and intensity. Turner's teasing of shy pianist Count, his longtime friend, during "Everyday I Have the Blues" draws a smile. (43:27/1989)

Stormy Monday (Pablo) ★★

Five blues and a standard, "Time After Time," essayed by Turner and four different groups of "cousins" at Pablo sessions between 1974 and 1978 fall short of expectations—as outtakes often do. Albeit charming, the singer isn't particularly vigorous, and guitarist Pee Wee Crayton, pianist Lloyd Glenn, and saxophonist Eddie "Cleanhead" Vinson are among those who flounder in loose arrangements. (45:10/1991)

Joe Turner and Roomful of Blues
Blues Train (Muse)   ★★★♪

With Roomful stoking the firebox, Turner engineers this run-away locomotive of a session with all the determination and derring-do of Casey Jones. Actually his strong vocals were taped separately from the eight-piece Rhode Island band, though he *was* present in the control room with producer Doc Pomus goading their progeny through nine delightful songs. Recorded in 1983 when Turner was a spry seventy-one.

(38:20/Reissue)

Joe Turner and T-Bone Walker
Bosses of the Blues, Volume One (RCA/Bluebird)   ★

Think twice before buying this obsolete late-1960s album that is split between singer Turner and guitarist Walker. Excruciatingly dumb soul/rock/R&B production sinks Turner's tracks; Walker, in turn, has to contend with electric saxophonist Tom Scott and other hacks decked out in love beads and dashikis.   (35:56/Reissue)

Troy Turner
Teenage Blues in Baton Rouge (Ichiban/King Snake)   ★★

Turner is a young Baton Rouge–based singer/guitarist whose debut is an attractive blend of blues, soul, gospel, and rock. The stylish Bob Greenlee production, however, can't hide the emotional callowness of a voice and electric guitar that dispense thrills without telling stories.   (37:35/1990)

Handful of Aces (Ichiban/King Snake)   ★★

Against another of Greenlee's stylish backdrops Turner's singing has become more forthright and his guitar has grown progressively serious in spite of its showiness. If only his songs, "Born in Louisiana" excepted, had a well-defined emotional outline. (34:44/1992)

Stevie Ray Vaughan
Texas Flood (Epic) ★★★↓

Vaughan's debut in 1984 showed off the Texas barroom flash he had honed in Austin clubs since leaving home at seventeen. He attacks a selection of songs that serve as a blueprint for every Vaughan album to come: hyperactive instrumentals ("Rude Mood"), blues classics ("Texas Flood"), and Jimi Hendrix–influenced ballads ("Lenny"). The real showcase here is "Pride and Joy," which presents the simultaneous lead and rhythm chops of Vaughan at his best. (J.G.)
(38:52/Reissue)

Couldn't Stand the Weather (Epic) ★★★★

This is the quintessential Stevie Ray album, originally released in 1984. Expansive versions of Jimi Hendrix's "Voodoo Chile" and the blues standard "Tin Pan Alley" showcase especially hot playing. "Cold Shot" is a concise bit of guitar work that recalls Magic Sam and set a standard for guitar-slingers everywhere. There are no throwaways, and nothing too ambitious, just blues rock played at its finest. (J.G.)
(38:11/Reissue)

Soul to Soul (Epic) ★★↓

A fairly routine (if spectacular) slice of Vaughan's rocking blues, released in 1985. He pays homage to Earl King and Jimi Hendrix simultaneously with "Come On (Part III)," rips through a wah-wah howler ("Say What!"), and puts down his only example of a straight soul ballad ("Life Without You"). (J.G.) (40:07/Reissue)

Live Alive (Epic) ★★♪

Best for fans. This is a fairly cursory survey of a Stevie Ray Vaughan concert, notable only for a cover of Stevie Wonder's "Superstition." Since Vaughan essentially played live on many of his studio albums, the playing isn't any more inspired than the studio versions. Fabulous Thunderbird Jimmie Vaughan guests on a few tracks, including the otherwise unavailable "Willie the Wimp." The performances date from 1985–86. (J.G.)   (71:26/Reissue)

In Step (Epic) ★★★

Stevie Ray's first album after giving up drugs and drink presents a healthy dose of blues. Covers of Buddy Guy's "Let Me Love You Baby" and "Leave My Girl Alone" showcase some serious guitar work. "Wall of Denial" weaves a Hendrix influence through a confessional tale about drug abuse, and some of his prettiest playing can be found on the jazzy instrumental "Riviera Paradise." Somehow the album is a bit flat: the sound is clean and a bit tinny, and Reese Wynan's keyboards always seem patched onto what is essentially a trio. (J.G.)   (41:11/1989)

The Sky Is Crying (Epic) ★★★★

It is ironic that a collection of outtakes issued posthumously is arguably Vaughan's finest work, but it is. These songs are all labors of love—offhand blues efforts that find him completely at ease. The opening cut, "Boot Hill," is a ferocious slide guitar workout that features one of Vaughan's finest vocals. The title cut explores the style of Albert King. "Wham!" burns with barroom energy and declares officially the Lonnie Mack influence that pervaded many of his previous instrumentals. "Life by the Drop" is his only instance of acoustic playing and proves that he is quite capable of working solo. (J.G.)   (38:48/1991)

The Vaughan Brothers
Family Style (Epic) ★★★✦

This disc marks the first collaboration between the brothers Vaughan and, unfortunately, Stevie Ray's last recorded work. While not the blues exploration one might expect, the guitar-slinging siblings present a winning collection of pop and R&B tunes that seem to reflect Jimmie's economy over Stevie's flash. (J.G.) (40:47/1990)

Maurice John Vaughn
Generic Blues Album (Alligator) ★★

Vaughn is a decent Chi-Town guitarist (and singer and saxophonist) best known for his work in A. C. Reed's band. As sessions leader he pushes beyond the wry claim of his album title only when providing his songs with refreshing lyrics (try "Computer Took My Job"). Alligator has remastered the album—first issued in 1984 on Vaughn's cost-effective Reecy label—and added a Vaughn track from their collection *The New Bluebloods*. (46:31/Reissue)

Eddie "Cleanhead" Vinson and Julian "Cannonball" Adderley
Cleanhead and Cannonball (Landmark) ★★★★

Eddie Vinson's historic 1961–62 studio meeting with the Cannonball Adderley Quintet is by and large eventful, compounded of soulful amiability and recreative ideas about how bebop mixed with blues should be played. The Houston alto saxophonist, prominent in jazz and blues circles since the 1930s, fires off biting, intelligent solos (notably on previously unreleased instrumentals) and sings stirringly (hear "Kidney Stew" and Jimmy Reed's "Bright Lights, Big City"). Of alto player Cannonball and the other musicians only cornetist Nat Adderley seems dispassionate. (45:33/1988)

Eddie "Cleanhead" Vinson and Roomful of Blues

Eddie "Cleanhead" Vinson and Roomful of Blues (Muse) ★★★↓

This perfectly decent 1982 blowing session has Vinson—fifty years into his estimable career—climbing aboard the Rhode Island jump blues juggernaut. His gingery, lean Texas alto makes it known that he's still a blues-and-jazz player of communicative warmth; and his vocals on three selections are rascally, just shy of being spent. The big little band gets plenty of space in which to celebrate the Southwestern blues and jazz tradition, especially during a T-Bone Walker salute titled "No Bones" and Earl Bostic's "That's a Groovy Thing."

(38:46/Reissue)

Eddie "Cleanhead" Vinson and Otis Spann

Bosses of the Blues, Volume Two (RCA/Bluebird) ★★★

The two Bosses headline eight songs apiece that were recorded in 1969 with Los Angeles sessionmen. Vinson, at this time enjoying semipopularity after some lean years, has sly fun reexamining juicy chestnuts such as "Alimony Blues" and "Old Maid Boogie." Spann, a fine singer and the archetypal Chicago blues pianist, acquits himself well, his serious demeanor undercut occasionally by a crapulous guitarist and an emotionally gauche reed player. Spann's paean to his creator, "Make a Way," is extremely poignant given his passing from cancer within a year. (58:04/Reissue)

• See also **Etta James and Eddie "Cleanhead" Vinson**

Joe Louis Walker
Cold Is the Night (Hightone) ★★★✔

The 1986 debut album of this excellent Bay Area guitarist isn't quite as assured as his subsequent Hightone efforts, but his crisp guitar and rich vocals are already in evidence. Relatively sparse production emphasizes the haunting feel of the pop-slanted title track, and the blues material sizzles. (B.D.)

(40:07/Reissue)

The Gift (Hightone) ★★★✔

Joe Louis Walker works through influences B. B. and Albert King to the essence of his songs with personal directness. Listening to the pained dignity in his singing and guitar playing one can believe that church work saved him from personal demons a few years back, and he's since made his peace with the blues. The production, alas, is watery. (42:41/1988)

Blue Soul (Hightone) ★★★★

No young blues guitarist has a better handle on the idiom than Walker, whose third Hightone disc confirms his rapidly rising status. Walker's incendiary combination of blues, rock, and soul is compelling on the crackling up-tempo "Prove Your Love" and "T.L.C." and the smooth "Personal Baby." "I'll Get to Heaven on My Own," the acoustic slide piece that closes the set, finds Walker remaining true to the source. (B.D.) (41:59/1989)

Live at Slim's Volume One (Hightone) ★★★★✔

Joe Louis Walker's first concert set outdoes his three previous studio efforts. Walker mixes fine new material with songs from his first album that show his confidence has risen markedly over the years, and he keeps the energy level sky high. His guitar playing is pyrotechnic but never stirs up a histrionic froth, and his pleasing vocals on the masterly slow blues "Don't Know Why" and the incandescent "Fuss & Fight" are delivered with extreme facility. It's not so high-flown to suggest his blues has the warm color and rhythmic motive of a lyrical Georgia O'Keeffe picture (the late artist sometimes drew her inspiration from music). Walker has as much to offer as any young blues artist currently active. (B.D./ F.J.H.)   (53:57/1991)

Phillip Walker
The Bottom of the Top (Hightone)   ★★★★✦

Out of print for too long after a short shelf life on the Playboy logo, this collection of 1969–72 Bruce Bromberg–produced masters presents the Los Angeles guitarist at his best. Walker's enduring Texas roots are prominent on electrifying tributes to Lightnin' Hopkins and Long John Hunter, and there's a scorching reprise of his rocking oldie "Hello My Darling." (B.D.)   (35:04/Reissue)

Someday You'll Have These Blues (Hightone)   ★★★✦

Originally released on Joliet and later reissued on Alligator, these pleasing mid-1970s sides by underrated guitarist and singer Walker have reverted to the Hightone label. Walker digs in on the Lone Star celebration "El Paso Blues" and the title track, also proving his versatility on the soul-slanted "Don't Tell Me" and a gospel piece, "When It Needs Gettin' Done." (B.D.)   (35:13/Reissue)

T-Bone Walker

The Complete Recordings of T-Bone Walker 1940–1954 (Mosaic) ★★★★★

Aaron Thibeaux "T-Bone" Walker's name is hallowed among the multitude of electric guitarists he held sway over (for starters, B. B. King, Albert Collins, Buddy Guy) and anyone at all who sincerely cares about blues and jazz. The Texan's electric guitar inventions—expert, well ordered, sophisticated, deceptively carefree, affluently swinging, sui generis—and his pleasing vocal style are fully displayed throughout these six discs. Classics "Call It Stormy Monday," "T-Bone Shuffle," and "I Want a Little Girl" are among the 144 songs (including twenty-six alternate takes) recorded for eight different labels. The first three discs and the bulk of the fourth (spanning 1940–47) offer the greatest rewards, supported as Walker is by jazz/blues notables such as Teddy Buckner, Bump Myers, and Jack McVea. Bonus: an attractive sixteen-page booklet filled with pertinent information and fine photographs. (6:44:00/1990)

The Complete Imperial Recordings, 1950–1954 (EMI) ★★★★✦

If you can't quite finance Mosaic's exhaustive T-Bone Walker box, get your feet wet with this classy two-disc collection that includes every title the electric blues guitar pioneer waxed for Imperial. With a roaring horn section, often featuring Maxwell Davis or Eddie Davis on tenor saxophone, Walker adapted his crisp, elegant guitar style effortlessly to the encroaching R&B era, and the classics are many—the lights-out "Cold, Cold Feeling," the swinging "Tell Me What's the Reason," and the torrid instrumental "Strollin' with Bones" are among the tastiest tracks Walker ever cut. With fifty-two titles on board, this is prime T-Bone. (B.D.) (2:19:06/1991)

I Want a Little Girl (Delmark) ★★★✦

Walker, who was honest as the day, cut this impressive little session in France in 1968. His talents are indeed imposing—what can't be said of ordinary pianist Georges Arvanitas or tenor saxophonist Hal Singer, a Tulsa native living in Europe whose swinging jazz ideas stint on persuasive force. The CD sound accentuates, to pleasing end, trouper S. P. Leary's drums and Jackie Samson's acoustic bass fiddle. (39:37/Reissue)

• See also **Joe Turner and T-Bone Walker**

Robert Ward
Fear No Evil (Black Top) ★★★

An influence on Lonnie Mack and Stevie Ray Vaughan, little-known Georgia guitarist Robert Ward—cherished by 1960s R&B buffs for his work with the Falcons—uses a Magnatone amplifier to transform his leads into spectral ectoplasms. Backed by reserved New Orleans and Austin musicians, he ably sings and plays fourteen blues and soul originals in pursuit of inner exultation. "Your Love Is Amazing" is catchy enough for a blues hit parade. (49:26/1990)

Washboard Sam
Washboard Sam (1935–1947) (Story of Blues) ★★★

Robert "Washboard Sam" Brown stirred prewar Chicago with a warm baritone voice, rhythmic scrubbing of a steel board, and songs that carried spry melodies and perceptive lyrics. No harm either that Bill Broonzy was frequently his guitarist, heard on all eighteen songs here. Pianists Blind James Davis, Roosevelt Sykes, and Memphis Slim, among others, make cameo appearances. Be on guard, because the CD sound is often dreadful. (54:10/Reissue)

Rockin' My Blues Away (RCA/Bluebird)

Brown has a secure sense of what makes his urban blues so popular, and these twenty-two Bluebird sides from the 1940s offer charactcristically superior musicianship and interesting lyrics (on women, city life, the work camps back home in Arkansas, etc.). Memphis Slim and Roosevelt Sykes share piano duties, and guitar mandarin Big Bill Broonzy is every-where. The sound quality is outstanding. (66:10/1992)

• See also **Big Bill Broonzy and Washboard Sam**

Dinah Washington
Mellow Mama (Delmark) ★★★★✦

Even at age twenty-one Dinah Washington (née Ruth Jones) was able to elevate conventional blues plaints to nearly heroic levels of richness and poignancy, intensity and concentration. Twelve Apollo sides cut in late 1945, about the time the Alabama-born vocalist departed thc Lionel Hampton orches-tra, also feature the complementary light tone of saxophonist Lucky Thompson and a small combo (with bassist Charles Mingus and vibraphonist Milt Jackson) acutely keen to timing and filling the spaces around her voice. (35:23/1992)

The Complete Dinah Washington on Mercury, Volume ★★★★✦
Five (1956–58) (Mercury)

The wonderful singer gets directly to the heart of blues and R&B material (from Bessie Smith, Fats Waller, Louis Jordan, etc.) in this fine three-disc installment in her seven-volume Mercury oeuvre. Her musical personality is dominating, with the freshness of accent and color in her phrasing taking listen-ers far from the mundane realities of the day. Washington's rapture can be explained in part by the presence of husband Eddie Chamblee, who heads up one of her swingiest bands. (3:31:00/1989)

Dinah Washington Sings the Blues (Mercury)　★★★✦

Dinah sings not only the blues but sultry ballads and swinging jazz as well on this pleasing disc. Best of all is the haunting hit "Soft Winds," cut with Hal Mooney's orchestra in 1954; other highlights include the brassy "Show Time," a romping 1956 remake of Louis Jordan's "Is You Is or Is You Ain't My Baby," and a sassy reading of Bessie Smith's "Backwater Blues." (B.D.)　(57:52/Reissue)

Walter "Wolfman" Washington
Sada (Pointblank/Charisma)　★★✦

The bromide about hearing a musician in concert to best appreciate his or her craft definitely applies to talented singer/guitarist Washington, an associate of vocalist Johnny Adams and leader since the mid 1980s of the Roadmasters. As on three blues-slanted Rounder albums and now a blues/funk/jazz effort for Charisma, Washington and his producers have difficulty getting his music across without forcing the excitement and derailing emotional directness. Immured in a Swiss studio, he's stuck with turgid "musical director" Craig Wroten and a mixed-bag repertoire that includes tunes every bit as vapid as their titles, e.g., "Share Your Love" and "Girl, I Wanna Dance with You."　(43:00/1991)

Benny Waters
Benny Waters—Freddy Randall Jazz Band (Jazzology)　★★✦

Honorary Parisian Benny Waters has been playing jazz and blues on reed instruments since the first world war. This 1982

London session has the ageless veteran of the Jimmy Lunceford and Roy Milton bands making playful and serious use of his clarinet in traditional jazz arrangements. When he glides from register to register in "St. James Infirmary," the set's most involving performance, a lifetime of blues knowledge tumbles out of the bell of his licorice stick. (48:52/1990)

Muddy Waters
The Chess Box (MCA/Chess) ★★★★★

No single artist was more important to the development of postwar Chicago blues than McKinley Morganfield, aka Muddy Waters—this lavish three-disc boxed set is eloquent testimony. The idiom's heyday and eventual decline are both mirrored in Waters's quarter century of recording for Chess, from his first hit "I Can't Be Satisfied"—his Delta-drenched slide guitar backed solely by Big Crawford's slapping upright bass—through seminal early-1950s band masterpieces such as "Hoochie Coochie Man" and "I'm Ready" to his inconsistent but still rewarding later work. This seventy-two-song box, complete with a thirty-two-page booklet, is a must for anyone seriously interested in the history of Chicago blues. (B.D.)
(3:36:01/1989)

The Best of Muddy Waters (MCA/Chess) ★★★★★

The Chess Box has eleven of the twelve songs programmed on this superb collection that spans the Waters epoch from 1948 to 1954. Still, blues novitiates looking for a tidy, inexpensive package of his singular artistry—a voice and guitar commanding in inflection, a penchant for lyrics that are barbed-wire sharp with insurgency, an uncanny feel for merging Delta and Maxwell Street incantation—shouldn't hesitate an instant in grabbing this single disc. Devotees weaned on "I Can't Be Satisfied," "Rolling Stone," and the rest will want to replace

their worn vinyl copy (first issued in 1955) or its LP alter ego
titled *Sail On* (a 1969 Chess release). (36:39/Reissue)

Rare and Unissued (MCA/Chess) ★★★★

With only four tracks that duplicate MCA's boxed set, this
assortment of Chess rarities is highly worthwhile. Spanning
1948–60, this is Waters at his best, surrounded by master
sidemen such as harpist Little Walter and guitarist Jimmy
Rogers, and Waters cranks his slide work on several cuts.
Even Waters's obscurities are treasurable. (B.D.)

(40:17/Reissue)

Trouble No More: Singles (1955–1959) (MCA/Chess) ★★★★

The assembling of twelve Chess sides from Waters's insuffi-
ciently appreciated late-1950s period is a great gift. As a
singer he is in his glory on the earliest tracks, using his mastery of phrasing and timbre to bring forth complex, deep
feelings; on the other hand at least three of the more recent
selections have him struggling with inexpressiveness. Heavyweights Little Walter, Otis Spann, James Cotton, and Pat
Hare, to list only some, provide melodic spontaneity, harmonic interplay, rhythmic drive, and enthusiasm that is exemplary. (34:30/1989)

Muddy Waters at Newport (MCA) ★★★✔

By 1960 Waters had captured the hearts and minds of English
audiences and his sights were set on white America. This
Newport Jazz Festival performance of old and new songs, in
stereo, endeared Otis Spann and the rest of the Waters band
to young jazz buffs, who cheered and hollered for a second
bewitching of "Got My Mojo Working." (34:56/Reissue)

Folk Singer/Muddy Waters Sings Big Bill Broonzy ★★★★✦
(MCA/Chess)

Waters salutes the source of his art on two albums set back to back. The magnificent *Folk Singer*, recorded in 1963, has him playing acoustic guitar and "crying" nine country blues that are throwbacks to his Mississippi plantation recordings for the Library of Congress in 1941. Accorded quietly stirring accompaniment by young guitarist Buddy Guy and on four songs a bare-bones rhythm section, he again brings light into the dark recesses of a proud Southern black man's anguished soul. *Sings Bill Broonzy*, a 1959 album, is his less compelling nod to the recently passed folk bluesman who had welcomed him to Chicago in the 1940s. Waters and his band give ten songs an urban blues thrust—by no means heretical, since Broonzy had often recorded with swinging small bands. (62:21/Reissue)

The Real Folk Blues (MCA/Chess) ★★★★✦

Waters and his cohorts are all business, turning twelve tracks from 1947–64 into sharp, bracing Chicago blues vignettes. Highlights of this 1966 release include the boastful "Mannish Boy" and the glorious 1950 rendering of "Rollin' and Tumblin'," which has Muddy's behind-the-beat, coarse-grained singing and hellfire slide guitar shadowed by Big Crawford's tubby string bass. All but two songs are duplicated on the Chess box. (34:54/Reissue)

More Real Folk Blues (MCA/Chess) ★★★

The listener doesn't get the choicest cuts of Waters's 1948–52 output, but eating low on the hog isn't so bad. His false soprano on Robert Johnson's "Kindhearted Woman Blues" is especially delectable. Of a dozen songs in this 1967 collection only "Train Fare Blues" shows up on the three-disc deluxe set. (35:09/Reissue)

Muddy, Brass and the Blues (MCA/Chess) ★

Chess ruined this 1966 session by dubbing beastly horns onto decent tracks laid down by Waters, James Cotton, Otis Spann, and confreres. "Betty and Dupree" is execrable beyond belief, the saxophonist visiting from some vile place. Seek out the brassless "Black Night" in the *Chess Box* to listen to the Waters band's plaintive grace uncontaminated. (36:29/Reissue)

They Call Me Muddy Waters (MCA/Chess) ★★★

Eight tracks from 1967, two from 1951, and one each recorded in 1959 and 1966 do not combine for anything better than a satisfactory Waters potpourri. Muddy's early bands—despite players such as Little Walter and Otis Spann—aren't on their mettle, and his latter-day aggregation with harp player Paul Oscher does not interact well enough to draw out the music's subtle eloquence. (34:48/Reissue)

The London Muddy Waters Sessions (MCA/Chess) ★★★

In addition to the grizzled dean's alluring vocals, it is the guitar bends of Irish rocker Rory Gallagher and Chicagoan Sammy Lawhorn that enrich nine songs recorded at a 1971 rock-with-my-British-kids date. Georgie Fame, Mitch Mitchell, and Steve Winwood could be tossed in the Thames for all they're worth. (36:07/Reissue)

Can't Get No Grindin' (MCA/Chess) ★★★★

A new band, a familiar sound. Returning—after several years of experimentation, mainstreaming, and all-star bands—to the Chicago electric blues that originally earned him his place in musical history. Waters assembled James Cotton, Pinetop Perkins, and a few more fresh faces and laid down one of his best albums in years. (J.T.) (36:13/Reissue)

Hard Again (Blue Sky) ★★★★

Waters's nobility of spirit and imperial constancy are on full display at the highly regarded mid-1970s session. James Cotton, Johnny Winter, and Pinetop Perkins are brawlers worth his time, and they superbly maintain a degree of control and reserve when shouting with pleasure or sorrow throughout the nine-song program, from the relumed "Mannish Boy" to the new anthem "The Blues Had a Baby and They Named It Rock & Roll (#2)." (45:41/Reissue)

I'm Ready (Blue Sky) ★★★

Harmonica men Walter Horton and Jerry Portnoy step in for James Cotton and guitarist Jimmy Rogers comes aboard for the follow-up session to the well-received *Hard Again*. This time the fervent rollin' and tumblin' isn't sustained and readings of milestones seem gratuitous. The new songs don't leave lasting impressions either. (40:32/Reissue)

Muddy Waters (LRC) ★

Not worth owning unless one perversely fancies grade-Z fare. Slipshod packaging, bootleg-quality sound, and solo noodling make this mid-1970s concert recording a stinker in Waters's vastly honorable discography. (58:55/1990)

Muddy Waters and Howlin' Wolf
Muddy and the Wolf (MCA/Chess) ★★✦

Not together on stage or in the studio, mind you. For a 1983 package, *Fathers and Sons* has been raided six times and *The London Howlin' Wolf Sessions* gives up seven songs. (43:00/Reissue)

• See also **Fathers and Sons**

Johnny "Guitar" Watson
Three Hours Past Midnight (Flair/Virgin) ★★★

Long before his whimsical muse led him down funk paths, Watson was a reputable Los Angeles–based blues guitarist. Dogged by the first-rate Maxwell Davis band, he has a good time singing and playing brusquely phrased guitar on fourteen songs made for Modern in the last half of the 1950s. (The addition of two pop-drenched Class sides is unwelcome.) The title track and the note-perfect rendering of Earl King's "Those Lonely Lonely Nights," both hits for the Houston native, are the premier pleasures of this Ace Records compilation that was originally released in Europe in 1986.
(45:45/Reissue)

Noble Watts
Return of the Thin Man (Alligator) ★★♪

Not the screenplay character but the R&B saxophonist who honked his way to moderate acclaim in the 1950s with a solo hit called "Hard Times." Energized by Bob Greenlee's Midnight Creepers band in 1987, Watts wallops instrumentals using his classic "big sound" (possibly an influence on King Curtis) and shows that at heart he is a swing jazz player well proud of having worked with Lionel Hampton. His singing is ragtag.
(39:12/Reissue)

Boogie Bill Webb
Drinkin' and Stinkin' (Flying Fish) ★★★

Recorded in the late 1980s, New Orleans singer/guitarist Bill Webb's primitive and thoroughly idiosyncratic blues threatens to run amok but doesn't. Drummer Ben Sandmel and Radiators bassist Reggie Scanlan maintain semiformal song structures that direct Webb's urban and country styles. An

accompanying booklet tells the interesting story of this early-
1950s Imperial recording artist, partly in his own words.
(44:45/1989)

Katie Webster

The Swamp Boogie Queen (Alligator) ★★★

The South Louisiana blues pianist also boasts a 1960s soul
influence, and she combines both genres on her Alligator
debut. Webster boogies through "Black Satin," struts her soul
style on two Otis Redding classics, and recalls her formative
years with the swampy "Sea of Love." Robert Cray, Kim
Wilson, and Bonnie Raitt have small roles. (B.D./F.J.H.)
(41:52/1988)

Two-Fisted Mama! (Alligator) ★★

The former Otis Redding sidelady does her most interesting
shouting, questioning, and breeze shooting through her blues
'n' boogie piano . . . not her voice box. The nine-minute-plus
"Red Negligee" is a prolonged and abhorrent tease.
(49:25/1989)

No Foolin'! (Alligator) ★★

Always synthesizing elements of blues, gospel, soul, and Louisiana R&B, Webster props up decent originals and cover
material with the refined exuberance of a top-flight entertainer. Yet her singing, as always, is imperfectly delivered and
borderline unctuous in both its sensuousness and sauciness.
Guitarist/singer Lonnie Brooks and accordion player C. J.
Chenier contribute to a song each, adding little of interest.
(45:06/1991)

Valerie Wellington
Million Dollar Secret (Rooster Blues)　　　★★✦

Chicago chanteuse Wellington, twenty-three years old at the time of her debut recording in 1983, takes a dozen songs by the collar and gives them a good shake. She possesses a fine instrument, trained in opera and classical music, and packs it with enough guttural grit to convey the meaning of the lyrics. Still, her vocals don't flow with the naturalness and understated might of Magic Slim and the Tear Drops and other supportive Windy City stalwarts.　　　　　(45:40/Reissue)

Junior Wells
1957–1963 (Paula)　　　★★★✦

Harmonica virtuoso Amos "Junior" Wells, formerly with Muddy Waters, recorded these twenty-three sides for Chief Records at a time when he and many more Chicago bluesmen were attempting to come to grips with the rock 'n' roll explosion. Keeping his harmonica in its case most of the time, he relies on the individuated tone of his singing voice to reveal shades of acute feeling. Eight different ensembles have widely varied degrees of success in achieving dramatic continuity; honors go to guitarist Earl Hooker and five cronies on the classic "Messin' with the Kid."　　　　　(59:06/Reissue)

Hoodoo Man Blues (Delmark)　　　★★★★★

Wells's excellent first long-player—one of modern Chicago blues' earliest—reaches across the years, from 1965, with its simple, direct disclosures of naked beauty. With clear thought and masterly control the harmonica magnifico takes his time scooping, stretching, and bending notes that pulsate for their tremendous hurt or sensual pleasure. His singing is no less stunning. Guitarist Buddy Guy is Wells's doppelganger, and bassist Jack Myers and drummer Billy Warren are completely under their spell. There are fourteen superb stereo tracks, including two alternate takes. (45:42/Reissue)

Coming at You (Vanguard) ★★

The team of Junior Wells and guitarist Buddy Guy too often confuses showiness with passion on this 1968 recording. Meanwhile the busybody horn section and rhythm section don't seem to care a whit about adapting their styles to the emotional demands of blues standards. (34:59/Reissue)

On Tap (Delmark) ★★★♪

In the 1970s, Wells was a habitué of Theresa's Tavern on Chicago's South Side, and this studio date approximates what happened when he and friends got the itch to rip up the joint. Tough and carnal bent tones heard in the night. For CD, Delmark has remixed the sound, resequenced the program, and changed the packaging of the 1974 release—all for the better. (44:52/Reissue)

• See also **Buddy Guy and Junior Wells**

T. J. Wheeler
Blue and Beige (Brassway) ★★★

T. J. Wheeler, a former pupil of Bukka White and Furry Lewis, travels the country holding school workshops that celebrate the message of hope found in the blues. A proficient country blues stylist, his burly low voice and nimble guitar fingerings resonate on originals and songs from Lewis, Blind Willie McTell, Robert Johnson, and Lightnin' Hopkins. Sometimes his zeal borders on sentimentality. (57:05/1991)

Artie "Blues Boy" White
Thangs Got to Change (Ichiban) ★★★

Veteran Chicago singer White has cultivated a Little Milton–by-way-of–Bobby Bland style on several Ichiban releases since the mid 1980s. Perhaps his most appealing contemporary blues album is this assortment of Milton, B. B. King, Lowell Fulson, and Brook Benton songs, where his deep voice unfolds adequate drama despite some labored phrasing. Agreeable help comes from Milton on lead guitar, Golden "Big" Wheeler on harmonica, and Cicero Blake's rhythm section. (33:11/1989)

Bukka White
Sky Songs (Arhoolie) ★★✦

Bukka White's *Sky Songs*, recorded in 1963, has been celebrated by some as the country blues equivalent of Homeric narrative poetry. Yet the Delta bottleneck guitar giant, a contemporary of Muddy Waters and Robert Johnson, runs far afield in thought and language improvising these l-o-n-g tales. The instructive charm and humanity of "My Baby," for instance, dissipates long before its arbitrary conclusion after fourteen minutes. Two of seven songs have him accompanying his talking or singing with piano rather than guitar. (64:10/Reissue)

Barrence Whitfield and the Savages
Barrence Whitfield and the Savages (Fan Club import) ★★★★

A most improper Bostonian, Barrence Whitfield (Barry White in a previous life) sings his lungs out on obscure blues and R&B songs learned from old 45s while his four feral musicians further incinerate this little-known 1984 Mamou release. Thoughts of Little Richard in his febrile prime pitched against a grungy garage band aren't farfetched at all. Recommended tamer fun with different Savages: 1989's *Live Emulsified* (Rounder CD). (27:52/Reissue)

Chris Whitley
Living with the Law (Columbia) ★★★♪

This is a rock album, but it's steeped in the imagery of the blues. Whitley plays slide on a National steel guitar that resonates throughout this ethereal Malcolm Burn production. He has a way with lyrics that are a contemporary extension of blues, too, on songs like "Phone Call from Leavenworth" and "Poison Girl." (J.G.) (46:59/1991)

The Wild Tchoupitoulas
The Wild Tchoupitoulas (Island) ★★★★♪

A New Orleans classic produced by Allen Toussaint for 1976 release. The *sine qua non* of this Mardi Gras Indian tribe, founded in the early 1970s by Big Chief Jolly (George Landry), is traditional chants. Jolly, in rich voice, spins melodies off the singsong harmonized so stirringly by his fellow Tchoupitoulas, while the Meters equal their jubilation with driving, syncopated rhythms of folk origin. "Hey Pocky Way" and "Meet De Boys on the Battlefront" edge out six others as the parade favorites. (34:53/Reissue)

Robert Wilkins
The Original Rolling Stone (Yazoo) ★★★★♪

Wilkins was an especially articulate, unassuming musician heard regularly in Memphis in the 1920s and 1930s. Fourteen solo sides from the time, recorded at four different sessions, bespeak a dreamy, graceful singer, a lyricist with tremendous power of reason, and a facile guitarist both rhythmically insistent and emotionally eventempered. Incidentally, after Wilkins became a minister he turned "That's No Way to Get Along" (found on this collection) into "Prodigal Son," which the Rolling Stones took as their own. (44:08/Reissue)

Big Joe Williams
Shake Your Boogie (Arhoolie)   ★★★★★

Two albums the legendary Delta singer/guitarist recorded for Arhoolie after his 1959 "rediscovery" share this single disc. *Tough Times* (1960) is amazing, its twelve songs about the artistic equal to his seminal 1930s and 1940s recordings, with or without Sonny Boy Williamson. His fresh, commanding singing and rhythmically powerful single-string guitar declaim new and old plaints, from a recent tangle with the police to the rigors of levee camp life. The numbers making up *Thinking of What They Did* (1969), three with harpist Charlie Musslewhite, provide only desultory flashes of his brilliance. (66:40/Reissue)

Nine String Guitar Blues (Delmark)   ★★★★

This early-1960s session finds Williams spearing to the heart of the Delta tradition. His full voice, at one instant a lion's roar and the next a mourning dove's cry, combines with his idiosyncratic playing of a modified six-string guitar to fill the air with suspense. (34:22/Reissue)

Classic Delta Blues (Milestone)   ★★★

The well-traveled guitarist pays homage to his Delta cohorts Charley Patton, Muddy Waters, and Robert Johnson (the latter four times) on solo six-string guitar. An enjoyable but not essential album recorded in Chicago in 1964. (B.D.) (36:01/Reissue)

Big Joe Williams (Optimism) ★★★

Late in the game, Williams nobly resisted weariness. Sixteen blues and spirituals recorded between 1973 and 1980 have the archdeacon's wrought iron voice and often imperfect guitar ready for more. When he sings of crying the whole night long or washing away his sins he is to be believed. (42:22/Reissue)

Big Joe Williams & J. D. Short
Stavin' Chain Blues (Delmark) ★★★

Big Joe Williams, always on the move, and his cousin J. D. Short made this informal St. Louis recording in 1958, a good twenty-five years after having established themselves in that urban center as leading exponents of raw, urgent Delta blues. As session producer Bob Koester points out in his liner notes, Short (on guitar, vocals, and harmonica) was somewhat unhinged by the recording process. On the other hand, Williams steers a comfortable and steady course through the fifteen songs. (51:18/Reissue)

• See also **Sonny Boy Williamson and Big Joe Williams**

Lucinda Williams
Ramblin' (Smithsonian/Folkways) ★★★★

Toting a twelve-string guitar, unknown singer/songwriter Lucinda Williams slipped into a Jackson, Mississippi, studio in 1978 and performed spirituals, blues, and country and western classics she had an intense liking for. Without affection or strain she establishes an emotional bond with Memphis Minnie, Robert Johnson, and Hank Williams, explicating the inherent exquisiteness and power of their songs on her own terms. The 1991 reissue has remastered sound. (44:22/Reissue)

Happy Woman Blues (Smithsonian/Folkways) ★★★★

In 1980 the Texas-based folkie posed a paradox with her second unheralded album. Williams's tenor had become as pure as a mountain stream, yet its colorful presence, its emotional expressiveness, was that of a contemporary blues lady. Twelve exceptional originals show her penchant for writing intelligent lyrics and strong melodies that perfectly suit the lilt of six not-so-traditional country and western musicians.

(35:47/Reissue)

Marion Williams
Strong Again (Spirit Feel) ★★★★★

By any measurement Marion Williams is one of the finest singers alive. Urgent, outgoing, and decisively sincere, she praises her God in pure terms while supported by expert musicians who amalgamate gospel and blues with an appropriate elation of spirit (Jonathan Dubose, Jr., is a *superlative* blues guitarist). When she stretches a syllable over numerous notes (melisma) and glides from note to note (portamento) a beautiful open sky is evoked—witness her stunning interpretation of Billie Holiday's "God Bless the Child" and nineteen more exemplars. Also deserving of highest praise: *Surely God Is Able* (Spirit Feel CD), a 1989 release. (61:56/1991)

Sonny Boy Williamson and Big Joe Williams
Throw a Boogie Woogie (RCA) ★★★★♪

This recent assembly of Bluebird sides from 1937–38 and 1941 by personages John Lee "Sonny Boy" Williamson and Big Joe Williams is worth a king's ransom. With Delta guitarist Williams's backing, Williamson metamorphoses jug band harmonica into an important new urban voice, wailing and cooing phrases that dovetail masterfully with his earnest, win-some, somewhat naive singing on classics "Good Morning School Girl," "Sugar Mama Blues," and four more. As fea-tured performer clear-sighted Williams displays to good ad-vantage his Delta bottleneck guitar and telling vocals on eight alluring tracks, with Sonny Boy present on "Highway 49" and "Baby, Please Don't Go." Furthermore, the virtuosic flat-picking guitarist Robert Nighthawk is on hand in 1937 to assist them in the shaping of Chicago blues. The digital remastering blanches some of the music's intrinsic warmth.   (46:29/1989)

Sonny Boy Williamson II
King Biscuit Time (Arhoolie)   ★★★★

The second Sonny Boy Williamson (Aleck or Alex "Rice" Miller) handled an amplified Delta/Texas-bred harmonica that momentously caught the spirit as well as the letter of urban blues. Sixteen Trumpet 78s, his first recorded in Jack-son, Mississippi, in 1951, witness to his larger than life talent, which also encompassed superlative, personally direct singing and songwriting. The star of "King Biscuit Time"—the KFFA (Helena, Arkansas) blues show—varies his phrasing from the exuberant and sensual ("Crazy About You Baby") to the plaintive (the famous "Nine Below Zero") with the aid of an able Memphis electric blues band. Bonuses: a fifteen-minute KFFA program from 1965, plus a historical Trumpet record-ing of "Dust My Broom" with the harp player in the august company of singer/slide guitarist Elmore James (60:19/Reissue)

One Way Out (MCA/Chess)   ★★★★

Fifteen important 1955–61 Chess sides from the wily harpist, including three from his first Checker session with Muddy Waters's band in staunch support. Also notable to the Rice

Miller legacy: the sly "Keep It to Yourself," with guitarist Robert Jr. Lockwood's supple licks; Williamson's soundalike tribute "Little Wolf"; and the often-covered title track. (B.D.)

(39:31/Reissue)

Down and Out Blues (MCA/Chess) ★★★★⧫

Williamson's first album, for Checker in 1959, collects twelve originals cut between 1955 and 1958 by the sometime Chicago resident. He invests all, from standard "Don't Start Me to Talkin' " to shuffle obscurity "99," with a pained lyricism and a rawly intelligent fireness seconded by *crème de la blooze* musicians such as Muddy Waters, Jimmy Rogers, Robert Jr. Lockwood, and Fred Below. (33:49/Reissue)

Bummer Road (MCA/Chess) ★★★★

Yes, this is the album with the infamous "Little Village" exchange between the irritable harp player and label owner Leonard Chess. But don't be deterred by the parental advisory sticker—Williamson is on top of his game throughout eleven songs from 1957–60, and he's backed by the cream of Chicago sidemen, notably magnificent guitarist Robert Jr. Lockwood. First released in 1969, this set remains important to the Williamson legacy. (B.D.) (39:30/Reissue)

The Real Folk Blues (MCA/Chess) ★★★★

Sonny-style electric blues, concise and ravaged, recorded across several sessions from 1957 to 1963. The pundit and his tight ensemble take "One Way Out," "Bring It on Home," and ten more under advisement. This set first appeared in record stores in 1966. (31:49/Reissue)

Keep It to Ourselves (Alligator) ★★★★

This acoustic set, originally released by Danish label Story-book Records, is from 1963. The sparse setting allowed Rice Miller—backed only occasionally by Matt Murphy on guitar, pianist Memphis Slim, and drums—to push the bounds of his music to incredible heights. (J.T.)   (47:50/Reissue)

More Real Folk Blues (MCA/Chess) ★★★★

Williamson is ever fluent with intimacy on this 1967 collection of a dozen tracks from 1960–64, with only Willie Dixon's yap-and-yelp fable "The Hunt" a distraction. One of many Sonny Boy songs covered extensively by blues rock bands, "Help Me" packs true back alley danger in spite of Lafayette Leake's mock-gothic organ.   (34:02/Reissue)

Sonny Boy Williamson II and the Yardbirds
Sonny Boy Williamson and the Yardbirds (Optimism) ★★★

These eleven tracks catch Williamson at a 1963 London gig with the "Most Blueswailing Yardbirds." The eighteen-year-old Eric Clapton adds tasty guitar fills behind the visiting dignitary's low-heat vocals and harp, covering fairly sophisticated emotional terrain in his modest, clean-toned solos.
(42:13/Reissue)

Chuck Willis
My Story (CBS)

Students of popular music know Atlanta singer/songwriter Chuck Willis as the late-1950s "King of the Stroll" who recorded for Atlantic. Blues devotees turn to this Okeh/Columbia collection of fourteen choice jump blues and ballads from his 1951–56 period. "Don't Deceive Me," "My Story," and the rest have his dry, sweet voice instinctively settling into keen-witted lyrics on separation and loss. A meticulous, swinging combo handles the arrangements without a trace of mawkishness or overkill. (40:48/Reissue)

Johnny Winter
Johnny Winter (Columbia) ★★★

Before Stevie Ray Vaughan there was Johnny Winter, the white Texas bluesman. This first major-label recording, from 1969, was as close to pure blues as Winter's albums were to be for many years—until Columbia gave up their desire to make Winter an American guitar-slinging rock hero to counter Eric Clapton. Winter is not yet fully developed here as a singer, but his slide work is among the first rank. Willie Dixon and Big Walter Horton contribute to "Mean Mistreater." (J.T.) (34:16/Reissue)

Nothin' but the Blues (Columbia) ★★★

While fronting Muddy Waters's band (with whom he had been gigging fairly regularly) Winter cut the 1977 album that set his future firmly with the blues—as opposed to the rock world he hated—and laid the groundwork for his subsequent "rediscovery" in the 1980s on Alligator Records. (J.T.) (34:44/Reissue)

Guitar Slinger (Alligator) ★★✦

On his Alligator debut, in 1984, the fearless Johnny Winter barrels his chariot of fire right to the precipice. Right behind him charge Albert Collins's rhythm team (Casey Jones and Johnny B. Gayden) and the Mellow Fellows' horn section. (39:37/Reissue)

The Winter of '88 (MCA) ★★

Blustery and frosty, except for Winter's rendition of Elmore James's "Stranger Blues," which is a tour de force of blitz-krieg riff–guitar and a forceful reminder of his blues affilia-tion. (54:32/1988)

Let Me In (Pointblank/Charisma) ★★★

Winter flails slow blues, shuffles, and breakneck rock numbers until they're raw. Happily, this time around it's apparent his conviction matches his virtuosity and energy level. No flies on this dinosaur. (49:52/1991)

Jimmy Witherspoon

Blowin' in from Kansas City (Ace import) ★★★★✦

The prolific Kansas City–style shouter was on a great number of labels during the late 1940s and early 1950s, including the Bihari brothers' Modern imprint, and Ace has assembled an impressive assortment of numbers (including rareties) from Witherspoon's early years. Typically laid back on many slower cuts, the brawny singer swings on, among others, the jump blues "Love My Baby" and "Who's Been Jiving You," which benefit from full-bodied saxophone improvisations by Maxwell Davis, Buddy Floyd, and Don Hill. (B.D./F.J.H.) (54:36/Reissue)

Spoon So Easy (MCA/Chess) ★★✦

The most interesting of these fourteen songs that Wither-spoon recorded for Chess in the mid 1950s are his rendition of James Oden's urban blues "Goin' Down Slow," where the Joe Turner–influenced singer captures the essence of melancholy, and "When the Lights Go Out," for his droll harmonies with label majordomo Willie Dixon. Most of the material suffers dreadfully from sluggish instrumental accompaniment. Nine of the songs went unreleased until recently.   (40:55/1990)

The 'Spoon Concerts (Fantasy)   ★★★★♪

After his initial popular and artistic success Witherspoon had to weather a lean period before the two 1959 performances documented on this disc (originally two albums, then a double-LP reissue) put him back in business. At both the Monterey Jazz Festival and a Los Angeles club appearance his river-deep voice is magnificent, a mix of empathy and sensitivity, jazz phrasing and blues gesticulation. His literate song selection—from the classic blues of Bessie Smith to urban stomps and from Joe Turner and Roy Brown to Count Basie staples—shows the breadth of his stylistic mastery. Trumpeter Roy Eldridge and saxophonist Ben Webster are among the jazz/blues experts providing him solos and obbligatos. Audio footnote: The original concert tapes were less than perfect.   (71:28/Reissue)

Midnight Lady Called the Blues (Muse)   ★★★♪

This relaxed, swinging 1986 soiree has sixty-two-year-old Witherspoon, his baritone dark, deep, and somewhat laborious, more mallet than sledgehammer, distilling the soulful meaning of songs jointly written by Dr. John and New York's late blues headman Doc Pomus. Saxophonists David "Fathead" Newman and Hank Crawford have a lot to say in their laconic solos, and drummer Bernard Purdie keeps time with characteristic flair. An undervalued little gem of a session.   (37:44/Reissue)

Rockin' L.A. (Fantasy)   ★★★♪

The grainy wrinkles in Witherspoon's voice carry shades of spontaneously created feeling to a lucky hotel bar throng during a 1988 quartet performance. On standards and the rare original he and saxophonist Teddy Edwards convey revelations with warmth and familiarity, swinging all the time. By the way, the singer would soon be treated successfully for throat cancer. (42:02/1989)

Mitch Woods
Solid Gold Cadillac (Blind Pig) ★★★♩

Woods is the Bay Area pianist/singer whose self-described "rock-a-boogie" sends dancers from Milan to Malibu (no kidding) into paroxysms of sweaty delight. He's a fine showman and a better-than-good musician, with a spirited band (the Rocket 88s) that shares his enthusiasm for Professor Longhair, Roy Milton, Louis Jordan, etc. Special guests Charlie Musslewhite, Ronnie Earl, and the Roomful of Blues horns are here to make the jump blues and boogie-woogie fun even more enjoyable than on Woods's earlier Blind Pig CD *Mr. Boogie's Back in Town*. (38:14/1991)

The Yardbirds
Blues, Backtracks and Shapes of Things, Volume Two ★★★★♩
(Sony Music)

The second volume in the excellent Sony/Columbia retrospective on the Yardbirds, a seminal 1960s rock band, devotes one of its two discs entirely to the group's propensity for blues, to wit seventeen tracks from a Crawdaddy Club performance with Sonny Boy Williamson (Rice Miller) in December 1963. Here fresh-faced Eric Clapton and four mates are more self-confident on their eight songs without the harp mogul than on the ten backing him. (There's also a studio demo rendition of John Lee Hooker's "Boom Boom.") Disc two is primarily concerned with innovative 1964–66 rock, but guitarist Clapton and his replacement Jeff Beck, along with singer/harpist

Keith Relf, do have ample room to show off the sincerity of their blues licks. (2:14:50/1991)

Johnny Young
Chicago Blues (Arhoolie) ★★★★

By the mid 1960s, Chicago blues was momentarily on the wane, but tragically under-recorded guitarist/mandolinist Johnny Young sounds lively indeed on these 1965 and 1967 sessions, backed by strong combos that feature powerhouse harp players James Cotton and Walter Horton as well as pianists Otis Spann and Lafayette Leake. (B.D.)

(65:23/Reissue)

Z. Z. Top
Greatest Hits (Warner Brothers) ★★★

This trio of blues-based rockers has usually been too eager to please the blotto arena crowd (several million strong), but by sifting seven albums for material the Texans came up with some tolerable grunge. "La Grange" is boogie John Lee Hooker could mash his boot heel to—more than can be said for most crawlin' kingsnake pretenders' megadecibels—and their extravagantly wrought tribute to blues entitled "My Head's in Mississippi" is respectable fun. (72:54/1992)

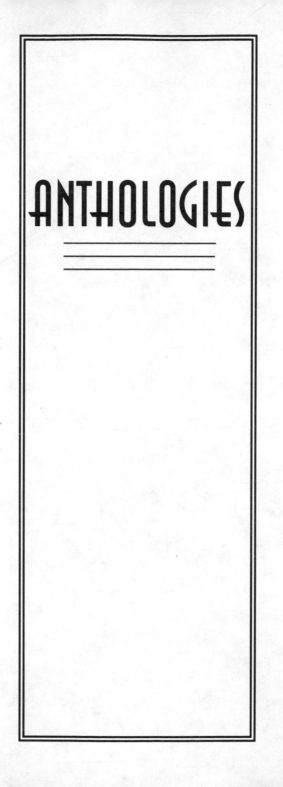

ANTHOLOGIES

The Alligator Records 20th Anniversary Collection (Alligator) ★★★

The premier American blues label, founded in Chicago on a shoestring by Bruce Iglauer, gives itself a hearty pat on the back with this handsome two-disc set. It works best as an introduction to the company's "Genuine Houserockin' Music," with thirty-five album tracks from as many label artists. There's a great deal of spare splendor, some dross. But why not include alternate takes and lost nuggets to give "payback" to longtime supporters? Why not program the selections chronologically and allow the listener to follow the label's stylistic drift from straight Chicago blues to more commercial variants? Accompanied by a twenty-two-page booklet with Iglauer's interesting essay on the history of the label.
(2:26:07/1991)

American Folk Blues Festival '62 (Optimism) ★★★★

In the early 1960s, after Muddy Waters pointed the way, blues notables faced east to Europe for work. The first AFBF

255

troupe, in 1962, was recorded (mostly in the studio) by tour sponsor Horst Lippmann on its Hamburg stop. T-Bone Walker, Memphis Slim, John Lee Hooker, Shakey Jake Harris, and Willie Dixon—all heard in electric band settings—are models of lyrical expressiveness and controlled energy. Dixon and Slim singing of their favorite racehorse in "Stewball" cut to the nub of charm.   (45:38/Reissue)

American Folk Blues Festival '63 (Optimism)   ★★★♪

A year later Big Joe Williams, Matt Murphy, Lonnie Johnson, Otis Spann, Sonny Boy Williamson, Muddy Waters, and Victoria Spivey rolled into Bremen, Germany, with holdovers Dixon and Slim. Guitarist/singer Johnson by his lonesome on "It's Too Late to Cry" gives the standout performance.
(45:55/Reissue)

American Folk Blues Festival '64 (Optimism)   ★★★

The Festival caravan now has a number of country blues players in its ranks. Lightnin' Hopkins is in good form, but John Henry Barbee and Sleepy John Estes have seen better times. Howlin' Wolf's furious intensity on "Dust My Broom" trivializes the efforts at sweat elsewhere by singer Sugar Pie DeSanto. Wolf and guitarist Hubert Sumlin are the victors of Hamburg this year.   (42:29/Reissue)

American Folk Blues Festival '66 (Optimism)   ★★★

No one exactly scintillates, but Robert Pete Williams, Junior Wells, Joe Turner, Sippie Wallace, and (at times) Otis Rush handle themselves decently on the Frankfurt stage. The Chicago rhythm section, though, is often ambiguous and unruly rather than declarative and kempt.   (45:00/Reissue)

American Folk Blues Festival '70 (Optimism) ★★★⸝

Another year and another blues zephyr blows through the Rhineland. The Chicago Blues All Stars, featuring fairly nimble harp player Big Walter Horton, share the concert program with a determined Bukka White, *wunderbund* pianist Champion Jack Dupree, and the ever-charming team of Sonny Terry and Brownie McGhee. Willie Dixon towers on several numbers bullying his bass fiddle. (74:30/Reissue)

American Folk Blues Festival '72 (Optimism) ★★★⸝

A passel of country and city blues players raise the audiences' spirits with their morally earnest music. The solo acts—Bukka White, Big Joe Williams, Roosevelt Sykes, Memphis Slim— have more to get off their chest than Chicago ensembles led by Jimmy Dawkins, Jimmy Rogers, and (pianist) T-Bone Walker. But not wronged-woman Big Mama Thornton, who declaims "Ball and Chain." Consumer note: There are eight more CDs in Optimism's "American Folk Blues Festival" series, all worth a listen. (67:31/Reissue)

Antone's: Bringing You the Best in Blues (Antone's) ★★★

This assortment of sixteen numbers taken from a dozen Antone's releases features the likes of Buddy Guy, Otis Rush, Matt Murphy, Lou Ann Barton, and Eddie Taylor having their way with the twelve-bar form, giving phrases and riffs a zestful boost on the Austin club's stage or in a nearby studio. (63:49/1989)

Antone's Tenth Anniversary Anthology: Volume One ★★★
(Antone's)

Clifford Antone's blues den threw a week-long party in 1985 that involved revelers named Albert Collins, James Cotton,

Eddie Taylor, Buddy Guy, Otis Rush, and twenty others. Even the rhetorical excess is enjoyable to hear. (64:33/Reissue)

Antone's Anniversary Anthology: Volume Two (Antone's) ★★★

The Antone's celebrations in 1986 and 1987 recruited Albert Collins, James Cotton, Buddy Guy, Otis Rush, Lazy Lester, and a swarm more. Enough shopworn licks whizz around the club to delight even the crankiest traditionalist. Few if any of the performers *feel* the music as clichés—an important distinction, that. (54:04/1991)

Antone's Women (Antone's) ★★★

On this sampler Austin ladies Angela Strehli, Marcia Ball, and Lou Ann Barton use the blues as a sumptuous, evocative song language, offering numbers either previously released or unavailable till now. More impressive yet is a track recorded especially for this disc by Barbara Lynn, the revenant whose 1962 smash "You'll Lose a Good Thing" is covered earlier in the program by Barton. Another new signee, Houston's gospel-trained Lavelle White, is a comer. The singing of young tigresses Sue Foley and Toni Price, in comparison, is gawky and forced. (48:01/1992)

Atlantic Blues: Chicago (Atlantic) ★★♪

Atlantic never established a Windy City presence, so this package is the weakest of the four in the *Atlantic Blues* series. There are a few solid sides, notably pianist Johnnie Jones's 1953 outing "Chicago Blues" with Elmore James on guitar and three tracks apiece by Freddy King and Otis Rush from their overlooked Cotillion days. But too many lame concert tracks by the likes of Howlin' Wolf and Muddy Waters make one suspect they're aboard for name recognition only. Jones's exciting "Hoy Hoy" is one of the four songs that have been deleted from the original program due to CD time restrictions. (B.D.) (74:31/Reissue)

Atlantic Blues: Guitar (Atlantic) ★★★✦

Plenty of sizzling rarities on this disc as well—country blues gems by Blind Willie McTell and Mississippi Fred McDowell and urban action from Stick McGhee, Texas Johnny Brown, and Chuck Norris. Mickey Baker, Johnny Heartsman (behind singer Al King), and Cornell Duprec are all welcome inclusions, but a few selections (e.g., B. B. King's "Why I Sing the Blues" and Stevie Ray Vaughan's "Flood Down in Texas") are totally superfluous concert recordings of more recent vintage that add little to the package besides big-name talent. The disc cuts four songs from the mid-1980s album. (B.D.) (72:27/Reissue)

Atlantic Blues: Piano (Atlantic) ★★★★✦

Probably the most consistent entry in the series (also available as a four-disc boxed set), this piano anthology features solid Chicago-style piano from Jimmy Yancey and Little Brother Montgomery, vintage Champion Jack Dupree, Professor Longhair representing New Orleans, and vastly underrated New York sessionsman Vann Walls. There's unissued Ray Charles, circa 1953, thundering boogies from Meade Lux Lewis, and more recent work by Jay McShann (great) and Willie Mabon (not). Six tracks missing. (B.D.) (73:33/Reissue)

Atlantic Blues: Vocalists (Atlantic) ★★★★✦

Although many of the featured artists aren't readily identified as blues singers, this anthology is consistently enjoyable, capturing everyone from obscure 1950s Jimmy Witherspoon and Wynonie Harris to searing 1960s soul by Otis Clay, Johnny Copeland, and Z. Z. Hill. Aretha Franklin's previously unreleased cover of Mable John's "Takin' Another Man's Place" is superb, as are Johnnie Taylor and Eldridge Holmes. Another half dozen tunes eliminated for the CD format. (B.D.) (74:33/Reissue)

Barrelhouse Boogie (RCA/Bluebird) ★★★★

The title can only mean paterfamilias Jimmy Yancey and his coroneted scions Meade "Lux" Lewis, Pete Johnson, and Albert Ammons. On this collection of 1936–41 RCA Victor recordings Lewis gets shortchanged with but two sides, yet the others have ample opportunity to "cut" their boogies or take it slow and easy. Johnson and Ammons battle to a draw in nine numbers. Don't miss the captivating liner notes by pianist Art Hodes. (58:28/1989)

Bawdy Blues (Bluesville) ★★

The mild naughtiness provided by late-1950s Prestige artists Tampa Red, Victoria Spivey, Memphis Slim, and four others isn't half as interesting as the overstuffed and dizzy liner notes of a Shakespearean scholar. Wonder what Slim thought about the pedant's musing that the Bard certainly would have smiled on his *"tour de force* on a phonemic four-letter acrostic"? Randy tip: For the *real* dirt hear *Copulatin' Blues* (Jass CD), twenty-two tracks from the shave-'em-dry jazz-blues 1920s and 1930s. (43:09/Reissue)

The Beauty of the Blues (Columbia/Legacy) ★

What's this claim by the Columbia "Roots 'n' Blues" series copywriters about *Beauty* being an "incredible eighteen-song collection" featuring "the biggest names in the blues"? And what does the highfalutin title refer to? The consumer gets a few superb blues by a couple masters—and some good archival Cajun music and straight gospel—along with many winsome nothings such as Hunter and Jenkins's "Lollypop," Buddy Woods's "Don't Sell It," and Bill Broonzy's "Horny Frog." Everything has been plucked off other discs in the series for no discernible reason other than hucksterism. Makes a lousy ashtray, too.   (54:04/1991)

The Best of the Blues Singers (LRC) ★★

Barely acceptable hodgepodge of twelve obscure tapings of Joe Williams, Ray Charles, Junior Parker, Joe Turner, Memphis Slim, and Muddy Waters. Don't let the miserable packaging fool you into thinking T-Bone Walker sings.

(53:03/Reissue)

The Best of Chess Blues, Volume One (MCA/Chess) ★★★★★

There is a large strongbox of singles that appeared on Chess and subsidiary labels during 1949–56, and respectful compiler Andy McKaie has picked the lock to pleasing end. The big guns—Muddy Waters, Howlin' Wolf, Sonny Boy Williamson, Little Walter—are all represented, and so too are minor miracle workers Robert Nighthawk, J. B. Lenoir, Lowell Fulson, Jimmy Rogers, Willie Mabon, and Eddie Boyd. A perfect introduction to the label's riches.   (35:28/1988)

The Best of Chess Blues, Volume Two (MCA/Chess) ★★★★

The focus is on the Chess 1960s, a less remarkable decade for the storied Chicago label. Selections include Elmore James's "Madison Blues," Muddy Waters's "You Shook Me," Howlin' Wolf's "Little Red Rooster," and John Lee Hooker's "One Bourbon, One Scotch, One Beer." A source point for those wondering where George Thorogood, Led Zeppelin, the Yardbirds, et al. found their inspiration, or what passed for such.   (36:39/1988)

Black Top Blues-a-Rama, Volume One (Black Top)   ★★★

What one hears is exactly what was encountered by frolickers at Tipitina's in New Orleans one April night in 1988. Pianist and singer Ron Levy supplies light entertainment, Grady Gaines shows off his lung power on saxophone, and Anson Funderburgh and the Rockets highlight this sampling of the six-hour spectacular with playing that has combustion and subtlety to match their fluency. Sam Myers's dust bowl–dry voice is the perfect counterpart to guitarist Funderburgh's endlessly communicative lines.   (38:11/1988)

Black Top Blues-a-Rama, Volume Two (Black Top)   ★★⌐

Hammond Scott's Black Top Records turns Tipitina's in New Orleans upside-down with performances by several label artists. Singer Nappy Brown is licentiously possessed, guitarist Ronnie Earl steamily scales improvisation against composition, singer James "Thunderbird" Davis revisits his Duke classic "Blue Monday Blues" with characteristic mettle, and Earl King on guitar sizes up local treasure "Things that I Used to Do."   (38:19/1988)

Black Top Blues-a-Rama, Volume Three (Black Top)   ★★★

The Black Top good times roll again at Tip's the following year. Thunderbird Davis, back again, has a penchant for reviving chestnuts, keyboardist Ron Levy leads the charge on two decent songs, then guitarist Bobby Radcliff (for a third of the disc) hurls phrases that sizzle and detonate in the ears of club attendees, turning the place into a shooting gallery of exalting tensions.   (46:09/1990)

Black Top Blues-a-Rama, Volume Four See **Grady Gaines**

Black Top Blues-a-Rama, Volume Five (Black Top)   ★★★

After his singer bows out, Ronnie Earl reaches a patrician level of expression in "I Found a New Love" that permits him to play his guitar lines with great solicitude. Local legend Earl King and Houston singer/guitarist Joe Hughes are no slouches as entertainers, further heating up the Napoleon Avenue club in May 1989.   (50:43/1991)

Black Top Blues-a-Rama, Volume Six (Black Top)   ★★★★

There wasn't an instant in this 1989 Tipitina's social when the music didn't sound fully realized and throb with life, thanks to Anson Funderburgh, Sam Myers, Snooks Eaglin, Hubert Sumlin, and attendants. Even the rampant clichés satisfy. The series continues in perpetuity.   (64:15/1992)

Blue Ballads (Blue Note)   ★★★★

This impressive collection of ruminations culled from the Blue Note 1950s and 1960s spotlights several jazz worthies' intimate understanding of blues terminology, its expressive properties, its creative possibilities. Moving performances include tenorman Joe Henderson shedding a blue tear in "Lazy Afternoon" and precocious trumpeter Lee Morgan conferring meaningful slurs and bends to "Since I Fell for You," probably the ultimate blues ballad.   (68:24/1991)

Blue Flames: A Sun Blues Collection (Rhino/Sun)   ★★★

Before Elvis, Sun Records was a blues label. This compilation presents a broad overview of that period. You'll find early Howlin' Wolf, James Cotton, and B. B. King, plus gospel and rock 'n' roll. But by covering so much ground with one album rather than concentrating on a few artists Rhino dilutes the force of what is here. (J.T.)   (51:41/1990)

Blue Ivory (Blind Pig)   ★★☆

Roosevelt Sykes, Henry Gray, Boogie Woogie Red, and Mr. B
(Mark Lincoln Braun) are the blues 'n' boogie pianists whose
Blind Pig recordings in the 1970s and 1980s are recycled for
this sixteen-song collection by that small San Francisco label.
The three veterans and young disciple Mr. B don't disappoint,
but none exactly surprises, either. The tracks by Sykes and
Red are otherwise unavailable.   (49:58/1991)

Blues Around Midnight (Flair/Virgin)   ★★★★☆

This sexy, sophisticated compilation of West Coast blues from
the 1950s and 1960s warmly illustrates the tenuous nature of
distinctions between blues and jazz. Taken from the Kent,
Flair, Modern, Crown, and RPM labels, contributing artists
include Jimmy Witherspoon, Lowell Fulson, B. B. King, Larry
Davis, Ray Charles, and T-Bone Walker, among others. (J.T.)
                                              (63:43/Reissue)

Blues at Newport (Vanguard)   ★★★★☆

Recorded at the Newport Folk Festivals from 1959 to 1964,
this release is one of the best "live" albums going. The recording quality is better than most studio recordings; the performances—selected by blues historian Samuel Charters—are all
sterling; and the artists, ranging from Sleepy John Estes to
John Lee Hooker to Skip James, are among the very best.
(J.T.)   (72:21/Reissue)

Blues Classics (K-Tel)   ★★★★

The title speaks the truth. This is a good place to start a love
affair with the blues, considering the presence of vintage
songs by Jimmy Reed, B. B. King, John Lee Hooker, Muddy
Waters, Slim Harpo, Brother Ray Charles, Howlin' Wolf, Gui-

tar Slim, Percy Mayfield, and Bobby Bland. A skinflint's running time, though. (29:11/1989)

Blues Cocktail Party! (Black Top) ★★✦

Satisfactory smorgasbord of leftover tracks from various 1982–89 Black Top sessions. The tastiest morsels are purveyed by Anson Funderburgh and Rod Piazza. Down the disposal goes Jimmy Don Smith's rancid "Jailbait."

(53:37/1991)

Blues from Dolphin's of Hollywood (Specialty) ★★✦

This assortment of Cash, Money, and Dolphin recordings from the 1950s is entertaining but hardly mandatory listening. Unable to locate the masters on Joe Houston's version of the Johnny Otis ballad "All Night Long" or other John Dolphin–produced gems, compiler Billy Vera makes do with material from seven artists who aren't at their best. Singers Memphis Slim and Jimmy Witherspoon act out the lyrics with a bit more assurance than either Pee Wee Crayton, Little Caesar, Percy Mayfield, Floyd Dixon, or Peppermint Harris. (66:57/1991)

Blues from the Montreux Jazz Festival (Malaco) ★★★✦

The Malaco Records entourage—five lead singers and eighteen accompanists—grooved a path across the Continent in 1989, recording at the internationally renowned festival near Lake Geneva. The blues gospel according to Bobby Bland, Denise LaSalle, and Johnnie Taylor is forever on the soul side, passionate and sonorous, and their tales of love tested and triumphant light up the Swiss night. Retrograde mistakes: LaSalle's dredging up "Don't Mess with My Tu Tu" and Sam Mosely of Sam & Dave fame trying to replicate sacrosanct harmonies with his post–Dave Prater partner, Bob Johnson.

(76:20/1991)

Blues in the Mississippi Night (Rykodisc) ★★★★

Suppressed at the time of its 1946 recording due to the misgivings of its participants, this fascinating disc contains the frank and often disturbing recollections of blues greats Big Bill Broonzy, John Lee "Sonny Boy" Williamson, and Memphis Slim on the origins of their music and the prejudices then inherent in their Delta homeland. Encouraged by interviewer/producer Alan Lomax, the three legends perform a few songs as well. (B.D.)   (50:50/1990)

The Blues, Volume One (MCA/Chess) ★★★★

This 1963 Chess array of valuable singles from the label's 1952–60 files includes two apiece from Muddy Waters, Little Walter, and Howlin' Wolf, plus one each credited to Chuck Berry, Buddy Guy, Sonny Boy Williamson, John Lee Hooker, Lowell Fulson, and Jimmy Witherspoon.   (33:05/Reissue)

The Blues, Volume Two (MCA/Chess) ★★★✓

A second 1963 Chess package isn't quite as strong from start to finish as *Volume One*. Still, some prime Little Walter ("Key to the Highway," "Blues with a Feeling") and prizes from Bo Diddley ("I'm a Man") and Howlin' Wolf ("Evil") invite repeated plays. Muddy Waters's concert performance of "Got My Mojo Working" has been truncated.   (32:33/Reissue)

The Blues, Volume Three (MCA/Chess) ★★★✓

The selections by Howlin' Wolf, Muddy Waters, Sonny Boy Williamson, and Elmore James (who provides an alternate take of "The Sun Is Shining") tower over those by Little Milton, Washboard Sam, and four others in the Chess 1950s and early 1960s. This third installment in the series originally appeared in 1964.   (34:43/Reissue)

The Blues, Volume Four (MCA/Chess) ★★★

Volume Four almost expires for Larry Williams's hideous "My Baby's Got Soul" and Memphis Slim's comatose ballad "I Guess I'm a Fool." Yet Eddie Boyd's 1953 chart hit "Third Degree," T. V. Slim's New Orleans gem "Flat Foot Sam," and eight other songs from a broader range of blues styles than on earlier volumes are small pleasures that breathe healthily.

(34:40/Reissue)

The Blues, Volume Five (MCA/Chess) ★★★★

Muddy Waters again proves his skill at revealing the most gripping idiomatic inflections, this time wreaking his vocal and slide wizardry in 1951's "Honey Bee." By comparison Howlin' Wolf, John Lee Hooker, Sonny Boy Williamson, Memphis Minnie, and several others belonging to the Chess 1950s seem like mere mortals. A solid set all the same, first heard in 1966.

(35:54/Reissue)

The Blues, Volume Six: '50s Rarities (Chess) ★★✦

Compilers Andy McKaie and Mary Katherine Aldin are genuinely concerned with quarrying sixteen Chess obscurities into the fresh air for everyone's enjoyment. Hearing microtone moguls Muddy Waters and Little Walter bind together performing "All Night Long," a single recorded at the close of 1951, produces the same ecstatic chills a cave explorer feels upon entering a previously unknown grotto. Floyd Dixon's "Alarm Clock Blues," a 1956 Checker single, furnishes modest pleasure. However, only *serious* blues hounds need attend to curiosities from Sonny Boy Williamson, Blue Smitty, Alberta Adams, Rocky Fuller, etc.

(44:52/1991)

Boston Blues Blast, Volume One (Tone-Cool) ★★★

With this attractive, considered anthology, producers Ron Levy and Richard Rosenblatt have made a strong case for Beantown as an honorable center of flatted-fifth ebullience. George Gritzbach, Paul Rishell, Luther Johnson, Jerry Portnoy, Sugar Ray, and George Mayweather—of eighteen featured artists—are the codfish aristocracy with abundant talent and personality. (67:55/1991)

Cajun & Zydeco Mardi Gras (Maison de Soul) ★★★★

Bayou producer Floyd Soileau rolls the dice and comes up with snake eyes fourteen times on a pre-Lenten collection that exalts "Louisiana's Best Performers," including Boozoo Chavis, Clifton Chenier, Rockin' Dopsie, and Lawrence Ardoin. (40:48/1992)

Chicago/The Blues/Today! (Vanguard) ★★★★★

Today! denotes 1965. The modern blues purveyed by Otis Spann, J. B. Hutto and His Hawks, and the Junior Wells Chicago Blues Band (with Buddy Guy, Jack Myers, and Fred Below) on this Sam Charters–produced album has the tough-grained texture of South Side ghetto reality. Indeed, the musicians have a special way with their subtle, rhythmic depictions of mood, at once nonchalant and vigilant to psychic pain, carnality, and life. Reportedly the inspiration for the Alligator *Living Chicago Blues* series some years later. (46:26/Reissue)

The Complete Stax/Volt Singles 1959–1968 (Atlantic) ★★★★★

Nine discs containing every A-side issued by Stax and its Volt subsidiary from 1959 to 1968 and selected flips make this boxed set a Memphis soul music bonanza, but there's plenty of interest for blues fanatics, too. Luminaries such as Rufus Thomas, Albert King, Johnnie Taylor, and even Otis Redding contribute blues-based material along with a host of undeservingly obscure artists. Rob Bowman's well-researched accompanying booklet is an added plus. All tracks are in mono. (B.D.)   (10:52:25/1991)

Dealing with the Devil (Sony Music)   ★★★

This recommended sampler of mid-1960s British blues, first released on Immediate, makes clear how doyens Cyril Davies, John Mayall, Eric Clapton, Jeff Beck, and Tony McPhee cared deeply for their American blues heroes and tried to move beyond imitation. *Devil* gets the nod over Sony Music's companion discs *Stroll On* and *Down and Dirty* for its stronger song selection and a well-reasoned essay written by Bruce Eder.   (46:03/1991)

Drop Down Mama (MCA/Chess)   ★★★★

First compiled in 1970, this late-1940s/carly-1950s Chicago anthology from the Chess shelves still packs a wallop. For instance, we get elegant slide guitar from Robert Nighthawk and Johnny Shines and brooding classics by Floyd Jones and Arthur "Big Boy" Spires, along with fleet-fingered picking by the elusive Blue Smitty. (B.D.)   (41:12/Reissue)

Genuine Houserockin' Music (Alligator)   ★★★

Alligator tries to induce a thirst for album shopping with an attractively priced assortment of tracks culled from its 1986 catalog. Among the tantalizers are Hound Dog Taylor, Son Seals, Koko Taylor, Jimmy Johnson, Fenton Robinson, and Lonnie Mack.   (43:31/Reissue)

Genuine Houserockin' Music II (Alligator) ★★★

Enough consumers made the trek to their local record stores to justify another collection. A few Young Turks (Lil' Ed and Little Charlie included) join the Old Guard (e.g., James Cotton, Albert Collins) on the 1987 "price buster." (66:50/Reissue)

Genuine Houserockin' Music III (Alligator) ★★

This mediocre 1988 installment in the series reflects an artistically sluggish year of label releases. The laudable tracks are by Roy Buchanan, the Kinsey Report, Lazy Lester, and the Paladins. Most of the rest should be tossed out with the bathwater. (61:13/1989)

Genuine Houserockin' Music IV (Alligator) ★★↙

The Alligator blues homestead has also become a blues rock haven over the past few years. Lonnie Mack, Elvin Bishop, Lonnie Brooks, and Roy Buchanan are among the acts represented on this generally entertaining disc. Lots of downward-slurred chords for the low price. (75:39/1990)

Good Time Blues (Columbia/Legacy) ★★★★

Almost all of the twenty-one songs performed by various folk blues ensembles radiate a frivolous innocence that blinks at the rigors of life for African-Americans dwelling in the Depression-era South and the years soon afterward. For instance, take the redoubtable Memphis Jug Band's "Gator Wobble," which is buoyed by piano, washboard, shouts, and percussion. Still, first-hand knowledge of harsh reality *is* omnipresent, whether it's in, say, Buddy Moss's harmonica or caught up with longing in Joe McCoy's singing voice. Another entry in the *Roots 'n' Blues* series with pleasing digital mono sound. (59:30/1991)

Great Blues Guitarists: String Dazzlers (Columbia/Legacy)　★★★★

Quite a glorious array of prewar guitar talent—three ground-breaking duets by Lonnie Johnson and Eddie Lang, seminal sides by Blind Willie Johnson and Blind Lemon Jefferson, and swinging efforts by Big Bill Broonzy, Blind Willie McTell, and Casey Bill Weldon are among the many highlights. (B.D.)
(61:31/1991)

Great Bluesmen/Newport (Vanguard)　★★★✦

Newport Folk Festival appearances by thirteen aging country blues artists between 1959 and 1965 please or come to naught. Skip James, until now missing for decades, mesmerizes with "Hard Time Killing Floor Blues." Son House and John Hurt also fare extremely well. On the other hand, Sleepy John Estes and a couple more veterans dawdle, while Robert Pete Williams has to compete with loud street and crowd noise. The CD doesn't have all the songs on the original two-record set.
(71:20/Reissue)

Grinder Man Blues: Masters of the Blues Piano (RCA)　★★★✦

The Bluebird vaults have been raided for this assemblage of tracks recorded by three of the blues's historically important pianists. Little Brother Montgomery's six acceptable tunes date from the mid 1930s; Memphis Slim dirties the dozens competently but less interestingly in 1940–41; and Big Maceo Mayweather highlights the program with a half dozen World War Two pièces de résistance, including the take-no-prisoners "Texas Stomp."
(51:33/1990)

Gulf Coast Blues, Volume One (Black Top)　★★✦

Enjoyable tour of the Gulf Coast blues/R&B landscape, with looks at the family team of singer Carol Fran and guitarist

Clarence Hollimon, saxophonist Grady Gaines, guitarist Joe Hughes, and singer/pianist Teddy Reynolds. Extensive local history in their bent tones. (33:09/1990)

Honkers and Bar Walkers, Volume One (Delmark) ★★★

The archives of Herald, Regal, States, and United Records yield twenty-two selections from a number of barroom orators of saxophone R&B in the late 1940s and 1950s. Jimmy Forrest, Tab Smith, Paul Bascomb, Jimmy Coe, and the lesser-knowns have little trouble going hog wild. They disappoint when they're heard troweling gobs of maudlin emotion. Better Delmark had reissued only the tunes full of ferocious bellowing and honking. (61:35/Reissue)

Honkers and Bar Walkers, Volume Two (Delmark) ★★★✦

The saxophonists generating a robust jazz in line with R&B plainspokenness on this collection of songs from the Apollo 1950s have a playful eye for larger-than-life gestures. King Curtis, Bill Harvey, and Morris Lane, among others, blow their tops, dealing excitedly in glibness not emotional authenticity. In addition to spouting merriment, Charlie Jefferson inches along dripping rubato molasses, and Hilton Jefferson—the ex-Cab Calloway altoist soon to hook on with Duke Ellington—merges romance with gentle heartbreak playing "Darkness on the Delta" under the banner of drummer/leader Panama Francis. Better-than-good fun. (59:54/1992)

How Blue Can You Get?: Great Blues Vocals in the Jazz Tradition (RCA/Bluebird) ★★★★

Longtime jazz benefactor Leonard Feather searched the dusty RCA Victor 1940–63 "jazz" shelves to assemble this commendable anthology. Exploiting the fast bond between jazz and blues, he presents the listener with good or excellent tracks (some of which he originally produced) featuring an array of notable singers such as Louis Armstrong, Leadbelly, Fats Waller, Jack Teagarden, Jimmy Rushing (with the Count Basie band), and Billy Eckstine (with Earl Hines's orchestra). Forgotten talents include Tiny Davis in front of the all-female International Sweethearts of Rhythm and Ruby Smith backed by gifted guitarist Al Casey and Gene Sedric's Orchestra. (62:05/1989)

Keys to the Crescent City (Rounder) ★★

On this survey of New Orleans keyboards, honorary citizen Charles Brown and locals Eddie Bo, Art Neville, and Willie Tee ostensibly carry the rich legacy into the 1990s. Pianists Bo and Brown do have local color to spare, but Tee's pleasant keyboard traversals have little geographical bearing and Neville's synthesizers could belong to a well-stocked music store in Des Moines. (43:44/1991)

The Legacy of the Blues Maxi-Sampler (GNP Crescendo) ★★★★

Fine introduction to the Hollywood label's twelve-disc series of Sonet recordings from the 1960s. Two songs each, country or urban blues, from a dozen mostly middle-aged gentlemen—Eddie Boyd, Lightnin' Hopkins, Memphis Slim, and Sunnyland Slim included. (71:24/1990)

Legends of Electric Blues Guitar, Volume One (Rhino) ★★★★✦

Guitar Player magazine's vastly enjoyable collection is a study in the triumph or near-triumph of personality over commanding technique. Insightful song selector Dan Forte sees to it that unheralded exemplars Wayne Bennett, Floyd Murphy, and Earl Hooker, to list but three, stand tall on a program shared with acclaimed players like B. B. King, Elmore James, and T-Bone Walker. These processions of mellifluous or mincing leads, chords, tremolos, and broken rhythms were recorded between 1948 and 1974 for a variety of labels.

(56:05/1990)

Legends of the Blues: Volume One (Columbia/Legacy) ★★★★✦

The perfect introduction to Legacy's *Roots 'n' Blues* prewar reissue series, with indispensible Blind Lemon Jefferson, Mississippi John Hurt, Blind Boy Fuller, Memphis Minnie, and much more. Nine of twenty tracks are previously unissued and all sound fine, thanks to the CEDAR sound restoration process. (B.D.)   (59:02/1990)

Legends of the Blues: Volume Two (Columbia/Legacy) ★★★★★

Taken from the Columbia 78s trove, this twenty-karat song collection chronicles the music's gradual transformation from its 1920s folk form into a fairly distinguishable 1940s city sound. Oak Cliff T-Bone (aka T-Bone Walker) and Texas Alexander are among the folk blues sages, Tampa Red and others belong to the outskirts of town, while Champion Jack Dupree and Curtis Jones are clearly urbanites. Yet another *Roots 'n' Blues* release having very clean mono sound.

(61:23/1991)

Living Chicago Blues, Volume One (Alligator) ★★★★★

Alligator's long-celebrated 1978–80 six-record survey of the Chicago scene, remastered expertly by Tom Coyne, is all the more enthralling a sonic experience in the CD format. The initial batch of shuffles and slow blues brings to the fore singer/guitarist Jimmy Johnson's acute musical intelligence and understated ache, ex–Howlin' Wolf henchman Eddie Shaw's mischievously sincere singing and driving saxophone, Left Hand Frank's rawboned guitar seriousness, and the vivid imagination of harmonica wonder worker Carey Bell. Each of the four Chicagoans' bands is intensely involved in its support role, save for Frank's awkward harmonica player and rhythm guitarist. (65:25/Reissue)

Living Chicago Blues, Volume Two (Alligator) ★★★★

The series continues in high style. Guitarist Lonnie Brooks vaults mettlesome lines across his songs, Johnny "Big Moose" Walker beats back despair singing and "dirtying the dozens," Magic Slim Holt's single-note guitar phrases caper through various tempos with ease, and, finally, pianist Pinetop Perkins achieves a state of ennobled ardency alongside four co-workers from the Muddy Waters band. (65:43/Reissue)

Living Chicago Blues, Volume Three (Alligator) ★★★♪

By today's measurement the name recognition dips—and so does the quality of the Chi-Town music. Still, A. C. Reed and the Spark Plugs, "South Side institution" Scotty and the Rib Tips, pianist Lovie Lee with harpist Carey Bell, guitar man Lacy Gibson, and the Sons of Blues (an informal group of upstarts) know a thing or two about sensual enjoyment and pained irony. (71:39/Reissue)

Living Chicago Blues, Volume Four (Alligator) ★★★★

Little Walter devotee Big Leon Brooks and guitarist Andrew Brown, two of the undervalued feature artists here, have since passed on, and a third, singing bassist Queen Sylvia Embry, has exchanged worldly truths for the Word. They deserve to be heard—better late than never. The same goes for Detroit Junior, showcasing his witty slant on life while singing and punctuating the piano, and guitarist Luther "Guitar Junior" Johnson (now a Bullseye artist) backed by a quintet schooled in Muddy Waters's emphatic terminology. As with all four series discs, the liner notes are excellent. (70:26/Reissue)

Louisiana Scrapbook (Rykodisc) ★★★

Eighteen tracks from fifteen Bayou State blues, R&B, and folk artists affiliated with Rounder Records in the late 1980s— Johnny Adams, Tuts Washington, Irma Thomas, etc.—fill you up like a bowl of good but not exceptional crawfish bisque. (62:46/1987)

Low Blows: An Anthology of Chicago Harmonica Blues ★★★★ (Rooster Blues)

A Windy City harmonica bonanza with Big Walter Horton, Big Leon Brooks, Good Rockin' Charles (Henry Bester), George "Mojo" Buford, Golden Wheeler, Big John Wrencher, Carey Bell Harrington, and Alex "Easy Baby" Randall. The spirit of the electrified 1950s lives on in twelve previously unreleased ensemble tracks recorded between 1972 and 1980 for partisan Steve Wisner and four record companies. Co-producers Jim O'Neal and Bob Corritore have painstakingly assembled the album, which has excellent liner notes. (42:23/Reissue)

Mardi Gras Party (Rounder) ★★★★

Some of the maskers tossing doubloons from the Rounder Carnival float are Bo Dollis, James Booker, Marcia Ball, Irma Thomas, the Dirty Dozen Brass Band, and Tuts Washington. Enjoyable any time of the year but especially during that special hedonistic season. (62:21/1991)

Masters of the Delta Blues (Yazoo) ★★★★

Charley Patton held sway over a number of early Delta greats, including Tommy Johnson, Son House, Bukka White, and Willie Brown, and some of their finest Patton-influenced performances are reproduced from 78s for this collection.

Johnson's "Button Up Shoes" and "Lonesome Home Blues" and House's "Walking Blues" in open-G tuning are recently discovered and previously unheard tests. (B.D.) (72:26/1991)

Mississippi Girls (1928–1931) (Story of Blues)   ★★★

Precious little is known about the five (or is it four?) early Delta blueswomen spotlighted on this compilation. Rosie Mae Moore and Mary Butler (apparently one and the same) benefit from the fretting of Charlie McCoy, while the other three provide their own guitar backing. Sound quality is quite impressive. (B.D.)   (51:23/Reissue)

Mississippi Moaners 1927–1942 (Yazoo)   ★★★★

Prewar classics (mostly from the late 1920s and early 1930s) from a variety of Delta mainstays, notably Charley Patton, Skip James, Son House (from his 1942 Library of Congress material), and Mississippi John Hurt, as well as the obscure Uncle Bud Walker and Isaiah "Mississippi Moaner" Nettles, whose alias gives this sterling collection (dubbed from 78s, some rough) its title. (B.D.)   (41:26/Reissue)

Mr. Santa's Boogie (Savoy Jazz)   ★★★♪

A sleigh-full of Christmas blues, R&B, and jazz songs from the 1940s and 1950s. Big Maybelle, Gatemouth Moore, and Alabama Slim are among those supplying blues cheer or heartache. Other unconventional Xmas CDs belonging under the tree? Try James Brown's *Santa's Got a Brand New Bag* (Rhino CD) and the collections *Hipsters' Holiday* (Rhino CD) and *It's Christmas Time Again* (Stax CD), the latter with Albert King squeezing down the chimney. (39:15/Reissue)

The New Bluebloods (Alligator) ★★½

Ten little-known young performers designated by Alligator Records as "The Next Generation of Chicago Blues" in 1986–87 contribute a song apiece to this showcase. Draw your own conclusions from the fact only Lil' Ed Williams, Maurice John Vaughan, and the Kinsey Report eventually released feature albums bearing the crocodilian imprint of the Chicago-based label. (39:45/Reissue)

News & the Blues: Telling It Like It Is (Columbia/Legacy) ★★★★

Twenty tracks that were topical at the time, all but the last three from the prewar era. Especially noteworthy is mesmerizing late-1920s work by Blind Willie Johnson and Mississippi John Hurt, Depression odes by Charley Patton and Big Bill Broonzy, and an unreleased 1946 side by Homer Harris, "Atomic Bomb Blues," with Muddy Waters on guitar. (B.D.)

(59:05/1990)

101 Proof Zydeco (Maison de Soul) ★★★★

Maison de Soul's bayou R&B jug packs a tremendous wallop with songs credited to Lynn August, Boozoo Chavis, Clifton Chenier, Major Handy, and eight more Louisiana/Texas entertainers. Only Jo Jo Reed, a horrendous singer, and the pompous Zachary Richard provide *fais do do* that's the equivalent of swamp water. (59:01/1990)

Piano Blues Rarities, Volume Two (1933–1937) (Story of Blues) ★★★

Interesting array of recordings by talented yet obscure singing pianists Ben Abney, Curtis Henry, Earl Thomas, and Whistlin' Rufus. The slightly better-known singer/guitarist Red

Nelson, supported by an unknown keyboard surveyor, is also represented. The material predates the boogie-woogie revival, and one shouldn't expect a plethora of delightful walking bass lines. Some of the 78s have crude sound. **(55:55/Reissue)**

Prime Chops (Blind Pig) ★★★

Succulent sampler featuring selections off fourteen Blind Pig records, spanning Yank Rachell's mandolin blues, Pinetop Perkins's and Mr. B's boogie piano, and the urban fire of James Cotton, Otis Rush, and Hubert Sumlin. **(51:16/1990)**

Raunchy Business: Hot Nuts & Lollypops ★★★✦ (Columbia/Legacy)

Rollicking prewar collection that delivers on its promise—double-entendre items that doubtless enlivened many a house rent party. Bo Carter and Lonnie Johnson are fine, but the raunchiest business comes courtesy of Lucille Bogan's "Shave 'em Dry II." (B.D.) **(61:34/1991)**

The RCA Victor Blues & Rhythm Revue (RCA) ★★★✦

RCA Victor's relatively small role in the flowering of R&B is born out on a Gregg Geller collection of twenty-five songs recorded by nineteen artists between 1940 and 1959. A fair amount of detritus (e.g., Cab Calloway, Delta Rhythm Boys) vies for room with good material from big bands (notably Erskine Hawkins's "After Hours," with sly dog pianist Avery Parrish), vocalists (unknown bluesman Little Richard included), and instrumentalists (especially King Curtis and Illinois Jacquet). **(71:21/1987)**

Regal Records in New Orleans (Specialty) ★★★★

Generous twenty-seven-track sampling of late-1940s and early-1950s New Orleans R&B from the Regal vaults. Pianist Paul Gayten's polished output dominates, his up-tempo romps and jumping instrumentals outshining his crooning ballads. Annie Laurie's half dozen tracks spotlight her strong pipes, and there are two previously unissued sides apiece by Crescent City legends (and singers) Dave Bartholomew and Roy Brown. (B.D.)   (73:34/1991)

A Riot in Blues (Mobile Fidelity) ★★★♪

This 1971 release gathers performances by artists that blues fan Bob Shad captured for posterity on his portable tape recorder during his travels in the South circa 1950. Lightnin' Hopkins elevates semiautobiographical tales with characteristic warmth, while Sonny Terry and Brownie McGhee offer traditional material in their uplifting manner. Young Ray Charles, in Florida, gives hints of his nascent genius; James Wayne, with his dry singing voice, performs his New Orleans R&B smash "Junco Porter" and some potboilers; and Arbee Stidham (in the studio) envelops a triad of likable blues with his Mammoth Cave–deep baritone.   (63:52/Reissue)

Roots of Robert Johnson (Yazoo) ★★★★

What were Robert Johnson's favorite platters? This innovative collection offers valuable insight into some of Johnson's principal influences, featuring early classics by Skip James ("Devil Got My Woman," "22-20 Blues"), Son House ("My Black Mama, Part One," "Preachin' the Blues, Part One"), Lonnie Johnson ("Life Saver Blues"), and others. (B.D.)
(42:21/Reissue)

Roots of Rock (Yazoo) ★★★★

Wonderful assortment of recordings from the 1920s and 1930s that are identified in their re-created forms with various contemporary folk artists and rock 'n' roll warriors. "Statesboro Blues," "Going Up the Country," "Shake 'em on Down," and eleven more didn't spring fully formed from the Zeus-like foreheads of, say, Bob Dylan, the Allman Brothers, Canned Heat, and Led Zeppelin. The debt, acknowledged or snubbed, is owed Blind Willie McTell, Hambone Willie Newbern, Bukka White, Tommy Johnson, and others.

(43:06/Reissue)

Shoutin' Swingin' and Makin' Love (MCA/Chess) ★★★

Singers Jimmy Rushing, Jimmy Witherspoon, Wynonie Harris, and Al Hibbler waxed these sides between 1947 and 1964, not caring a whit whether their music was pigeonholed as jazz or blues. Highlights include Witherspoon rocking into his baby's arms in "I Can Make It with You" (1954) and Jimmy Rushing belting out three songs in 1953 with formidable emotional largesse in spite of indifferent instrumental backing.

(41:14/Reissue)

The Slide Guitar: Bottles, Knives & Steel (Columbia/Legacy) ★★★★

With the exception of the last two selections, this set concentrates on prewar slide tracks, notably by Charley Patton, Blind Willie Johnson, and Bukka White. As in most of the *Roots 'n' Blues* series, sound quality has been greatly improved through state-of-the-art restoration. (B.D.)

(57:38/1991)

Soul Shots, Volume Four: Urban Blues (Rhino) ★★★★

Crackling 1960s urban anthology with an interesting mixture of hits and obscurities, notably Otis Rush's rare 1962 Duke single "Homework." Little Richard, Little Milton, and Z. Z. Hill justify the soul tag, surrounded by classic Bobby Bland, B. B. King, Junior Parker, and Tommy Tucker. (B.D.)
(54:36/1989)

Sound of the Swamp: The Best of Excello Records, ★★★★♪ Volume One (Rhino)
Southern Rhythm and Rock: The Best of Excello Records, ★★★★ Volume Two (Rhino)

Nashville's Excello Records was the 1950s and 1960s company that championed the southern Louisiana swamp blues of dexterous and facile exponents Slim Harpo, Lightnin' Slim, Lazy Lester, and Lonesome Sundown. The first volume of Rhino's ambitious label retrospective examines J. D. Miller–produced bayou blues from the aforementioned, as well as appealing lowland pop and rockabilly. The second collection centers up north in the Tennessee capital and is more varied, sporting blues from Arthur Gunter, Louis Brooks, and the hilarious Jerry McCain, along with R&B, doo-wop, rockabilly, and even hillbilly numbers. (B.D./F.J.H.)   (Vol. One 44:51/1990)
(Vol. Two 45:23/1991)

The Stax Blues Brothers (Stax) ★★

Jimmy McCracklin and Johnnie Taylor fare the best on this loose survey of releases by Stax male rhapsodists in the late 1960s and early 1970s. Only label loyalists need spend time with Little Sonny Willis, Mighty Joe Hicks, Albert King, and the rest.   (48:12/1988)

Sun Records Harmonica Classics (Rounder) ★★★⌐

Blues harp buffs will want to savor this carefully prepared
Colin Escott compilation of rare Sun recordings from the
Memphis early 1950s. Doctor Ross, Joe Hill Louis, Big Walter
Horton, and Coy "Hot Shot" Love all bend their reeds *con
brio*. Even casual fans should listen to Horton's epic, "Easy."
(38:30/1989)

Superblues: All-Time Classic Blues Hits, Volume One (Stax) ★⌐

This gallimaufry of singles has real or imagined "classics" by,
among other strange bedfellows, Lightnin' Hopkins, Howlin'
Wolf, Ike and Tina Turner, Jimmy Reed, and Little Johnny
Taylor. (44:23/1990)

Superblues: All-Time Classic Blues Hits, Volume Two (Stax) ★⌐

Compiler Kirk Roberts places giants such as Sonny Boy Williamson, Joe Turner, and Percy Mayfield alongside homunculi
named Gene Allison, Donnie Elbert, and Joe Hinton. We get
Chicago blues, Southern soul, New Orleans R&B . . . the
kitchen sink. The capricious unifying theme is, again, "All-
Time Classic Blues Hits." (52:33/1991)

Super Soul Blues, Volume One (Paula) ★★★

A number of blues and soul blues artists who have recorded
for Shreveport's Jewel, Paula, and Ronn labels in the 1960s,
1970s, and 1980s (plus the rare acquisition act) parade their
talent on this appealing collection. Cicero Blake, John Lee
Hooker, Frost Frost (his Jimmy Reedesque "My Back
Scratcher" probably comes from the mid 1960s), and Artie
"Blues Boy" White (performing his 1985 single "Jimmie")
belong to the peaks, while only Tina Turner, with the badly

dated "Shake a Hand," wallows in a fetid valley. Sessions information and liner notes are conspicuously absent.

(55:43/1991)

Super Soul Blues, Volume Two (Paula) ★★★✦

Most of these sixteen archival songs lie stylistically at the confluence of Southern R&B and blues. One long stretch is a sort of low-rent heaven, proceeding from Little Johnny Taylor (his two-timer classic "Everybody Knows About My Good Thing") and B. B. King through Peppermint Harris and Jimmy Reed to John Fred and Toussaint McCall (his striking late-1950s ballad "Nothing Takes the Place of You"). No annotation.

(53:49/1991)

Texas Piano Blues (1929–1948) (Story of Blues) ★★★★

Compressing seventeen New Deal–era sides and three from just after World War II, this compilation points out the pathos basic to cool, calm, and collected Texas blues singers and pianists. Joe Pullum, with his fantastically pitched voice, is the center of interest, besting vocalists Whistlin' Alex Moore, Nick Nichols, and two others. Moore, Big Boy Knox, Robert Cooper, and Andy Boy proficiently man the playful, peekaboo keyboards. The CD sound is only as good as the 78s: fine to fair.

(63:48/Reissue)

Tuesday's Just as Bad (K-Tel) ★★★✦

Better-than-good selection of ten modern blues evergreens from Bobby Bland, Muddy Waters, Junior Wells, Slim Harpo, B. B. King, and five other heavyweights. Sessions information would have made this an even more enticing introduction to the music.

(37:51/1991)

Wrinkles: Classic and Rare Chess Instrumentals (MCA/Chess) ★★★✦

Varied and fascinating lineup of 1950s and early-1960s instrumentals from the Chess vaults, ranging from label mainstays Little Walter, Chuck Berry, and Bo Diddley to searing Chicago guitarist Jody Williams and rolling pianists Lloyd Glenn, Paul Gayten, and Otis Spann. (B.D.)   (27:43/1989)

Zydeco: The Early Years (Arhoolie) ★★★

Folklorist-slanted zydeco compilation captured by Arhoolie founder Chris Strachwitz around Louisiana and Texas in 1961–62. Herbert Sam offers the wild R&B-influenced "They Call Me Good Rockin'." Also present are both sides of Clifton Chenier's 1954 debut single for Elko and guitarist Clarence Garlow's classic 1949 rocker "Ton Ton Roulet," which isn't zydeco but is welcome anyway. (B.D.)   (64:33/Reissue)

Zydeco Shootout at El Sid O's (Rounder) ★★★

The dancers in El Sid O's, the popular Lafayette club, are swept up by powerful, swinging Creole R&B like surfers gyrating in a great wave. Good times indeed, with outfits headed by veterans Lynn August and Warren Caesar carousing in casual competition with young hellions Zydeco Force, Pee Wee and the Zydeco Boll Weevils, Morris Ledet and the Zydeco Playboys, and Jude Taylor and the Burning Flames.   (55:50/1991)

Addendum

The inevitable lag between the author's deadline and the book's publication date sees the release of many new titles and CD reissues, a surprising garden of fresh flowers and weeds ever expanding and needing attention. Below are listed just a few of the recordings introduced to the stores during this period. The next edition of the *Guide* will find each accorded a star rating and otherwise given its due. Note: Ten discs in Rhino's grand *Blues Masters: The Essential Blues Collection*, reportedly a fifteen-volume series, should be available for purchase before spring 1993.

Recommended (with varying degrees of enthusiasm):
Lynn August: *Creole Cruiser* (Black Top)
The Bluzblasters: *Sooner or Later* (Flying Fish)
Eric Clapton: *Unplugged* (Reprise)
Papa John Creach: *Papa Blues* (Bee Bump)
Larry Davis: *Sooner or Later* (Bullseye Blues)
John Delafose and the Eunice Playboys: *Pere et Garcon Zydeco* (Rounder)

Dr. Hector and the Groove Injectors: *Emergency* (Ichiban)

Honeyboy Edwards: *Delta Bluesman* (Earwig)

Sleepy John Estes: *Brownsville Blues* (Delmark)

Sue Foley: *Young Girl Blues* (Antone's)

Mike Griffin and the Unknown Blues Band: *Back on the Streets Again* (Waldoxy)

Buddy Guy and Junior Wells: *Live in Montreux* (Evidence)

Son House: *Father of the Delta Blues* (Columbia/Legacy)

Elmore James: *King of the Slide Guitar—The Fire/Fury/Enjoy Recordings* (Capricorn)

Blind Lemon Jefferson: *Blind Lemon Jefferson* (Milestone)

Luther "Georgia Boy" Johnson: *Lonesome in My Bedroom* (Evidence)

Louis Jordan: *I Believe in Music* (Evidence)

Eddie Kirkland: *All Around the World* (Deluge)

Robert Jr. Lockwood: *Steady Rollin' Man* (Delmark)

Branford Marsalis: *I Heard You Twice the First Time* (Columbia)

Andrew "B.B." Odom: *Goin' to California* (Flying Fish)

Pinetop Perkins: *On Top* (Deluge)

Ma Rainey: *Ma Rainey* (Milestone)

Roots of Rhythm and Blues: A Tribute to the Robert Johnson Era (Columbia)

Eddie Shaw: *In the Land of the Crossroads* (Rooster Blues)

Specialty Legends of Boogie Woogie (Specialty)

Koko Taylor: *South Side Lady* (Evidence)

Texas Blues Guitar (1929–1935) (Story of Blues)

Jimmy Witherspoon: *The Blues, the Whole Blues and Nothing But the Blues* (Indigo import)

Under suspicion:

Anson Funderburgh and the Rockets: *Thru the Years: A Retrospective* (Black Top)

Screamin' Jay Hawkins: *Live and Crazy* (Evidence)

Smokey Hogg: *Angels in Harlem* (Specialty)

John Lee Hooker: *Graveyard Blues* (Specialty)

Luther "Guitar Junior" Johnson: *It's Good to Me* (Bullseye Blues)

Little Mike and the Tornadoes: *Payday* (Blind Pig)

Taj Mahal: *Taj's Blues* (Columbia/Legacy)

Professor's Blues Revue: *Professor Strut* (Delmark)

Otis Rush: *Mourning in the Morning* (Atlantic)

Muddy Waters: *Blues Sky* (Columbia/Legacy)

Zora Young: *Travelin' Light* (Deluge)

Index

291

About the Author

_____
_____
_____

Frank-John Hadley has written about blues, jazz, and other types of music for several major music magazines since 1979, when his work first appeared in _Down Beat_. He is currently a contributing writer at _Down Beat_ and _Jazziz_ (where he has been the "Blues & Rhythm" columnist), and his freelance writing has appeared in a number of newspapers, including the _Boston Globe_. Hadley is a former critic for _Living Blues_. He has done liner notes for record companies and co-produced concerts featuring artists Dizzy Gillespie, Carrie Smith, Tiny Grimes, and Luther "Guitar Junior" Johnson.